Older Men's Lives

RESEARCH ON MEN AND MASCULINITIES SERIES

Series Editor:
MICHAEL S. KIMMEL, SUNY Stony Brook

Contemporary research on men and masculinity, informed by recent feminist thought and intellectual breakthroughs of women's studies and the women's movement, treats masculinity not as a normative referent but as a problematic gender construct. This series of interdisciplinary, edited volumes attempts to understand men and masculinity through this lens, providing a comprehensive understanding of gender and gender relationships in the contemporary world. Published in cooperation with the Men's Studies Association, a Task Group of the National Organization for Men Against Sexism.

Volumes in this Series

Other series volumes in preparation

Older Men's Lives

Edited by
Edward H. Thompson, Jr.

*Published in cooperation with the Men's Studies Association,
A Task Group of the National Organization for Men Against Sexism*

SAGE Publications
International Educational and Professional Publisher
Thousand Oaks   London   New Delhi

For my dad, and for my children's Papa, my stepdad

For information address:

HＱ
10 64
.U S
O 419
1994
may 1995

 SAGE Publications, Inc.
2455 Teller Road
Thousand Oaks, California 91320

SAGE Publications Ltd.
6 Bonhill Street
London EC2A 4PU
United Kingdom

SAGE Publications India Pvt. Ltd.
M-32 Market
Greater Kailash I
New Delhi 110 048 India

Printed in the United States of America

Library of Congress Cataloging-in-Publication Data

Main entry under title:

Older men's lives / edited by Edward H. Thompson, Jr.
    p. cm.—(Research on men and masculinities series ; 6)
    Includes bibliographical references and indexes.
    ISBN 0-8039-5080-2.—ISBN 0-8039-5081-0 (pbk.)
    1. Aged men—United States—Social conditions. 2. Aged men—United States—Psychology. I. Thompson, Edward H. II. Series.
HQ1064.U50419 1994
305.31—dc20
                                          94-7209
                                            CIP

94 95 96 97 10 9 8 7 6 5 4 3 2 1

Sage Production Editor: Yvonne Könneker

Contents

Foreword

"Will you still need me," ask the Beatles in their memorable song, "when I'm 64?" Fears of aging have long animated the human quest for immortality, and recently we have begun to draw the connection between age and gender. Only rarely, though, has that connection been focused on the meaning of aging to men. But what could be more central to men's sense of themselves than being needed, being of use, and being valued? Yet that sense of ourselves is precisely what we feel is most threatened by aging.

How is the aging process experienced by men? How do different groups of men react to this process? What types of strategies do men develop to handle aging, less as an unexpected crisis and more as a process of life? These are the questions that Ed Thompson set for himself in organizing this collection.

This is the sixth volume in the **Sage Series on Research on Men and Masculinities**. The purpose of the series is to gather together the finest empirical research in the social sciences that focuses on the experience of men in contemporary society.

Following the pioneering research of feminist scholars over the past two decades, social scientists have come to recognize gender as one of the primary axes around which social life is organized. Gender is now seen as equally central as class and race, both at the macro, structural level of the allocation and distribution of rewards in a hierarchical society and at the micro, psychological level of individual identity formation and interpersonal interaction. Social scientists distinguish gender from sex. Sex refers to biology, the biological dimorphic division of male and female; gender refers to the cultural meanings that are attributed to those biological differences. Although biological sex varies little, the cultural meanings of gender vary enormously. Thus we speak of gender as socially constructed: the definitions of masculinity and femininity as the products of the interplay among a variety of social forces. In particular, we understand gender to vary spatially (from one culture to another), temporally (within any one culture over historical time), and longitudinally (through any individual's life course). Finally, we understand that different groups within any culture may define masculinity and femininity differently, according to subcultural definitions. Race, ethnicity, age, class, sexuality, and region of the country all affect gender definitions. Thus it is the goal of this series to explore the varieties of men's experiences, remaining mindful of specific differences among men and aware of the mechanisms of power that inform both men's relations with women and men's relations with other men.

As the chapters collected in this volume make clear, the convergence of life course processes and gender issues is particularly piquant for men. And, of course, different men—differently situated in other social hierarchies—experience this convergence differently.

Some issues do remain constant, and among the most persistent is the sense of loneliness and isolation that men face as they age. Of course, it need not be that way. "You'll be older, too," the Beatles remind us. "And if you say the word, I could stay with you."

MICHAEL S. KIMMEL
Series Editor

Acknowledgments

No scholarly work, especially an edited work, is constructed alone. Thanks are due to Susan Ostrander and John Harney for the encouragement to take on this project and the advice and suggestions. In men's lives, short face-to-face conversations can have lasting effects. Also, I want to acknowledge the enthusiastic support that Michael Kimmel has provided throughout the project. As series editor, Michael made several contributions and offered further assistance if needed. At Sage, Mitch Allen, Frances Borghi, and Yvonne Könneker took control and moved the project from idea to print. I also want to acknowledge the suggestions from Stephen Ainlay (Holy Cross College) and Jetse Sprey (emeritis, Case Western Reserve University) that sharpened my sensitivity to the discourses on older men; Cathy Pojani for her technical assistance in preparing chapters; and the unconditional, unwavering "being there" that Ruth Mendala-Thompson gave.

Introduction

Especially outside, but even inside, the field of gerontology, there has been a tendency to view the elderly population as a homogeneous mass of older people whose lives take place in contexts that differ markedly from the middle-aged and the young. However commonplace this image, it was constructed in error. The elderly population in the United States is not a unified mass, and it has not been for centuries. This population differs conspicuously by gender as well as by birth cohort. Inside the population are older men and older women, very elderly men, and very elderly women. There are more women, and now many theorists postulate that a feminization of "the aged" has begun. But there are elderly men whose masculinities, relationships with intimates, developmental trajectories, worries, work and leisure activities, material resources, age-related limitations, and health concerns differ from other older men and women in their communities.

As much as we know that the elderly population is neither homogeneous nor exclusively female, we have not established much information about elderly men. The research communities in gerontology, family studies, and gender studies have not studied older men as men. Basic to this volume is the distinction between *sex* and *gender.* Sex is fundamentally biological, gender is fundamentally social. Biological males grow and age; men mature and change throughout life. Much of the gerontological literature has introduced us to older biological males by virtue of describing a sex difference in aging. The 13 chapters in this volume begin a process in which elderly men are studied through a lens that emphasizes gender as much as age.

In much the same way that the gerontological literature treats men as if they are genderless, the gender studies literature has unwittingly presented adult men as ageless. Without a wide-frame, life course perspective and an appreciation of aging as a social process, much of the research on men failed to recognize that numerous masculinities coexist for older men, and that these individuals are not living equally by the same standard. Theorizing the presence of multiple masculinities means that old men of different birth cohorts, ethnicity, class, and sexual orientation could have their own age-specific standards of masculinity. The authors contributing to volume, although drawing on different discourses, have begun to help clarify the principle that older men also exhibit masculinities in their relations with others. The authors' work uniquely contributes to men's studies and gender studies.

The collective effort presents no one perspective as the authentic "older men" viewpoint. This collection effectively demonstrates the diversity within the academy. Nonetheless, one cannot help but wonder whether the diverse visions of what it means to be both a man and an elder presented in this volume can ever be concurrent and woven together.

1

Older Men as Invisible Men in Contemporary Society

EDWARD H. THOMPSON, JR.

As the 21st century approaches, academic researchers, journalists, professional caregivers, and other opinion makers are beginning to see a shortcoming in our discourse on class, race, and gender. We have ignored age. Marginalization of elders might feel wrong and yet be in perfect accord with ongoing discussions. The collective effort in this book is to call attention to one group of elders: older men. It is timely, acknowledging that "older men" are a distinct group of men and elders. Their gendered experiences and social lives are different from women their age as well as younger men. It is timely also to look inside the elderly male population to appreciate the diversity among older men when generations are studied separately, class differences become well known, or family status, ethnicity, and race are considered. Taking the point position, my introductory chapter was designed to make the study of elderly men more customary and theoretically interesting.

The basic question is, Why have elderly men been relatively invisible? Four assessments are offered. Beforehand, Bureau of the Census information is used to develop profiles of the men (and women) within the age band "65 and over." These demographic sketches are constructed to call attention to the presence of older men in the United States, as well as the diversity among elder males. The sketches provide a necessary window into objective reality. Following this demographic overview, the question of older men's invisibility is addressed systematically in an effort to grasp the problem of such invisibility as one generated in conventional practices

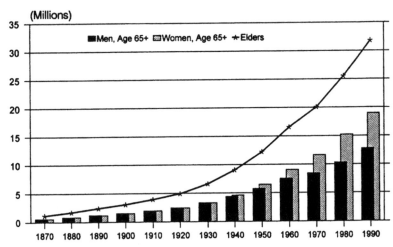

Figure 1.1. Number of Elders in the United States, 1870-1990
SOURCE: U.S. Bureau of the Census (1976, 1993a).

of reality and knowledge production. Seeing older men's invisibility as built into the maintenance of core values and the rules of knowledge production helps reveal how social constructions about "old men" and theories addressing the interaction of gender and age pose intriguing research agendas and policy questions.

Daguerreotypes

We are all somewhat aware of the remarkable restructuring of the shape of the age pyramid that has occurred in the United States over the last century. We also are somewhat aware of the remarkable shifts that are forecasted to take place between 2010 and 2025. These are the years when the age cohort of baby boomers will begin their march into the "Third Age" (Laslett, 1987) and their lives as elders. This march of the baby boomers will prove to be both historic for the nation and for older men's lives.

A century ago in 1890, just 4% of the U.S. population was aged 65 and older. The entire elder population numbered approximately 3 million. By 1930, the group had doubled in size to 6.7 million. It more than doubled in size again by 1960, and by the early 1990s nearly doubled once more (Figure 1.1). Currently, there are 32 million men and women age 65 and older. They represent 12% of the nation and include more than 3 million

Table 1.1 Life Expectancy at Birth (in years)

| | Males | | Females | |
	White	Black	White	Black
1900	48.2	32.5	51.1	35.0
1929-1931	59.1	47.6	62.7	49.5
1959-1961[a]	67.6	61.5	74.2	66.5
1990	72.6	66.0	79.3	70.3

SOURCE: U.S. Bureau of the Census (1976, 1993a).
a. Black and other nonwhite "races."

Table 1.2 Proportion of Populations Surviving to Age 65 (in percentages)

| | Males | | Females | |
	White	Black	White	Black
1900	39	19	44	22
1929-1931	53	29	61	31
1959-1961[a]	66	51	81	61
1990	76	58	86	75

SOURCE: U.S. Bureau of the Census (1976, 1993a).
a. Black and other nonwhite "races."

elders over age 85, an age many now identify as "very elderly" rather than the twice stigmatizing tag "old-olds" (U.S Bureau of the Census, 1993b).

Implicit in these changes and hinted at by the growing size of the nation's elder population is what each individual man experiences: It is much more common for men to at least celebrate their 65th birthday. A long life has become ordinary and predictable. Life expectancy at birth has increased for white males from 48 years in 1900 to 73 years in 1990, and for black males from just 32 years to 66 years (see Table 1.1 for more detail). The proportion of males surviving from birth to age 65 has similarly increased: from 39% to 76% for white males, and from just 19% to 58% for black males (Table 1.2; U.S. Bureau of the Census, 1978, 1993a). The narrowing of the marked racial disparity in men's life expectancy witnessed from the beginning to the end of the century is most often attributed to improved nutrition and the less toxic physical environment in

Table 1.3 Growth of Older Male Population, 1970-1992 (in thousands)

	1970	1992	% Increase
65-69 years old	3,125	4,478	43.3
70-74 years old	2,317	3,643	57.2
75-79 years old	1,562	2,538	62.5
80-84 years old	876	1,446	65.1
85 and over	489	911	86.3
Males, 65+	8,369	13,016	55.5

SOURCE: U.S. Bureau of the Census (1993a, 1993b).

which people work and reside, particularly for African-Americans (McKinlay & McKinlay, 1977). For these very same "health" reasons, the life span for males to be born in the first decade of the 21st century is forecast to be virtually the same for all ethnic and racial groups, and not much greater than found for white males currently (U.S. Bureau of the Census, 1993b). But this prediction for greater equality in life span is debatable. Manton and Soldo (1985) forecast increasing divergence. They observed substantial variation in the timing of death when standard deviations of death rates are examined, rather than the median number of years of survival, and this variability in mortality has increased over the last two decades.

With many more men routinely living to and beyond age 65, there has been an emerging consciousness of the distinct age groups that exist among elder men (Neugarten, 1975). Formerly, all men aged 65 and older were categorically the same: "old." Distinct elder age groups are now regularly identified (see Table 1.3). The male population aged 65 to 74, for example, is part of what is called the "young elderly." This group is perhaps the most widely recognized, partly because of these older men's sheer numbers and presence and partly because of the research attention given to their retirements. But as each year passes, this age cohort represents a smaller and smaller proportion of all elder males. In 1990, for instance, the young elderly group, as a percentage of all males aged 65 and older, constituted 62% of older white males and 63% of the elder black males (U.S. Bureau of the Census, 1993a). By comparison, young elders accounted for nearly three of every four elderly white and black males in 1930. Projections for 2050 indicate that young elders will represent just 47% of elder white males and 52% of elder black males. The key point is that the population of elders is itself aging, with increasing numbers of men in the 85-and-over population. What are the experiences, social worlds, concerns, opportunities, and views of the "over 75"? How do faith experiences change images of self? What opportunities do older men have in their families?

Most striking about the information in Figure 1.1 is the gender difference in mortality over time. Men and women were equally represented in the growing elder population until the 1930s. Then men's morbidity and mortality became measurably distinct from women's. The size of the elder population has since reflected these different mortality rates and, increasingly, the disproportionate number of males to females within the elder population. Today the minority of elderly are men: 13.0 million versus 19.2 million women (U.S. Bureau of the Census, 1993b). Because of the sex and gender differentials in life expectancy, men are increasingly the minority population as age advances. It is still remarkable for men to reach age 85: The 911,000 men who survived to age 85 in 1992 may well be the fastest-growing cohort, but they represented just 7% of all elderly men (review Table 1.3). By comparison, one in eight elderly women has reached age 85 (U.S. Bureau of the Census, 1993b).

The importance of gender to aging is more visible in Figure 1.2. As presented, the plotted sex ratio of men to women aged 65 and older was balanced at virtually 1:1 until the 1930s. For the next 60 years, however, the sex ratio turned downward and thus a "feminization" of the elder population has been ongoing since the 1930s (Arber & Ginn, 1991; Verbrugge, 1989). By the early 1990s the nation's elders were represented by three women for every two men. During this 60-year history, improvements in nutrition, work, and living environments, as well as medical therapies had multiplied the proportion of elder men from nearly 4% to 10%. However, because gendered morbidity and mortality risk factors paced the deaths differently (Harrison, Chin, & Ficarrotto, 1992; Waldron, 1976; Wingard & Cohn, 1990), the proportion of older women increased at a quicker rate and now approaches 15%.

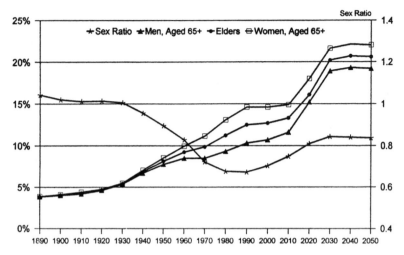

Figure 1.2. Proportion of Older Men and Older Women in the United States, 1890-2050
SOURCE: U.S. Bureau of the Census (1976, 1993a, 1993b).

The often-cited gender gap in longevity, which steadily widened for the last 60 years, may have peaked. Projections for the next 60 years (Figure 1.2) suggest two stunning trends: (a) the sex ratio will tighten considerably, and (b) the proportion of elders will stabilize just above 20% of the nation's population. This means many more men are expected to live to fully experience and extend the normal male life course deep into the Third Age, and, much more so than previously, women will face the life-shortening risks associated with paid employment. By 2030, it is unlikely that older men could continue to be invisible in the population: They will represent one of every five men in the nation, and among elders there will be, on average, four men per five women. Put differently, older men will account for 20% of all males, twice the shadow they now cast, and this older male population will be the size of today's entire elderly population, a tenacious 32 million. What are the implications for elderly men's (and women's) lives? The forecasts further suggest that women's prior "advantage" in longevity will decrease and within 60 years the numerical ratio of women over men in later life will diminish considerably, particularly for the population under 85.

Although these changes are imminent and will amend the past 60 years' feminization of the elder population, there is no need to wait until the baby boomers march into old age or until elderly men cast off their demographic invisibility before scholars begin to study older men's lives. There are already nearly 13 million men age 65 and older. The minority among elders, and especially the minority among the very elderly, 13 million older men is still a sizeable population. It is greater than the number of all undergraduates enrolled full-time in 4-year colleges in 1992 (U.S. Department of Education, 1992), greater than the number of children living in single-parent families in 1980, and nearly three quarters the size of group of children in 1990 (Thompson & Gongla, 1983; U.S. Bureau of the Census, 1992), nearly 20 times greater than the number of physicians practicing medicine in 1993 (Roback, Randolph, & Seidman, 1993) and 10 times the number of people incarcerated in correctional institutions in 1990 (U.S. Bureau of the Census, 1993a). Mainstream journals and opinion makers have made us much more familiar with these folks, however smaller their population size.

Reasons for Invisibility

Older men have remained invisible for reasons beside their smaller number. For one, gerontologists have not encouraged the distinction between the concepts of "sex" and "gender." *Gender* is often accepted as if synonymous with *sex,* serving fundamentally as a categorical construct for grouping the aged. Consequently, the literature introduces us to older biological males by virtue of describing a sex difference in aging. However, what surely distinguishes older biological males, as a group, is their cohort-specific, gendered social lives. As much as research has treated all men as if they were genderless (Kimmel & Messner, 1992), fewer researchers have paid attention to the masculinities that older men encounter or those they disclose.

Another reason for older invisibility is that aging and ageism do not affect men and women equally. From a political economy perspective, it is true that older men have a more comfortable, privileged life compared to older women of the same generation. Consequently, when gender is taken into consideration, elderly women have a much higher profile in gerontological research because the view of aging places women in double jeopardy relative to older men (Sontag, 1972) and because sociological research on "advantaged" groups has traditionally attracted less sustained attention than studies of the disadvantaged (Berger, 1963). In this frame, the pernicious concept of "the aged" is synonymous with a disadvantaged group and thus more synonymous with the providence of older women than older men.

Similarly, the organizations, interest groups, industries, professional societies, and political bodies that make up "the aging enterprise" and serve the elderly in one capacity or another (Estes, 1979, 1993) also furnish ideas about aging and images of elder men. These are elaborately constructed images pressed into public consciousness, and the images the aging enterprise has fabricated are just that—"constructed." To illustrate, for two decades the medical-industrial complex has profited handsomely by medicalizing elderly men's lives more than meeting elderly men's and women's needs. Cardiac catheterization laboratories, fourth- and fifth-generation ventricular pacemakers, arthroscopic surgical technology, and cardiac bypass surgery all derive great profit by "servicing" the elderly male population's health problems and yield much greater profit for the enterprise than would programming to raise the standard of living and health status of all elders. The socially constructed image of elderly men—former breadwinners and national leaders—as "old" and by definition in poor health fuels compassion and, of course, greater profit than the image of most elderly men (and women) as having poor access to health and medical care services. This "compassionate ageism" (Binstock, 1983) is also sexist. It has medicalized elderly men's lives and their perceived well-being, perhaps more than elderly women's. One unintended consequence, for example, of the "compassion" and profiteering is that older men's nonmedical needs become frivolous. The everyday needs of healthy elder males, as well as elder men's need for services other than medical interventions, become remote concerns when compared to the life-and-death emphasis.

In much the same way that gerontologists have inadvertently homogenized elders to make older men genderless, scholars working in the field of gender studies have not paid much notice to men in late life. Older men's masculinities are couched as an invisible part of the dynamics of hegemony or, more simply, ignored. Whether in the research traditions or contemporary theorizing "about men," age is truncated. To illustrate, Daniel Levinson and his colleagues (1978) discuss men's late adulthood in their landmark *The Seasons of a Man's Life* in just seven pages (pages 33-39) and characterize this age in "discontinuous" imagery, as if aging is a negation of masculinity: "A primary developmental task of late adulthood is to find a new balance of involvement with society and with the self. A man in this era is experiencing more fully the process of dying and he should have the possibility of choosing more freely his mode of living" (p. 36). The widely praised second edition of *Men's Lives* that

Kimmel and Messner organized for gender scholars has not one article among the 56 that directly probes older men's masculinities. At this point in the development of gender studies, the masculinities of older men have been subordinated to the concerted effort to understand middle-aged and younger men's lives, who are, as Ortega y Gasset (1958) suggests, "the dominant" group. Even when a life course perspective is recognized (e.g., Connell, 1992; Segal, 1990), the theoretical discourse on masculinities has concentrated on social practices of young to middle-aged men and, by default, marginalized the masculinities of elderly men. But, meta-theoretically, has the marginalization of older men in the scholarship on gender contributed to the preservation of conventional discourses on masculinity? Failing to acknowledge elderly men as a distinct group of men may have homogenized not only adulthood but also theory on masculinity.

One can see, with retrospective clarity, how these four initiatives have helped conceal older men's lives. My interest is to examine them collectively in greater detail. The task is to advance the conceptual and theoretical underpinnings for a more long-term discussion of older men as men and as elders.

The Relative Comfort of Older Men's Lives

They are often pictured as poor, standoffish, persnickety, and of ill health. Often they are imagined to be living alone, following singular paths. But as a group, and compared to both older women and younger men, they are more likely to have fewer financial liabilities and more assets, enjoy good health, lead active lives unhindered by disability, and experience few distressing "turning points" or "life events" in this age of the life span.

Although the incomes of elder males, as a group, are lower than younger men's, in a peculiar way "less is more" (Lazer & Shaw, 1987). Older men spend little of their assets. They are more likely to have paid off their home mortgage, and they spend less on the necessities—household operations, food, clothing—as well as discretionary items (Lazer & Shaw, 1987). In fact, older men would seem to be at a quality-of-life advantage, for they may face fewer emotionally wrenching life events than younger males, who cope with the work and family conflicts of two-income households, the downsizing of corporate America, intermittent periods of unemployment, state governments that have gotten out of the education business and children's educational needs, and so on (Chirboga, 1989).

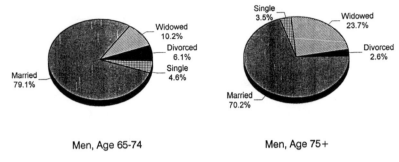

Figure 1.3. Marital Status of Older Men, 1992
SOURCE: U.S. Bureau of the Census (1993b).

Older men, compared to older women, would also seem to be at a quality-of-life advantage even though they are at a mortality disadvantage; their deaths may come sooner, but later life for older men presents fewer troubles (Kaplan, Anderson, & Wingard, 1991). Consider, for example, older men's living arrangements and marital status. Excluding elders who make up the institutional population, such as those living in nursing homes or other places providing custodial care, elderly men are much more likely than elderly women to live with their spouses. Nearly three quarters of elderly men today are both married and living with their spouses. Barely 1 man in 10 aged 65-74 is a widower, and by the time they are age 75-84, just 2 in 10 are widowed (U.S Bureau of the Census, 1992). Aging does not oblige many older men to recast their lives and go it alone after the death of a spouse.

By comparison, fewer than 40% of the older women in the nation are both married and living with their spouse. Half of all elder women are widowed, and the vast majority of widows (71%) do not live with others. They, rather than men, follow singular paths. As many as one third of all women aged 65-74 and about one half aged 75 and older lived alone in 1992 (see Figures 1.3 and 1.4 for details). The proportions for older men, by comparison, were 13% and 22%, respectively. The point is not men's earlier deaths. Rather, it is their relatively nonplussed lives, compared to older women of the same age, when living arrangements and marital status are compared. Men are not obliged to bury their spouses and live alone as often as women. It is also because elderly men as a group are more likely to be married and less likely to live alone that they derive several other late-life advantages.

Thus for the vast majority of older men, the company of a spouse affords greater opportunity to enjoy the extension of the life span into the Third Age. Older men rely on their spouses and report greater satisfaction

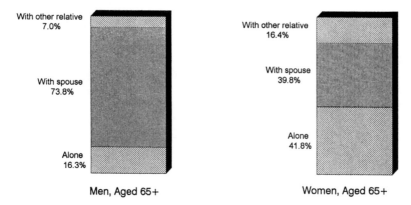

Figure 1.4. Living Arrangements of Older Men and Women, 1992
SOURCE: U.S. Bureau of the Census (1993b).

with marriage than do older women (Antonucci & Akiyama, 1987). And as Shumaker and Hill (1991) noted, the protective role of social support is consistently demonstrated for marrieds and white men. For older men, assets—and not just their income and pension—are greater, allowing them greater autonomy. Personal care tasks are maintained by two adults, not just one. Life is experienced in the company of another.

Not surprisingly, the relative advantages to everyday morale and well-being that the community of a spouse affords elderly men does not apply equally to all older men. We need to anticipate and be sensitive to the diversity among elder men. Elderly black men are much less likely to live with a spouse than are white men or men of Hispanic origin. Among the "young elders" aged 65 to 74, the married proportions for each group are 58%, 79%, and 77%, respectively. Add 10 years to compare men aged 75 and older, and the proportions drop roughly 10% to 46%, 70%, and 67%, respectively. This variance in older men's marital status across ethnic and racial lines may be a result of the greater proportion of black men who never marry (U.S. Bureau of the Census, 1992) and the higher levels of marital disruption among blacks. Whatever the reasons, the proportion of elderly men who live alone is higher for blacks (29%) than whites (15%) or men of Hispanic origin (11%).

Socially Constructed Images of Aged Men

Visualize the image. The men hold themselves upright and proud—these middle-aged men whose time of life is shifting from "early" to "middle adulthood" and who are perhaps at a peak in their impact on the world outside the home. They are the "dominant" generation, as Ortega y Gasset defined the age 45-60. They make their ideas and aims the pivotal ones in every sector of society: business, politics, religion, science. But soon they take up wearing bifocals, their skin wrinkles more, their hair turns silvery, they become grandparents, they stoop, and they embrace the season of life that Levinson and his colleagues (1978) call "late adulthood" and, for some, "late, late adulthood."

In the popular culture men in late adulthood no longer occupy center stage. Their generation is no longer the dominant one: It has been displaced by a younger, "Pepsi" generation. Men in late life are classed as "senior" or "old." They become "socially opaque" (Green, 1993). They are presumed to have completed the major part—perhaps all—of their life work. The older man sees himself living in his shadow or death's (Levinson et al., 1978). Writing in *Esquire,* novelist Thomas Morgan (1987, p. 162) describes a memory of his father's 60th birthday: "I do not remember his exact words, only that he seemed to be telling me he was conceding at sixty, perhaps welcoming at sixty that he need not be a part of the future. . . . As it happened, he worked ten more years, but lived, I'm sorry to say, as though it were all an anticlimax."

Television commercials, newspaper presentations, and magazine advertisements fully impart this image, too. No longer in control, wealthy, and urbane, old men are pictured as living neither in the city nor the suburbs but in a small rural town or in the country, near the pasture. Homes are smaller, more plain, without gadgets and machines. Bodies are not virile, rather pleasantly plump. Checked, flannel shirts have replaced the dark blue suit. As part of the "grandparent" generation, advertisements will show that the older man's soft lap cat has replaced the younger man's spirited black labrador retriever. Lemonade is now the drink of choice (Buchholz & Bynum, 1982; Ferraro, 1992; Kaiser & Chandler, 1988; Powell & Williamson, 1985; Swayne & Greco, 1987). Such images seem inflated to the point of parody. Perhaps, as Wernick (1987, p. 283) would maintain, when advertisers and other opinion makers become interested in speaking to and about older men, the more conventional construction of masculinity as a symbolic term will have weakened, and we can then expect a disappearance of what one might call the *metaphorical* old man.

Until then, it seems that the constructed images of older men leave these elders with two strikes against them. First is the prejudice within public (and professional) attitudes regarding "old age" in general (Butler, 1969;

Walsh & Connor, 1979). Elders—in particular, elderly men—are thought to suffer significant losses: Their occupational role, their livelihood and community of co-workers, their health and independence, and their masculinity are commonly thought to be displaced by aging. The traditional discourses of masculinity and aging separate adult men into two categories: old and all others. The older man is depicted in a yo-yo fashion, with both positive and negative content (Hummert, 1990). He is portrayed as interactively and psychologically involved in more expressive and caring roles within the family. He is also, by default, contrasted with an image of the younger, justly preoccupied father and husband whose primary concern is with productive labor and power management. The underlying core values in the discourse extol youth, independence, and economic productiveness and an aversion to aging and anything feminine (Cole, 1986; Fischer, 1978; Green, 1993, p. 53).

By displacing elder men from the mainstream, one result of contemporary cultural coding is the oppression of older men. As Fischer (1978) observed when he reviewed American cultural documents and chronicled the development of a "cult of youth" from 1770 to 1970, the definition of elder men as oppressors provided a symbol for all other echelons among men to unite against gerontocracy.

The second strike is older men's perceived genderlessness. Ask people to complete the sentence "An old man . . . " and then listen to ungendered ageism and his feminization. Older men are depicted as sedentary, resting on a park bench, passing time, asexual. Images of older men basically portray diminished masculinity (Kite, Deaux, & Miele, 1991; Puglisi & Jackson, 1980-81; Silverman, 1977). To many people, aging is a negation of masculinity, and thus older men become effeminate over time. Given this cultural assumption, older men are used, however unwittingly. The degendered imagery of the older man keeps afloat a masculinity and a discourse that sustains younger men. The conventional discourse describes gender in simply binary terms, wherein aging diminishes men's masculinity and, by default, heightens their femininity over time. Framed this way, images of age-specific and cohort-specific masculinities never rise to a threshold of public consciousness. Rather, the social construction maintains that "old men" are not men at all.

Discourses in the Academy

As the size of elderly female population increased between 1930 and 1990, the importance of gender and aging commanded greater and greater attention among academics and policy makers (Haug, Ford, & Sheafor, 1985; Herzog, Holden, & Seltzer, 1989; Lesnoff-Caravaglia, 1984; Markson, 1985; Matthews, 1979; also see Coyle, 1989). Ironically, as older women's lives and their profound needs gained visibility, older men became more marginal and invisible. In fact, being elderly appears in some quarters to have become synonymous with being female. For example, in *Gender and Later Life,* Arber and Ginn (1991, p. vii) state, "Later life is primarily an experience of women." Their first chapter is powerfully titled "The Feminization of Later Life," because the demographics of aging show that elderly women outnumber elderly men in later life, especially as age advances. The message that is constructed, however, goes beyond making note of a sex differential in longevity. Rather, as women's experience in later life is brought to the foreground, older men's fade from attention. Arber and Ginn's otherwise very fine work makes "later life" as synonymous with women as "gender" has become.

Homogenizing elders—as reflected by midcentury discourses on "the aged" or the new academic discourse on feminization—was once said to be akin to "tabloid thinking" (Binstock, 1983, p. 140). Homogenizing sets the stage to ignore individual differences and to think about "the elderly" only at the collective level as disadvantaged individuals beset by common problems. Kalish (1979) warned that this construction was a form of "new ageism." The new discourse of feminization of the aged goes beyond the devaluation of diversity (Butler, 1969) to thwart discussion of the ways in which the population of older men is itself devalued and the ways in which men's personal experiences of age are challenged by cultural double binds and structurally induced conflicts about masculinities—conflicts such as about their work ethic and their diminished social significance as men, or their relative social opaqueness as individuals versus a collective.

Although the core value behind older men's invisibility is academics' "compassionate ageism" for older women (Binstock, 1983), knowledge production in gerontological studies currently makes for blinds spots and a lack of understanding of older men. As Cook (1992, p. 293) warned in an editorial in *The Gerontologist,* "If we want the public and the media to abandon the oversimplifying generalities they often make about age and aging and look instead at the diversity among older people, then gerontologists must stop asking attitudinal and factual questions about 'the elderly' as if they were a homogeneous group."

In the sociologies of the life course and family life, elderly men were not often studied as men but served as the referent point to better understand late-life families, elderly women's lives as caregivers, or younger men. Small wonder then that as much as "wives' sociology" once informed us about family life (Safilios-Rochschild, 1969), there is a "midlife sociology" that has tried to theorize about older men's lives. To illustrate, role-theory sociologies directed attention to the rolelessness of late life. Retired men were envisioned outside the "normal" work spaces, and, by default, they were invading their wives' space—the family home (see literature review in Brubaker, 1990, and Chapter 8 in this volume). This early sociological discourse of older men defined their lives as a period of indispensable disengagement from former, power-brokering statuses. Older men were portrayed as obsolete currency in a culture that cherishes power; in disengagement terms, the spotlight was on younger men's welfare. Later discourses of activity theory similarly emphasized the core values of a masculinity that best fits younger employed men's lives. Neither did these theoretical accounts reveal much about older men as a group or about subgroup and individual differences.

Logically, the diversity among young and middle-aged men does not disappear at age 65, 70, or 75, when older men leave the workplace to take up more assiduously their semipublic and private social worlds. Their gendered lives continue. Their relationships with institutions, women, other men, and children press on. Dannefer (1988) pointed out that as men grow older, their accumulated decisions about life course options produce increased differentiation among them. But in what ways? Do age and gender interact to affect older men's thoughts, feelings, behaviors, and relations with others? Do the two interact to affect men as a group?

Aging and Masculinities

Over the last 30 years a body of theoretical literature on men's character in late life (or the postparental years) has emerged to explain the psychological comfort of the individual man as he ages (e.g., Deutscher, 1964; Gutmann, 1987; Livson, 1983; Lowenthal et al., 1975; Vaillant, 1977). By far the greatest common denominator in these accounts is the focus on the individual and his gender orientation. Gender is conceptualized as the "male role" and visualized as the institutionalized practices of men. The common discourse also proposes a single masculinity for each developmental stage that men confront in their life span; thus any diversity in masculinities is age-specific and accounted for by the underlying developmental processes. This theorizing targets the men who "do gender," not the masculinity ideologies (Thompson, Pleck, & Ferrera, 1992) or the structure of gender relations that organize the way men do gender (Connell, 1987; West & Zimmerman, 1987).

Neugarten and Gutmann (1958) and Neugarten, Moore, and Lowe (1965) envision individual aging as a life journey through socially scheduled role entries and exits. Strong age and gender norms structure the march across the life course, and changes in men's (and women's) gender relations are normative for each transition point. However, agreement among theorists ends on this point. When the literature discussing older men is examined, two fundamentally different views have been constructed on the "continuity" of gender across the life span. One viewpoint has proposed a general "discontinuous model" of gender across the life span and a formulation wherein the older man is emasculated by aging. But the common discourse even among these authors breaks up. First, these models offer different assumptions about what determines the changes. Some theorists (such as Gutmann and Huyck—see Chapter 4 in this volume) emphasize an ontogenetic basis for the behavioral, personality, and spiritual changes; others (such as Payne—see Chapter 5 in this volume) attribute distinct life stage differences in men's experiences to structurally induced conflicts and men's accommodations to changes in expectations. Second, discontinuity models present different nuances of discontinuity. Some theorists visualize men experiencing dramatically different gendered worlds in contiguous life stages. In Gutmann's scheme, for example, at the onset of parenthood adult men engage in highly polarized gender relations and exhibit gender-congruent personalities; on exiting this life stage, however, men experience a "nomic rupture" by facing a crossover toward a more feminine world (Sinnott, 1984).

Third, the discontinuity models introduce quite different masculinities for older men. Sinnott (1982, 1984) and Gutmann (1975, 1977, 1987), for instance, theorized a convergence of conventional masculinity and femininity in late life. This pattern of gender convergence in older men's and women's lifestyles and personalities, however, has failed to find much empirical support (McCreary, 1990). Others do not agree with the assertion that either diminished masculinity or increased femininity parallels men's aging; instead they propose that there is greater consistency to masculinities over time (McCrae & Costa, 1982).

The other representation emphasizes the continuity of gender experiences across the life span, particularly as men enter late life. According to the continuity models, becoming an older man might mean adapting to a new masculinity, but one not too different from the previous (Neugarten, 1977; Solomon, 1982; Solomon & Swazbo, Chapter 3 in this volume;

Gradman, Chapter 6 in this volume). The continuity perspective suggests that men's gendered social worlds do not appreciably change throughout the life course; rather, older men continue to participate in the "institutionalized" practices that significant others expect (Brubaker, 1985; Szinovacz, 1980) and continue to reveal consistency in their self-conceptions (Marsiglio & Greer, Chapter 7 in this volume).

Within the available literature on aging and masculinities, change in men's character or institutionalized practices is at times thought to be ontogenetic, at other times triggered by the individual man's psychological discomfort with aging. Consistency also is thought to be generated by individual monitoring of psychosocial norms. The discourse is a biographical stage of life and not the masculinities within gender relations or the masculinity ideologies in the culture. Attention is directed to individual experiences with a stage-specific conventional masculinity without deciphering the matrix of masculinities that older men exhibit, the dynamics generated within gender relations, or the kind of masculinity that would be consistent with a (historical) change in the structure of gender relations.

Little has been said about the social conditions under which the different masculinities older men live with are constructed. For example, there is no evidence to suggest that the older men who were familiar with the Depression and who adopted a two-income family model (and thus elected not to be sole breadwinners) practice a different masculinity than sole breadwinners. Could both men participate in the public world of hegemonic masculinity in sports? Are they equally interested? Can they both return home to resume the full caregiving responsibilities of supporting a wife with Alzheimer's?

More work is also needed to address older men's lives in masculine spheres—such as when visiting with friends, whether on the golf course, in a cafeteria, in a veterans' bar, over the back fence (Duneier, 1992; Halle, 1984), or in gender relations (see Chapters 9 through 12 of this volume). What has emerged to date is an ambiguous image of elderly men in families and society. Are older men in fact marginal and nonessential, perhaps in the way of their wives and younger men? Is their experience one of exclusion? Is it one of rekindling the gerontocracy (see Chapter 13 in this volume)? The scope of theorizing and research both need to expand from examining only conventions of gender to understanding the ways in which older men's practices support and change gender relations broadly.

The merit of examining ordinary men's lives has become more widely acknowledged (Diamant, 1992; Heller, 1993), but in the investigations of masculinities, older men have not been the men studied. Age distinctions in how adult men embrace manhood, generational differences in masculinity, attention to gender presentations when similarly aged men engage in a common sphere of activity, and the meaning of being a man in the Third Age are largely outside what is understood and need to be brought in theoretically and placed on research agendas.

References

Antonucci, T. C., & Akiyama, H. (1987). An examination of sex differences in social support among older men and women. *Sex Roles, 17,* 737-749.

Arber, S., & Ginn, J. (1991). *Gender and later life: A sociological analysis of resources and constraints.* London: Sage.

Berger, P. L. (1963). *Invitation to sociology: A humanistic perspective.* New York: Anchor.

Binstock, R. H. (1983). The aged as scapegoat. *The Gerontologist, 23,* 136-143.

Brubaker, T. H. (1985). *Later life families.* Beverly Hills, CA: Sage.

Brubaker, T. H. (1990). Families in later life: A burgeoning research area. *Journal of Marriage and the Family, 52,* 959-981.

Buchholz, M., & Bynum, J. E. (1982). Newspaper presentations of America's aged: A content analysis of image and role. *The Gerontologist, 22,* 83-88.

Butler, R. N. (1969). Age-ism: Another form of bigotry. *The Gerontologist, 9,* 243-246.

Chirboga, D. A. (1989). The measurement of stress exposure in later life. In K. S. Markides & C. L. Cooper (Eds.), *Aging, stress and health* (pp. 13-41). New York: John Wiley.

Cole, T. R. (1986). "Putting off the old": Middle class morality, antebellum Protestantism, and the origins of ageism. In D. van Tassel & P. N. Stearns (Eds.), *Old age in a bureaucratic society* (pp. 49-65). Westport, CT: Greenwood Press.

Connell, R. W. (1987). *Gender and power.* Stanford, CA: Stanford University Press.

Connell, R. W. (1992). A very straight gay: Masculinity, homosexual experience, and the dynamics of gender. *American Sociological Review, 57,* 735-751.

Cook, F. L. (1992). Ageism: Rhetoric and reality. *The Gerontologist, 32,* 292-293.

Coyle, J. M. (1989). *Women and aging: A selected, annotated bibliography.* Westport, CT: Greenwood Press.

Dannefer, D. (1988). Differential gerontology and the stratified life course: Conceptual and methodological issues. In G. L. Maddox & M. P. Lawton (Eds.), *Annual review of gerontology and geriatrics* (Vol. 8, pp. 3-36). New York: Springer.

Deutscher, I. (1964). The quality of postparental life: Definitions of the situation. *Journal of Marriage and the Family, 26,* 52-59.

Diamant, A. (1992, December 14). Academia tackles masculinity: Male studies courses booming on campus. *Boston Globe,* pp. 17, 24.

Duneier, M. (1992). *Slim's table: Race, respectability, and masculinity.* Chicago: University of Chicago Press.

Estes, C. L. (1979). *The aging enterprise.* San Francisco: Jossey-Bass.

Estes, C. L. (1993). The aging enterprise revisited. *The Gerontologist, 33,* 292-298.

Ferraro, K. F. (1992). Cohort changes in images of older adults, 1974-1981. *The Gerontologist, 32,* 296-304.

Fischer, D. H. (1978). *Growing old in America* (expanded ed.). New York: Oxford University Press.

Green, B. S. (1993). *Gerontology and the construction of older age: A study in discourse analysis.* Hawthorne, NY: Aldine.

Gutmann, D. (1975). Parenthood: A key to the comparative study of the life cycle. In N. Datan & L. Ginsberg (Eds.), *Life-span developmental psychology: Normative life crises* (pp. 167-184). San Diego, CA: Academic Press.

Gutmann, D. (1977). The cross-cultural perspective: Notes toward a comparative psychology of aging. In I. J. Birren & K. W. Schaie (Eds.), *Handbook of the psychology of aging* (pp. 302-321). New York: Van Nostrand Reinhold.

Gutmann, D. (1987). *Reclaimed powers: Toward a new psychology of men and women in late life.* New York: Basic Books.

Halle, D. (1984). *America's working man.* Chicago: University of Chicago Press.

Harrison, J., Chin, J., & Ficarrotto, T. (1992). Warning: Masculinity may be dangerous to your health. In M. Kimmel & M. Messner (Eds.), *Men's lives* (2nd ed., pp. 271-285). New York: Macmillan.

Haug, M., Ford, A. B., & Sheafor, M. (1985). *The physical and mental health of aged women.* New York: Springer.

Heller, S. (1993, February 3). Scholars debunk the Marlboro man: Examining stereotypes of masculinity. *Chronicle of Higher Education,* pp. A9-A11, A15.

Herzog, A. R., Holden, K. C., & Seltzer, M. M. (1989). *Health and economic status of older women.* Amityville, NY: Baywood.

Hummert, M. L. (1990). Multiple stereotypes of elderly and young adults: A comparison of structure and evaluation. *Psychology and Aging, 5,* 182-193.

Kaiser, S. B., & Chandler, J. L. (1988). Audience responses to appearance codes: Old-age imagery in the media. *The Gerontologist, 28,* 692-699.

Kalish, R. A. (1979). The new ageism and the failure models: A polemic. *The Gerontologist, 19,* 398-402.

Kaplan, R. M., Anderson, J. P., & Wingard, D. L. (1991). Gender differences in health-related quality of life. *Health Psychology, 10,* 86-93.

Kimmel, M. S., & Messner, M. A. (1992). *Men's lives* (2nd ed.). New York: Macmillan.

Kite, M. E., Deaux, K., & Miele, M. (1991). Stereotypes of young and old: Does age outweigh gender? *Psychology and Aging, 6,* 19-27.

Laslett, P. (1987). The emergence of the third age. *Aging and Society, 7,* 133-160.

Lazer, W., & Shaw, E. H. (1987). How older Americans spend their money. *American Demographics, 9,* 36-41.

Lesnoff-Caravaglia, G. (1984). *The world of the older woman: Conflicts and resolutions.* New York: Human Sciences Press.

Levinson, D. J., Darrow, C. N., Klein, E. B., Levinson, M. H., & McKee, B. (1978). *The seasons of a man's life.* New York: Knopf.

Livson, F. B. (1983). Gender identity: A life-span view of sex-role development. In R. Weg (Ed.), *Sexuality in the later years* (pp. 105-127). San Diego, CA: Academic Press.

Lowenthal, M. F., Thurnher, M., Chiroboga, D., & Associates. (1975). *Four stages of life: A comparative study of women and men facing transitions.* San Francisco: Jossey-Bass.

Manton, K. G., & Soldo, B. J. (1985). Dynamics of health changes in the oldest old: New perspectives and evidence. *Milbank Memorial Fund Quarterly/Health and Society,* *63*(2), 206-285.

Markson, E. W. (1985). *Older women: Issues and prospects.* Lexington, MA: Lexington Books.

Matthews, S. H. (1979). *The social world of old women: Management of self-identity.* Beverly Hills, CA: Sage

McCrae, R. R., & Costa, P. T. (1982). Aging, the life course, and models of personality. In T. M. Field (Ed.), *Review of human development* (pp. 602-613). New York: Wiley.

McCreary, D. R. (1990). Self-perceptions of life-span gender-role development. *International Journal of Aging and Human Development, 31,* 135-146.

McKinlay, J. B., & McKinlay, S. A. (1977). The questionable contribution of medical measures to the decline of mortality in the United States in the twentieth century. *Milbank Memorial Fund Quarterly/Health and Society, 55,* 405-428.

Morgan, T. B. (1987, May). What does a sixty-year-old man see when he looks in the mirror? *Esquire,* pp. 161-167.

Neugarten, B. L. (1975). The future of the young-old. *The Gerontologist, 15*(1), 4-9.

Neugarten, B. L. (1977). Personality and aging. In J. E. Birren & K. W. Schaie (Eds.), *Handbook of the psychology of aging* (pp. 626-649). New York: Van Nostrand Reinhold.

Neugarten, B. L., & Gutmann, D. (1958). Age-sex role and personality in middle age: A thematic apperception study. *Psychological Monographs, 470,* 1-33.

Neugarten, B. L., Moore, J. W., & Lowe, J. C. (1965). Age norms, age constraints, and adult socialization. *American Journal of Sociology, 70,* 710-717.

Ortega y Gasset, J. (1958). *Man and crisis.* New York: Norton.

Powell, L., & Williamson, J. B. (1985). The mass media and the aged. *Social Policy, 16,* 38-49.

Puglisi, J. T., & Jackson, D. W. (1980-81). Sex role identity and self esteem in adulthood. *International Journal of Aging and Human Development, 12,* 129-138.

Roback, G., Randolph, L., & Seidman, B. (1993). *Physician characteristics and distribution in the United States.* Chicago: American Medical Association.

Safilios-Rochschild, C. (1969). Family sociology or wives' family sociology? A cross-cultural examination of decision-making. *Journal of Marriage and the Family, 31,* 290-301.

Segal, L. (1990). *Slow motion: Changing masculinities, changing men.* New Brunswick, NJ: Rutgers University Press.

Shumaker, S. A., & Hill, D. R. (1991). Gender differences in social support and physical health. *Health Psychology, 10,* 102-111.

Silverman, M. (1977). The old man as woman: Detecting stereotypes of aged men with a femininity scale. *Perceptual and Motor Skills, 44,* 336-338.

Sinnott, J. D. (1982). Correlates of sex roles of older adults. *Journal of Gerontology, 37,* 587-594.

Sinnott, J. D. (1984). Older men, older women: Are their perceived sex roles similar? *Sex Roles, 10,* 847-856.

Solomon, K. (1982). The older man. In K. Solomon & N. B. Levy (Eds.), *Men in transition: Theory and therapy* (pp. 205-240). New York: Plenum.

Sontag, S. (1972). The double standard of aging. *Saturday Review, 55*(39), 29-38.

Swayne, L. E., & Greco, A. J. (1987). The portrayal of older Americans in television commercials. *Journal of Advertising, 16*(1), 47-54.

Szinovacz, M. E. (1980). Female retirement: Effects of spousal roles and marital relationships. *Journal of Family Issues, 1,* 423-440.

Thompson, E. H., & Gongla, P. A. (1983). Single parent families: In the mainstream of American society. In E. D. Macklin & R. H. Rubin (Eds.), *Contemporary families and alternative lifestyles: Handbook on research and theory.* Beverly Hills, CA: Sage.

Thompson, E. H., Pleck, J. H., & Ferrera, D. L. (1992). Men and masculinities: Scales for masculinity ideology and masculinity-related constructs. *Sex Roles, 27,* 573-607.

U.S. Bureau of the Census. (1976). *Historical statistics of the United States: Colonial times to 1970.* Washington, DC: Government Printing Office.

U.S. Bureau of the Census. (1978). *Demographic aspects of aging and the older population in the United States.* Current Population Reports, Series P23, No. 59. Washington, DC: Government Printing Office.

U.S. Bureau of the Census. (1992). *Marital status and living arrangements: March 1992.* Current Population Reports, Series P20, No. 468. Washington, DC: Government Printing Office.

U.S. Bureau of the Census. (1993a). *Statistical abstracts of the United States, 1992.* Washington, DC: Government Printing Office.

U.S. Bureau of the Census. (1993b). *Population projections of the United States, by age, sex, race, and Hispanic origin: 1992 to 2050.* Current Population Reports, Series P25, No. 1092. Washington, DC: Government Printing Office.

U.S. Department of Education. (1992). *Projections of education statistics to 2003.* Washington, DC: Government Printing Office.

Verbrugge, L. M. (1989). Gender, aging and health. In K. S. Markides (Ed.), *Aging and health: Perspectives on gender, race, ethnicity, and class* (pp. 23-78). Newbury Park, CA: Sage.

Vaillant, G. E. (1977). *Adaptation to life.* Boston: Little, Brown.

Waldron, I. (1976). Why do women live longer than men? *Social Science and Medicine, 10,* 349-362.

Walsh, R. P., & Connor, C. L. (1979). Old men and young women: How objectively are their skills assessed? *Journal of Gerontology, 34,* 561-568.

Wernick, A. (1987). From voyeur to narcissist: Imaging men in contemporary advertising. In M. Kaufman (Ed.), *Beyond patriarchy: Essays by men on pleasure, power, and change* (pp. 277-297). Toronto: Oxford University Press.

West, C., & Zimmerman, D. (1987). Doing gender. *Gender and Society, 1,* 125-151.

Wingard, D. L., & Cohn, B. A. (1990). Variations in disease-specific sex-morbidity and mortality ratios: United States vital statistics data and prospective data from the Alameda County study. In M. G. Ory & H. R. Warner (Eds.), *Gender, health, and longevity: Multidisciplinary perspectives* (pp. 25-37). New York: Springer.

2

"Successful Aging" and Psychosocial Well-Being

Evidence From a 45-Year Study

GEORGE E. VAILLANT

As we go through life, we see vigorous, happy, generative octogenarians, and we ask, What were the relevant antecedents? A definitive answer is not possible. But if gerontology is to understand successful adaptation to aging as well as it understands unsuccessful aging, then the parameters and antecedents of successful aging must be addressed.

Aging must always be studied as a process, for aging conveys change. Older men have a past and a future. Longitudinal study is also necessary to assess predictive validity, the closest we will ever have to a "gold standard" with which to assess value-laden judgments such as relative "success in life." For this reason, the present chapter will discuss a 45-year prospective study of socially favored men. It will seek to identify the most promising predictors of successful later life adaptation among 204 Harvard University sophomores followed since 1940 (Vaillant, 1977).

Successful aging, no matter how humanely defined, is a value judgment. So are the concepts of forward motion and velocity. All three— velocity, forward motion, and successful aging—depend on the vantage

AUTHOR'S NOTE: Preparation of this chapter was supported by research grants KO5-MH00364 and MH42248. Part of the chapter was published in P. B. Baltes and M. M. Baltes (Eds.), *Successful Aging: Research and Theory*, Cambridge University Press, 1991. Reprinted with permission.

point of the observer. But if we wish to understand our own lives in time and space, these are nevertheless judgments worth making. What Leo Kass (1975), a research professor of bioethics, said of health can be applied to successful aging as well. "Health," he wrote, "is a natural standard, a norm—not a moral norm, not a 'value' as opposed to a 'fact,' not an obligation but a state of being that reveals itself in activity" (p. 28). If successful aging is to be empirically validated, it needs to be looked at in terms of objective "activity."

The Study

As a means of assessing "successful" aging, two general outcomes— physical health and psychosocial health—will organize my multidimensional model. With the passage of time, progressively diminished physical reserves are an inevitable part of aging, but the rate at which these diminished reserves occur is variable. One can be young or old for one's chronological age. Biological health and longevity are two different ways of assessing the multifaceted process associated with declining biological reserves. Thus biological health and length of life can be considered dimensions of the physical health component of successful aging.

Psychosocial health is the other complex, multidimensional aspect of successful aging. For this chapter, psychosocial health will encompass three dimensions: mental health, psychosocial efficacy, and life satisfaction. Positive evidence of mental health underlies adaptation and successful aging, because mental health reflects the capacity to master life changes and stress, such as loss and grief, conflict, and past failure. In addition, good self-care (Rowe & Kahn, 1987) and self-esteem, close correlates of mental health, often make the difference in being "old" or "sick."

Positive evidence of psychosocial health is also reflected by relatively sustained psychosocial efficacy or physical and mental vigor. Continued capacity for success at working and loving are reflections of this dimension of psychosocial efficacy. Finally, psychosocial health involves an individual regarding the present period of life as being somewhat more than satisfactory—ideally, the subjectively best period of one's life. Life satisfaction constitutes an important dimension of successful aging.

For this chapter, therefore, physical health and psychosocial health are conceptualized as two separate but intercorrelated elements of successful aging. On the one hand, this chapter will focus on the antecedents of men remaining in excellent physical health at age 63 to 65. On the other hand, it will also focus on the antecedents of men who, at age 65, are experiencing superior psychosocial health as defined by life satisfaction, mental health, and showing clear ability to play, work, and love. A final part of successful aging will be addressed only in passing. This dimension includes those tasks that individuals can do better after age 60 than before. These ill-defined processes come under such headings as *experience, wisdom,* and *keepers of the meaning.* Older individuals' skills often manifest increased capacity to conserve and transmit cultural heritage. Liberated from personal allegiances, older individuals are more likely to be trusted by both sides to mediate conflict. The mean age for genealogists, high court judges, church leaders, and trustees is often beyond the retirement age for most occupations.

The Sample

The cohort that this chapter describes consists of a 10% sample of three consecutive college classes. The sample was created between 1940 and 1942 when the Harvard University Health Services under Arlie Bock, M.D., began a longitudinal study of Harvard University sophomores (Heath, 1945). The men were originally selected for intensive multidisciplinary study because their freshman health service physical exam had revealed no mental or physical health problems, and their college deans saw the men as becoming promising adults (Heath, 1945). This cohort, also known as the Grant Study, has been prospectively followed from age 18 to age 65, from 1940 to 1988 (McArthur, 1955; Vaillant, 1984). In college, the men received 20 to 30 hours of multidisciplinary assessment. The men were reinterviewed at ages 25 and 30 and again between ages 47 and 57. For 45 years or until their death, the men have also been followed by means of annual or biennial questionnaires. In addition, physical exams have been obtained every five years. By design, important outcome ratings at each period have been made by raters blind to other ratings.

Of those 204 men originally in the sample, 6 had dropped out in college, 5 died in combat in World War II, and 5 died young from deaths unrelated to identified mental illness. As indicated in Table 2.1, of the remaining 188 middle-aged men who had complete data sets at age 47, 173 remained alive and active in the study until after age 60. Of the missing 15, 13 men had died before age 60, and 2 had incomplete data sets.

Before discussing the findings, we will put the cohort into historical perspective. Born just after 1920, these men were adolescents during the Depression. They virtually all saw active military service in World War II and on return benefited from high employment, a valuable dollar, and the

Table 2.1 Attrition Within the Sample

1940-1942	204 19- to 20-year-old college sophomores selected for study
1968-1970	188 still had complete data sets (10 died young, 6 dropped out)
1985- ?	173 men still had complete data sets (13 died; 2 incomplete data sets)

"G.I. Bill," which virtually guaranteed these successful college students a graduate education. Having forgotten the pacifism that many of them had shared in 1940 and 1941, these combat veterans were confronted—and often dismayed—by their "baby boom" children who came of age in the 1960s, children who protested U.S. military involvement in Vietnam, cohabited before marriage, and smoked marijuana. The men themselves were young enough to benefit from the secular trends of 1960-1980 toward middle-aged fitness and smoking cessation.

Among other longitudinal studies, the Oakland Growth Study cohort from the Institute of Human Development at Berkeley described by Glen Elder (1974) captures the historical times of these men well. But in contrast to Elder's cohort, through their Harvard degree the men of the Grant Study, whatever their social origins, were given a ticket of entry to the upper middle class.

Physical Health

Among the difficulties of longitudinal studies are halo effects. Thus physical health, like all the major variables discussed in this chapter, was assessed by raters blind to all other major variables and hypotheses. Approximately every five years the study obtained physical exams from the men—preferably by an internist—including chest x-rays, routine blood chemistries, urinalysis, and an electrocardiogram. An internist, blind to psychosocial adjustment, rated these examinations on a 5-point scale of objective physical health. Table 2.2 summarizes the two physical health dimensions of successful aging—"length of life" and the progressive decline in the physical health of these men—until age 63 ± 1. At this point in the men's lives, morbidity, not mortality, is the dominant problem. At age 50, very few of the men had been chronically ill. But at nearly 65, few are still completely well. Of the 188 men alive at age 45, only 22% were still in excellent health at age 63 ± 1 (that is, revealed no evidence of significant irreversible illness or physical defect). The men who fell in the category of "minor problems" had experienced potentially progressive difficulties such as reversible hypertension, hypercholesterolemia,

Table 2.2 Progression of Physical Health in 188 Men Surviving Until
Age 45

	Excellent Health (%)	Minor Problems (%)	Chronic Illness (%)	Chronic Illness With Disability (%)	Dead (%)
Age 25 years	96	4	0	0	0
Age 40 years	80	17	2	1	0
Age 50 years	48	35	13	2	2
Age 65 years	22	42	22	4	10

NOTE: The table excludes the 6 men who dropped out and 10 men who died before age 45. In quantifying relative physical health, the following scale was used: 1 = excellent, 2 = minor problems, 3 = chronic illness, 4 = disabled, 5 = dead.

hearing loss, or moderate arthritis. The category "chronic illness" refers to illnesses that could be expected to be progressive, that would shorten life or significantly affect daily living. Examples are coronary thrombosis, diabetes, multiple sclerosis, and hypertension not fully controlled by medication. Chronic illness with disability includes men whose irreversible illnesses have led to significant restrictions in daily living.

Psychosocial Health

Table 2.3 summarizes the findings for the three dimensions of psychosocial health at age 65. American psychiatrist Roy Grinker pleaded for "operational referents" to make the concept of psychosocial health less metaphysical (Grinker, Grinker, & Timberlake, 1962). Table 2.3 tries to provide such operational referents for three of the more general (or Platonic) indications of "successful aging": psychosocial efficacy, mental health, and life satisfaction. But in so doing, we acknowledge that operationalizing psychosocial health and assessing the three selected dimensions are each more controversial and value-laden than was physical health. The global measure and the 10 individual items used are set forth in Table 2.3. The calibration closely follows the measure originally designed to assess positive mental health at age 47 (Vaillant, 1975, 1979). The points assigned to each item are indicated to the right of each item in the table. (A low score was favorable.)

Table 2.3 Measure of Psychological Health in Later Life

| | Psychosocial Health Score | | | |
| | Best[c] (%) | Mid (%) | Worst (%) | Interrater |
Individual Scale Item (Range)[a]	(n = 37)	(n = 99)	(n = 37)	Reliability[d]
Psychosocial efficacy				
Early retirement (1-3 points)	3	25	46	.70
Career declined (1-2 points)	0	9	60	.47
Career not enjoyed (1-2 points)	0	15	70	.54
Less than 3 weeks vacation[b] (1-2 points)	19	33	43	.64
Failed marriage (1-3 points)	0	34	57	.80
Few social activities (1-2 points)	54	62	92	.54
Mental health				
10+ psychiatric visits (1-2 points)	0	9	32	.87
Use of mood-altering drugs (1-3 points)	0	9	32	.87
5+ days of sick leave per year (1-2 points)	3	11	41	.55
Life satisfaction				
Observer-rated dissatisfaction (1-5 points)	0	5	73	.60

a. Only the most unfavorable category for each outcome is illustrated.
b. Only variable not significantly associated with the global outcome variable at $p < .001$.
c. The group with the best psychosocial health received scores of 10-12, the middle group ranges from 13-17, and the worst group from 18-26.
d. Kendall's Tau b.

Six items operationalize the psychosocial efficacy dimension. The initial two assess work. Were the men:

still working full-time at 65 (1 point)
cut back (2 points) or
retired (3 points)?

Next, were their occupational responsibilities after age 60 at least as great as they had been at age 50 or had they become less effective?
Two items were then chosen to reflect the men's ability to play. One item asked:

Did they appear to regard work or retirement as enjoyable? (1 point)

Was their enjoyment ambiguous? (2 points)

Did they regard their work or their retirement as demeaning or boring?
(3 points)

Although in identifying overall psychosocial adjustment the second item—presence or absence of an enjoyable three-week vacation—did not seem as important at age 65 as it had at age 47, it was retained to maintain symmetry with the age 47 scale (Vaillant, 1975).

Two items assessed social relationships. On three occasions after age 50, the subjects, and on two occasions their wives, were asked a variety of scaled questions about both the stability and their enjoyment of their marriage. These scores were averaged, and cutting points were chosen to indicate a marriage that over the 15-year period of observation was:

consistently and mutually enjoyable (1 point),

of ambiguous stability (2 points), or

clearly unhappy or terminated by divorce during the period or nonexistent for reasons other than widowhood (3 points).

The item "few social activities" indicated that the individual did not engage in regular group activities with friends—for example, golf, bridge, or charitable enterprises. However, the men were by no means as socially isolated as the rater's strict interpretation of this item makes it appear.

The next three items reflect efforts to operationalize the mental health dimension. During the 15-year period from age 50 to 65, had the men

never visited a psychiatrist? (1 point)

made 1 to 10 visits? (2 points)

made more than 10 visits? (3 points)

Second, during the same period, had the men

never used mood-altering drugs (hypnotics, minor tranquilizers, antidepressants)? (1 point)

used such drugs for less than 30 days? (2 points)

used such medicine for more than a month? (3 points)

Third, because at age 47 the number of days of sick leave taken each year had been more highly correlated with mental than with physical health (Vaillant, 1975, 1979), this item was retained. The cutting point was five or more days of sick leave a year.

Finally, life satisfaction, the last dimension of psychosocial health, is a clinical assessment of the subject's own attitude toward his life between 55 and 65 and his expressed attitude toward growing older. An effort was made to discount the effects of either alcoholism or poor physical health per se. Greatest weight was given to the subject's own responses to the question asked at age 56 and again at age 64: Did he see the present decade as:

the happiest decade of his life? (1 point)
intermediate in happiness relative to the rest of his life? (3 points) or
the unhappiest decade of his life? (5 points)

Although it may be argued that subjective happiness cannot be accurately measured by a simple 5-point scale, a simple face-valid measure may be the best we can hope for. Certainly, the enormous literature (e.g., Diener, 1984; Hoyt & Creech, 1983; Larson, 1978) on life satisfaction in the elderly suggests little evidence that complexity of measure offers greater validity. Assessment of relative happiness will always reflect the crudest of approximations.

The values from the 10 items in Table 2.3 were summed to provide a global assessment of psychosocial adjustment, scores ranging from 10 to 26. The purpose was not to provide an arbitrary definition of psychological "health" and "successful" aging but to provide an empirical rank ordering of the men. Clearly, the presence or absence of predictive validity of such a scale must be assessed at some later date. Table 2.3 demonstrates that it was possible to identify 37 men who at 65 had experienced virtually none of the negative criteria. It was possible also to identify 37 men who had experienced negative outcomes in all three domains—life satisfaction, mental health, and psychosocial efficacy.

To make the ratings in Table 2.3, the independent raters had to integrate data from seven questionnaires, two wives' questionnaires, and interview material; therefore, their judgments on individual items showed modest variation. The right-hand column of Table 2.3 indicates the interrater reliability for each item. Interrater reliability for the total measure was 0.72 (Kendall's tau B).

Signs of Successful Aging

The sample's physical and psychosocial health having been outlined, Table 2.4 looks at the intercorrelations between several of this chapter's

Table 2.4   Intercorrelation of Different Dimensions of Successful Aging

	Physical Health, Age 63	Psychosocial Health, Age 47	Career/ Retirement Enjoyment, Age 65	Mood- Altering Drug Use, Age 65	Observer- Rated Life Satisfaction, Age 65
Global variables					
Physical health (age 63)	—	.23*	.13	.27*	.33*
Psychosocial health (age 65)	.36*	.51*			
Psychosocial Health Scale (age 65)					
Age at retirement	.13	.10	.31*	.15	.19
Career success	.23*	.25*	.37*	.18	.47*
Career/retirement enjoyment	.16	.25*	—	.16	.50*
Length of vacation	.01	.07	.16*	.02	.14
Marital satisfaction	−.13	.38*	.16*	.23*	.33*
Social activities	.21	.21	.11	.10	.18
Psychiatric visits	.20	.34*	−.02	.42*	.12
Use of mood-altering drugs	.27*	.41*	.16	—	.37*
Sick days	.19	.17	.19*	.34*	.31*
Observer-rated life satisfaction	.33*	.36*	.50*	.37*	—

NOTE: For this table, all variables have been scaled as if the most favorable score was low (e.g., little mood-altering drug use correlated positively with little evidence of physical illness).
*$p < .001$ (Spearman's rho).

operational dimensions of successful aging. In general, the individual facets of physical health and psychosocial health were only modestly associated with one another. Even the two global outcomes variables of physical and psychosocial health correlated at only $r = .36$. Internal analysis showed, for example, there were only 16 men who were included among the 41 men with excellent physical health and among the 37 men with the best psychosocial adjustment. By age 65, poor physical health was present in 16% of men with the best psychosocial health, and 51% of the men with the worst psychosocial health had either become chronically ill or died.

Physical health, after all, reflects only one dimension of successful aging. Table 2.4 also examines the interrelationships among the measures of psychosocial adjustment. In Column 2, the global psychosocial health scores derived 15 years earlier showed a significant relationship with the score at age 65 and with most of the individual items. The two exceptions were early retirement and long vacations. In this sample early retirement was a relatively poor indicator of overall adjustment; and at age 65 the capacity to take enjoyable vacations no longer reflected the discriminative power that it had shown at age 47.

Columns 3, 4, and 5 detail interrelationships among the three dimensions of psychosocial health at age 65. Two of the individual items—career and retirement enjoyment (Column 3) and tranquilizer use (Column 4)—were selected for this table as the best representatives of the dimensions of psychosocial efficacy and mental health respectively. Both showed the highest correlations with their respective dimensions. Even these variables, however, showed relatively modest correlation with the other variables in their set and even weaker correlations with the variables in the other sets. In contrast, observer-rated happiness (Column 5) showed a strong positive relationship with nearly every facet of successful aging.

Predictors of Successful Aging

As already noted, current physical health is moderately correlated (r = .36) with current psychosocial health. For this reason the association of antecedent predictor variables with psychosocial health was calculated only after physical health at age 63 was partialed out. In Table 2.5 ancestral longevity was estimated by computing the age at death of the subject's parents and four grandparents. Surprisingly, long-lived ancestors only weakly predicted good physical health at late midlife and psychosocial health not at all (see Vaillant, 1991). Indeed, even in a replication study on 90 of the now 75- to 79-year-old women in the Terman Study (Sears, 1984), ancestral longevity was only weakly correlated with vigorous late-life adaptation (unpublished data).

Assessment of childhood environmental strengths was provided by two independent raters blinded to the future, but with access to all data gathered at age 18 on several facets of the men's childhood. These data included several psychiatric interviews with the men and home interviews with their parents (Vaillant, 1974). Rater reliability was 0.71. Despite its crudity and its dependence on subjective clinical judgment, the scale's predictive validity over three to four decades has been as robust as the best measures from reviews of other prospective studies (Kohlberg, LaCrosse, & Ricks, 1970). Over the years the most powerful predictive subscales of the childhood environmental strengths scale were cohesiveness of the home and whether the boy's relationships with his mother and father were

Table 2.5 Correlation of Significant Antecedents With Successful Aging

	Good Physical Health (n = 172)[a]	Good Psychosocial Health (n = 173)[b]	Psychosocial Health Controlling for Physical Health (n = 172)
Predictors < Age 20			
Ancestral longevity	.15*	.10	.06
Childhood environmental strengths	.27***	.25***	.17*
Closeness to siblings	.22**	.26***	.20**
College pulse rate	-.09	-.30***	-.28***
Exercise in college	.14*	.22**	.18**
Predictors < Age 50			
Regularity of promotions	.15*	.28***	.24***
Use of mood-altering drugs	-.36***	-.47***	-.37***
Psychiatric visits	-.19**	-.37***	-.33***
Physiological symptoms with stress	-.16*	-.23**	-.18*
Alcohol abuse < age 50	-.28***	-.27***	-.17*

a. Health of one man unclassified.
b. So that the zero-order correlations could be calculated in the same manner as the partial correlations in the righthand column and in Table 2.7, Pearson's product-moment coefficient was used.
*p < .05; **p < .01; ***p < .001.

conducive to trust, autonomy, and initiative. What was also particularly interesting to observe in Table 2.5 was that at age 65 the simple 0-to-2 closeness-of-siblings subscale (2 = destructive relationship with siblings or no siblings, 1 = ambiguous data or no siblings, 0 = close to at least one sibling) proved as powerful a predictor of psychosocial health at age 63 as the full 20-point childhood environment scale or, for that matter, as any other single variable assessed before age 30.

A low standing-pulse rate during the men's college physical exam provided another predictor of "successful" aging. Previous work (Phillips, Vaillant, & Schnurr, 1987) has shown that for this sample this association was independent of physical fitness. We speculate that the predictive power of an elevated pulse rate may reflect social anxiety (see Kagan,

Reznick, & Snidman, 1988). Consistent with this, mental health evaluations between ages 30 and 50 were the best predictors of successful aging outcome. The number of psychiatric visits, the use of tranquilizers, and the presence of few physiological symptoms with stress between ages 20 and 50 (Vaillant, 1978) were significantly correlated with late physical and psychosocial health. None of the 21 men who were ever diagnosed as significantly depressed before age 50 (i.e., meeting *DSM-III-R* criteria for either dysthymic disorder or major depressive reaction) fell in the top quartile of psychosocial adjustment at age 65.

Other studies have suggested that income should be a powerful predictor of life satisfaction in old age (e.g., Diener, 1984). The present findings suggest that in future studies it would be important to control for mental illness and alcoholism that exert strong negative effects on income, before taking such findings at face value.

Table 2.6 illustrates that many other potential predictor variables known to be important in adolescence and young adulthood were not associated with successful aging. For example, childhood social class (lower middle to upper), stability of parental marriage, childhood parental loss, and college scholastic aptitude—variables often found to be associated with adjustment in young adulthood—were uncorrelated with long-term outcome. Similarly, extroverted personality variables assessed in college failed to predict healthy adjustment in later life (Heath, 1945; Wells & Woods, 1946). For example, "sociable" (i.e., general ease in social relationships) correlated with good psychosocial health in college ($r = .24$, $p < .001$) and at early midlife ($r = .13, p < .05$), and "vital affect" correlated with good adjustment in college ($r = .31$, $p < .001$) and in young adulthood ($r = .18$, $p < .02$). Neither is an important predictor by age 65. Perhaps most dramatic was the fact that the trait "psychopathic" (the psychiatrist's estimate of categorical psychological impairment in college) that correlated negatively with global college adjustment ($r = -.35$) correlated only $r = -.08$ with poor adjustment at age 65. Clearly people change over time.

Other variables in Table 2.6 were associated with either physical health or psychosocial health, but not both. For example, ancestral longevity assessed in a variety of ways was a better predictor of decline in physical health than of psychosocial health. By contrast, variables associated with good late-life psychosocial adjustment only included the absence of emotional problems in childhood, early adult psychosocial health, and the more surprising association between college standing pulse and outcome (Phillips et al., 1987) depicted in Table 2.5.

Table 2.6 Theoretically Important Variables That Did Not Predict
Successful Aging Outcomes

	Physical Health at Age 63 (n = 172)	Psychological Health at Age 65 (n = 173)
Neither physical nor psychological health		
Childhood social class	.01	.02
Stability, parental marriage	.05	.10
College scholastic aptitude	−.02	.07
"Sociable" in college	.02	.03
"Vital affect" in college	.01	.06
"Psychopathic" in college	.03	−.08
Not with physical health		
Childhood emotional problems	.05	−.14*
College psychosocial health	.05	.15*
Age 29 psychosocial health score	.01	.21**
Not with late midlife psychosocial health		
Ancestral longevity	.16*	.09
Number of octogenarians	.18**	.11
Death of a parent in childhood	−.15*	.03

*p < .05; **p < .01 (Spearman's rho).

Discontinuities

Table 2.7 illustrates that over time there was a diminishing concordance of adult psychosocial adjustment with that in earlier time periods. At four points in the men's lives (age 21, age 29, age 47 and age 65) independent assessments were made of relative psychosocial health. This global assessment was always the most powerful predictor of psychosocial health at the next age period. With the passage of time, not surprisingly, clear shifts occurred that could not be explained by simple chance variation.

That shifts in psychosocial health occur over time was perhaps most dramatically illustrated by the following observation (Vaillant & Schnurr, 1988). Of the 188 men still active participants at age 47, only 16 were consistently in the top quartile of adjustment during all periods of observation. Eighty-seven of the 188 men in this cohort could have been described as psychiatrically impaired in college or at age 29, 47, or 62 or

Table 2.7 Association of Psychosocial Health at Earlier Periods of Adult Life With Health in Late Life

	Age 21	Age 29	Age 47
Age 65 psychosocial health[a]	.16*	.29**	.44**

	Psychosocial Health at Previous Ages for the 37 Men With the Best Psychosocial Health at Age 65 (%)		
Top quartile	41	49	54
Middle half	57	38	45
Bottom quartile	3	13	11

	Psychosocial Health at Previous Ages for the 37 Men With the Worst Psycho ocial Health at Age 65 (%)		
Top quartile	27	25	8
Middle half	51	40	27
Bottom quartile	22	35	65

a. Partial correlation coefficient controlling for physical health at age 63.
*$p < .05$; **$p < .001$.

by meeting the *DSM-III* criteria for alcoholism or for some other *DSM-III* Axis I diagnosis. Only 10 of these 87 "impaired" men, however, fell in the bottom quartile of psychosocial adjustment at every point of observation. Perhaps the two most important variables in causing shifts from good to poor psychosocial health were the onset of poor physical health or of alcoholism. Of the 12 men who were in the top quartile at age 29 yet who were in the bottom quartile at age 65, 7 had developed alcoholism or poor health.

Case History

Most men in the Grant Study sample are still too young to be at risk for the major negative outcomes of unsuccessful aging—mortality, institutional living, need for multiple aids to daily living, and conflictual dependence on others for basic needs. Only two of our subjects have experienced Alzheimer's disorder, and none has yet been confined to a nursing home. But adaptation to these more melancholy aspects of aging must be addressed in any discussion of "successful aging." For the concept of successful aging can be valuable if we see it as process rather than product. Indeed, the concept of "successful aging" will be demoralizing to both subject and observer if successful aging is seen only as being "better" than others or being healthy all of one's days.

Successful aging must also reflect vital reaction to change, disease, and environmental imbalance. Indeed, the contemplation of successful aging forces us to reflect on human dignity. One of the subjects in the study described in this chapter expressed the dignity of aging and mortality a little differently when he wrote:

> What's the difference between a guy who at his final conscious moments before death has a nostalgic grin on his face, as if to say, "Boy, I sure squeezed that lemon" and another man who fights for every last breath in an effort to turn time back to some nagging unfinished business? Damned if I know, but I sure think it's worth thinking about. (Vaillant, 1977, p. 357)

Because the social sciences lack adequate metrics for assessing human dignity and "squeezed lemons," let me substitute a case of a Grant Study member, Dr. Eric Carey (a pseudonym), who died young.

Dr. Carey began life as a gregarious member of a close family. Both his parents were social workers in the spirit if not the letter of the phrase, and as a 13-year-old, Dr. Carey also had made a commitment to a life of service to others. The general experience of the Grant Study has been that Eriksonian tasks of intimacy, career consolidation, generativity, and keeper of the meaning are mastered in sequential order (Erikson, 1959; Vaillant, 1993; Vaillant & Milofsky, 1980). But if Dr. Eric Carey illustrates a life that violates such principles, there was no one else in the study quite like him. Indeed, Dr. Carey even violated the principle that good physical health per se has something to do with successful aging. For Dr. Carey is dead, but while dying he demonstrated a capacity to make meaning for himself and to keep meaning for others. Thus his late-life psychosocial adjustment put him among the most successful outcomes. For Dr. Carey's life suggests that death and retirement by no means reflect failure, that the capacity while alive to remain productive and generative provides pleasure and meaning.

Early on, Carey collected a sense of himself, consolidated it, and shared it with discretion throughout the 45 years that he revealed himself to the study. But all life events—and there were severe setbacks for this man—were moderated by his relationship to people, both on a personal and professional level. At age 23, when asked about his "fitness for his present work" (medical school), Dr. Carey wrote:

> Children fascinate me; I enjoy playing and working with them. . . . I get along well with children, enjoy taking the time to amuse them or circumvent their distrust of doctors; . . . I'm patient enough to do with children what many other people do not have time or patience to do.

Dr. Carey described what a pediatrician does, but there was also a sense of self-content in his words. It was not just a career, but the relationship and the skill in the relationship that came through. Later, at age 26, when Dr. Carey was asked what was stimulating or interesting about his career, he replied, "the opportunity for aid to children through increasing parental understanding" and that the meaning of his work was "to make a contribution to the community."

Dr. Carey had not only begun the work of generativity young, but also begun the work of growing old early. At age 26, the not-yet-crippled Dr. Carey had already told the study his "philosophy over rough spots": "That no matter what personal difficulty I struggle with others have survived worse; and that, fundamentally, there is a force of events that will carry us through even though at personal sacrifices."

At age 32 Dr. Carey developed poliomyelitis. Newly liberated from six months in an iron lung and knowing that he would never walk again, Dr. Carey responded as follows to a Thematic Apperception Test card:

> Here is a young boy who . . . started out in college with brilliant prospects, a bright future but becomes disillusioned with life, morose, despondent . . . and decides to end his life. He is apprehended in the process of jumping from a tall building. As he does so, he closed his eyes. Before them flashes a panorama of his past life, hopes aspirations, sadness of . . . failure, realizing then the agony of being cornered . . . the despondency to end his own life.
>
> He'll be examined by a psychiatrist and placed in a hospital for therapy. After months, his goals will be altered. After being in therapy a little longer, he'll get what he wants. He'll be able to be of use to society again, to go on to achieve that which . . . in later years will be satisfying.

By age 35, crippled by polio, Dr. Carey continued as both a pediatrician and a teacher. Confined to a wheelchair, he did not use his academic success as an excuse to withdraw from being a full-time clinician. His generativity was not derived from the old saw "Those who can, do; those who can't, teach." Nor did his pleasure in teaching come from didactic instruction, from self-aggrandizing telling. His success as a teacher came from enabling others, from, as it were, giving the self away. This process probably is vital to successful aging. Dr. Carey wrote that the nurses and the medical students he taught "seem to respond to increased participation and responsibility, in contrast to the passive roles they often play in our clinics." Later in the same questionnaire, he wrote of the fact that he worked as an active clinician from a wheelchair: "Others can get not only professional help but some measure of comfort from my carrying on as if nothing happened." Mentorship means to show and to share, not merely to tell.

Almost 20 years later, the progressively crippled Dr. Carey again expressed the challenge of old age: "The frustration of seeing what needs to be done and how to do it but being unable to carry it out because of physical limitations imposed by bedsores on top of paraplegia has been one of the daily pervading problems of my life in the last four years." But three years later at age 55, Dr. Carey answered his own challenge: "I have coped . . . by limiting my activities (occupational and social) to the essential ones and the ones that are within the scope of my abilities."

At 57, although he was slowly dying from pulmonary failure secondary to 20 years of muscular paralysis, Dr. Carey wrote that the last 5 years were the happiest of his life. "I came to a new sense of fruition and peace with self, wife, and children." He spoke of peace, and his actions portrayed it. During this time he had "let go" of his stamp collection, which had absorbed him for half a century; he had given it to his son. A year before his death, in describing to an interviewer his "risky anesthesia" and recent operation, Dr. Carey said, "Every group gives percentages for people who will die: 1 out of 3 will get cancer, 1 out of 5 will get heart disease—but in reality '1 out of 1 will die'—everybody is mortal."

At age 32, Dr. Carey had written of his work motivations: "to add an iota to pediatric knowledge, the sum totals of which may ultimately aid more than the patients I see personally." But it takes a longitudinal study to differentiate between real life behavior and facility with pencil-and-paper tests. That Dr. Carey's words were not pious good intentions but rather intimations of immortality was confirmed by the fact that when Dr. Carey died an endowment for a professorship in his name was raised to perpetuate his lifelong contribution to pediatrics. Throughout his life, his wife, children, colleagues, and patients loved him.

Generativity and keeper of the meaning are tasks to be mastered in the second half of life (Vaillant, 1993). But what does the term "keeper of the meaning" mean? Generativity and its virtue, care, require taking care of one person rather than another (Erikson, 1959). Keeping of the meaning and its virtue, wisdom, involve a more nonpartisan and less personal approach to others. Wisdom, unlike care, means taking sides impersonally. The focus of keeper of the meaning is with the collective products of mankind—the culture in which one lives and its institutions—rather than in the development of its children. Kotre (1984) separates the two components by observing that the targets of Eriksonian generativity must be both "the culture and the disciple, and the mentor must hold the two in balance" (p. 14). If the mentor puts too much into his mentees (i.e., "generativity"), "he neglects and dilutes the culture's central symbols. But if the preservation of culture is paramount [i.e., "Keeper of the Meaning"] he makes anonymous receptacles of disciples" (Kotre, 1984, p. 14). I believe that Dr. Carey mastered both tasks.

Summary

Ultimately, in any study of life span development the dependent variables for one phase of life must become the independent variables for evaluating the next stage. Thus the validity of this chapter's outcome measures must in part depend on their ability to predict the future. Put differently, how adequately might this chapter's definition of successful aging at age 65 serve as an intermediate variable on the developmental path toward becoming engaged, vigorous, and happy octogenarians? Clearly, it is too soon to tell.

Another criterion of an outcome measure is replicability. Replicability touches on one of the few real shortcomings of longitudinal research. Both cost and the vagaries of history make it not feasible to repeat a 40-year longitudinal study. An effective strategy will be to try to examine the same measures in this chapter in secondary analysis (Vaillant, 1993) of the Terman sample of women (Sears, 1984) and of an inner-city sample that has also been followed for 40 years (Glueck & Glueck, 1968; Vaillant, 1993).

Certainly this sample of 173 men was a biased one, and biased toward successful aging. The study members were white and male, and they had been selected for good physical health and high academic achievement. Most men received some graduate education and had forged their occupational careers during a time of American economic growth and prosperity. They had access to good medical care, practiced good nutrition, and had opportunities for exercise. On a more positive methodological note, such homogeneity of background allows their lives to cast light on certain variables associated with late midlife aging without interference from undue environmental adversity.

Perhaps the most striking finding was that absence of psychiatric vulnerability in young adulthood, absence of psychiatrist and tranquilizer use, and absence of depressive disorder were the most important variables predicting later psychosocial health. Other, more obvious potentially negative causal variables—shortened ancestral longevity, bleak childhoods, and alcoholism—appeared if anything more associated with physical decline. Still other variables, those in which common sense might have been picked as a predictor variable, were uncorrelated with outcome. Indeed, it was perhaps instructive that extensive exercise habits in college should predict psychosocial adjustment at 65 better than they did good physical health at 65, and that a warm childhood environment should predict late-life physical health better than it predicted happiness and psychosocial vigor. If we are to understand successful aging, we must learn to expect such surprises and to conceptualize the mind and body as a whole.

References

Diener, E. (1984). Subjective well-being. *Psychological Bulletin, 95,* 542-575.

Elder, G.H. (1974). *Children of the Great Depression.* Chicago: Chicago University Press.

Erikson, E. (1959). Identity and the life cycle. *Psychological Issues, 1,* 1-171.

Glueck, S., & Glueck, E. (1968). *Delinquents and nondelinquents in perspective.* Cambridge, MA: Harvard University Press.

Grinker, R., Grinker, R. R., Jr., & Timberlake, J. (1962). "Mentally healthy" young males (homoclites). *Archives of General Psychiatry, 6,* 405-453.

Heath, C. W. (1945). *What people are.* Cambridge, MA: Harvard University Press.

Hoyt, D. R., & Creech, J. C. (1983). The life satisfaction index: A methodological and theoretical critique. *Journal of Gerontology, 38,* 111-116.

Kagan, J., Reznick, J. S., & Snidman, N. (1988). Biological bases of childhood shyness. *Science, 240,* 167-171.

Kass, L. R. (1975). Regarding the end of medicine and the pursuit of health. *Public Interest, 40,* 11-42.

Kohlberg, L., LaCrosse, J., & Ricks, D. (1970). The predictability of adult mental health from childhood behavior. In B. Wolman (Ed.), *Manual of child psychopathology* (pp. 1217-1284). New York: McGraw-Hill.

Kotre, J. (1984). *Outliving the self.* Baltimore: Johns Hopkins University Press.

Larson, R. (1978). Thirty years of research on the subjective well-being of older Americans. *Journal of Gerontology, 33,* 109-125.

McArthur, C. (1955). Personality differences between middle and upper classes. *Journal of Abnormal and Social Psychology, 50,* 247-254.

Phillips, K. A., Vaillant, G. E., & Schnurr, P. (1987). Some physiological antecedents of adult mental health. *American Journal of Psychiatry, 144,* 1009-1013.

Rowe, J. W., & Kahn, R. L. (1987). Human aging: Usual and successful. *Science, 237,* 143-149.

Sears, R. R. (1984). The Terman gifted children study. In S. A. Mednick, M. Harway, & K. M. Finello (Eds.), *Handbook of longitudinal research* (Vol. 1, pp. 398-414). New York: Praeger.

Vaillant, G. E. (1974). Natural history of male psychological health: II. Some antecedents of healthy adult adjustment. *Archives of General Psychiatry, 31,* 15-22.

Vaillant, G. E. (1975). Natural history of male psychological health: III. Some antecedents of healthy adult adjustment. *Archives of General Psychiatry, 32,* 420-426.

Vaillant, G. E. (1977). *Adaptation to life.* Boston: Little, Brown.

Vaillant, G. E. (1978). Natural history of male psychological health: IV. What kinds of men do not get psychosomatic illness? *Psychosomatic Medicine, 40,* 420-431.

Vaillant, G. E. (1979). Natural history of male psychological health: Effects of mental health on physical health. *New England Journal of Medicine, 301,* 1249-1254.

Vaillant, G. E. (1984). The study of adult development at Harvard Medical School. In S. A. Mednick, M. Harway, & K. M. Finello (Eds.), *Handbook of longitudinal research in the United States* (Vol. 2, pp. 315-327). New York: Praeger.

Vaillant, G. E. (1991). The association of ancestral longevity with successful aging. *Journal of Gerontology, 46,* P292-P298.

Vaillant, G. E. (1993). *The wisdom of the ego.* Cambridge, MA: Harvard University Press.

Vaillant, G. E., & Milofsky, E. M. (1980). Natural history of male psychological health: IX. Empirical evidence for Erikson's model of the life cycle. *American Journal of Psychiatry, 137,* 1348-1359.

Vaillant, G. E., & Schnurr, P. (1988). What is a case? A forty-five-year follow-up of a college sample selected for mental health. *Archives of General Psychiatry, 45,* 313-319.

Wells, F. L., & Woods, W. L. (1946). Outstanding traits: In a selected college group with some reference to career interests and war records. *Genetic Psychology Monographs, 33,* 127-249.

3

The Work-Oriented Culture

Success and Power in Elderly Men

KENNETH SOLOMON
PEGGY A. SZWABO

Visualizing the relationships between work, success, and power, we have consciously focused on one type of masculinity, what we call the "traditional masculine gender role." Although some individuals argue that behaviors of American men have been changing over the past two decades or so, that argument largely ignores cohort differences and perhaps racial, socioeconomic, and geographic differences as well. The cohort effect is particularly important, because the older men we are writing about in this chapter were generally born and grew up before the Great Depression and often before World War I. Gender definitions were different then than they are today. These men learned their "sex role" (as did the women), and, as they became older, the effect of decades of reinforcement has led not only to few changes in the behaviors of these men but also, at times, to an entrenchment into more rigid gender-defined attitudes and behaviors. As a result, we use for our framework the traditional masculine gender role as it was experienced by the population of contemporary older men.

Our emphasis on this framework is based on theoretical and clinical considerations. Based on Rosow's (1967, 1973, 1974, 1976) and Atchley's (1982a, 1982b, 1988) work on continuity theory, we believe that an individual's personality, the core of which is set in childhood, remains

EDITOR'S NOTE: Kenneth Solomon died suddenly on April 12, 1994. This work was his last outlining his conception of the continuity of a masculinity for a cohort of men.

relatively stable throughout life. The specific social factors that shape many aspects of the individual's personality, including but not limited to gender, are rooted in the individual's age cohort. Thus, when a man is faced with different "opportunities for affirming [his] manhood" (Thompson, personal communication, December 6, 1993), the man's responses will be primarily based on factors relevant to his age cohort rather than on factors that derive primarily from the social forces at play at that time.

Of course, it is possible that behaviors may change; indeed, this is the goal of both psychotherapy and of one's adaptation to life. In a previous work, Solomon (1982b) noted that many of the behaviors that seem to represent a change in the masculinity of older men actually represent a change in surface behaviors and not in self-concept. Several authors have suggested that masculine roles dedifferentiate as men become older (e.g., Gutmann, 1976, 1991), and early research based on the simple observation of the behaviors of a cross-sectional cohort of older men seemed to support this view (Ames, 1975; Barrows & Zuckerman, 1976; Douglas & Arenberg, 1978; Gutmann, 1969, 1970; Keith & Brubaker, 1979; Lowenthal, Thurnher, & Chiraboda, 1977; Neugarten & Gutmann, 1968; Ryff & Baltes, 1976; Singer, 1963; Strong, 1943). However, some recent studies (clinical and nonclinical) that examine the self-perceptions and identity of older men suggest that the cores of the roles learned in a given age cohort of men do not significantly change as men age (Goldmeier & Fandetti, 1992; Jackson, 1974; Solomon, 1991; Vaillant, 1977, 1988).

In this chapter, we will discuss power, success, and work issues in relation to our belief that "masculine gender roles" are specific to one's age cohort and remain quite stable throughout life. We will also theorize that external experiences may change the outward behaviors of many men but that their self-concept is consistent with the role they integrated early in life. (We are aware of the few men who are able to make significant changes in their behaviors and self-perceptions of their roles, but they will not be the focus of this chapter because we believe that they are a minority in the age cohort we are discussing.) This chapter will focus on men born between the end of the Victorian era and the onset of the Great Depression. In it we first provide an overview of the relationship between work, power, success, and the traditional masculine gender role for one age cohort of older men. We will then examine the relationship between work and developmental issues and well-being in older men. We will particularly examine the importance of restricted opportunities for the expression of this traditional masculinity in the development of psychopathologic patterns of behavior in older men.

Manhood and Work

A primary descriptor of manhood for this age cohort was the man's work. The importance of work has been well documented in both research and theoretical publications for many decades (Astrachan, 1986; Brenton, 1966/1976; Bucher, 1976; Crites & Fitzgerald, 1978; David & Brannon, 1976; Emerson, 1985; Fasteau, 1974; Franklin, 1984; Gaylin, 1992; Goldberg, 1977, 1979; Gould, 1973/1976; Levinson, Darrow, Klein, Levinson, & McKee, 1978; Morgan, Skovholt, & Orr, 1979; Morse & Weiss, 1955; Nichols, 1975; Ochberg, 1987; Olson, 1978; O'Neil, 1981, 1982; Pasick, 1990; Pleck & Sawyer, 1974; Shostak, 1969/1976; Solomon, 1982a; Tausky, 1969; Tolson, 1977; Weiss, 1990; Wesley & Wesley, 1977; Williams, 1951/1976). Issues of success and power have also dominated much of the research and theoretical publications on masculinity. All the authors cited above have noted that there is a close relationship between men's work, success, and power. The literature clearly establishes this relationship for younger and middle- aged men (e.g., David & Brannon, 1976; Solomon, 1982a).

Perhaps this association was best described by O'Neil (1982), who noted that work, as part of the "masculine mystique," defines many of the boundaries of both success and power. The assumptions of the masculine mystique include the following beliefs:

1. "Men's work and career success are measures of their masculinity."
2. "Self-definition, self-respect, and personal worth are primarily established through achievement, success . . . on the job."
3. "Male power . . . [is] the primary means to becoming a success."
4. "Men's power, dominance . . . are essential to proving one's masculinity."
5. "Men's success in relationships with women is contingent on subordinating females by using power, dominance."

Recently, O'Neil, Helms, Gable, David, and Wrightsman (1986) identified men's experiences and worries with success, power and competition as the dominant component of their gender role conflict. Eisler and Skidmore's (1987) masculine gender role stress scale also recognizes interpersonal power issues and concerns, with success as prominent in men's well-being.

A decade ago, Solomon (1982a, 1982b) introduced a life span perspective to the discussion of the success and power dimension. His observation was that men's gendered behavior and identity do not change throughout life unless a conscious effort is made to do so. Men's outward behavior may change but for reasons other than a change in gender expectations and relations. Rather their outward behaviors represent a shift from participating in institutionalized roles to informal ones. These informal relations with people with whom older men are comfortable and intimate maintain well-established interpersonal strategies and patterns of interaction. Unless the immediate community and family members change their expectations and demand otherwise, older men do not change their behavior, and they are as masculine in their self-concept as they were when they were younger.

Most of the research on and theory about masculinity are primarily based on data collected from White, young or middle-aged, middle-class or working-class, urban or suburban American men. Because of an almost total lack of information about elderly men, the methodological problems with the published research on elderly men and work, and the unclear operational definitions of success and power—either as psychological or sociological constructs—extrapolation of the available data and thinking to the contemporary population of elderly men is fraught with problems. However, using what has been published in this area and drawing from our clinical experience, we can construct an image of the importance of work, success, and power for older men. Our clinical experiences suggest, for example, that non-White elderly men face many of the same issues and developmental tasks as do White elderly men, in spite of a cultural milieu that provides for different adaptive strategies. Therefore we will generalize the published data to all elderly men, knowing full well that this generalization may prove to be inaccurate once adequate research data are collected. This is unfortunate, but the paucity of data from other populations, as well as the paucity of data on the possibility (and probability) of multiple masculinities in elderly men, makes other frameworks impossible to use.

In addition, when discussing older men, we recognize that we are talking about several different age cohorts. As was clearly noted by Neugarten (1976, 1979), it is difficult to make generalizations for men aged 85 years that would be valid for the cohort of men aged 65 years. It is our clinical impression that individuals become less like their age peers throughout life. This enhances the probability that there are many masculinities in elderly men. Again, the lack of data precludes us from offering a discussion of these hypothetical gender definitions and behaviors and how they relate to elderly men and work.

Older Men and Work

Although it is true that the majority of older men are retired, it is equally true that a large minority of American men over the age of 65 remain in the workforce. In 1986, 43.3% of individuals aged 60 to 64 years and 10.9% of individuals 65 years old or over were in the workforce (U.S. Senate Select Committee on Aging, 1988). There were considerable gender and racial differences at all ages, but we will review only those data for men. Of men between the ages of 60 and 64 years, 54.9% were working. However, there were more white men than black men (55.7% compared to 45.9%) in this age group working. Although 16% of men aged 65 years or more were working, a rapid decline in work in this age group accounted for this number. Of those between the ages of 65 and 69 years, 25.3% of White men and 21% of Black men were working. From age 70 years, only 10.7% of White men and 7.2% of Black men were still in the workforce. The jobs held by men who continued to work were most likely to be in services industries, wholesale and retail trade, and agriculture, in that order. The occupations of older men were most likely to be professional or managerial, technical, sales, administrative, or service occupations. In other words, men who work in jobs that require physical labor were more likely to leave the workforce as they aged. The importance of this fact is that maintaining the traditional masculine gender role in the workplace is probably less of an issue for elderly blue-collar men than for other elderly men.

Not all elderly men work full-time. According to the U.S. Senate Select Committee on Aging (1988), only 52% of working men aged 65 years or more were working full-time in 1986. The other 48% were working part-time. Another unknown percentage of men also continues to work part-time in the "underground economy." For example, they may work as handymen, gardeners, chauffeurs, or in-home child care or adult care workers, and they may be paid in cash without any reports being made to Social Security and without any taxes being paid. These men are rarely counted as members of the workforce in official statistics.

Similar data were reported by Harris and Associates (1981). In addition, as noted by Rix (1990), older men who continue to work may shift jobs from those that require considerable physical labor to more managerial and administrative positions or to jobs that allow more flexible, creative, or shared hours and responsibilities. Other men may actually start a second career in old age, a career that may be the kind of work they had always wanted to do but could not pursue for various reasons. These changes in work activities have also been noted in many other societies around the world. For example, as noted by Gutmann (1991), older men may no longer work tending herds or farming, but they may work as chieftains, judges, and religious leaders in many rural areas of less-developed countries.

Multiple studies have noted that the performance of men in the work environment generally improves with aging. Although there may be some performance decrements related to physical changes, increased knowledge and an expanded repertoire of work-related techniques tend to more than offset these decrements. Studies by McEvoy and Cascio (1989), Waldman and Avolio (1986), and Avolio, Waldman, and McDaniels (1990) clearly demonstrate the increased productivity of elderly workers. However, this effect is noted only in jobs in which experience and problem-solving skills are needed. A diminished productivity of older workers was noted in jobs that require the repetitive performance of identical tasks (Avolio, 1991).

Another form of work for elderly men is that of unpaid employment. These worklike roles adopted by elderly men often require a regular schedule and a commitment to the completion of specific tasks. They also require a longitudinal commitment over time. Many of these roles come under the rubric of traditional volunteer tasks. Thus a man might be involved in his religious community or working at the front desk of a hospital 3 half-days a week. Although he may not get paid in cash, he may receive some form of compensation, such as a free lunch at the hospital cafeteria whenever he works. Other men may create new worklike roles for themselves, as Hochschild (1973) observed. We know, for example, of one 73-year-old retiree who functions as a chauffeur for many older men and women in his senior citizen's apartment complex. He maintains a busy schedule of driving them to doctor's appointments, supermarkets, the airport, etc. His only compensation is that they pay for gasoline. Occasionally, one or another of his "clients" treats him to lunch or dinner for compensation. He has remarked that his obligations and schedule are just as busy now as they were when he worked in paid employment. Few data are available on the frequency of unpaid (volunteer) work performed by older men.

Herzog and Morgan (1992) have attempted to develop a methodology to assess the value of all productive work, including volunteer work, in the elderly. They noted that elderly people aged 65 to 74 years were more likely to be engaged in productive activities than were individuals aged 75 years or more. They also noted that men were more likely to be engaged in these activities than were women. Individuals living alone had a higher probability of being involved in work-related activities. The same was true for individuals with a higher level of education. Finally, individuals at the lowest and the highest income levels were the ones most likely to continue to be involved in productive activities. By estimating the dollar value of unpaid work and adding it to the value of paid employment, they found that men aged 65 to 74 years averaged more than $11,000 per annum in the value of productive activities and that men aged 75 years and older averaged more than $4,000 per annum in the value of productive activities.

That so many older men continue to be active in work—the paid workforce, the underground economy, and volunteer work—is not difficult to explain. Many men must continue to work to assure financial survival either because they have no source of pensions or because they need to supplement their income (Herzog & Morgan, 1992; Howard, 1986; Mor-Barak & Tynan, 1993). These men often work in service industries. For example, one 67-year-old man continues to work full-time at his airport shoeshine stand. He does not want to work, but the amount of money he earns on the job is greater than the amount of money he would receive from Social Security. To maintain his standard of living, work is a necessity.

However, many men do not require the financial compensation from continued employment. These men choose to continue to work, some because of a desire to continue their productive involvement in society (Hayward, Grady, & McLaughlin, 1988). A 78-year-old physician spends approximately 4 hours weekly teaching medical students and residents. He is financially secure and does not require the modest stipend he receives. He stated that he feels obligated to continue these activities so that the young generation of physicians can make use of the knowledge and expertise that he has accumulated through more than 50 years of professional activities. Rubinstein (1986) noted that many men who were living alone wanted to be involved in part-time employment but refrained from doing so because of their belief that such employment was not available. He noted that the men who were most socially active were also those who were most likely to be involved in paid employment or volunteer work.

In spite of these factors, we believe that for many men, the reasons for their continued emphasis on worklike activities may be related, at least in part, to a strong cohort belief in the traditional masculine role. Some men simply never develop any interests outside of work, so their identity is wrapped up in their occupation (Solomon, 1982a). Other men become workaholics, an exaggeration of the work-oriented aspects of traditional masculinity. The interface between work, success, and power is an integral part of masculinity for younger men; it is likely to be no different for older men in the age cohorts discussed in this chapter. For those men who give reasons for continued work other than financial need, we believe that the underlying acceptance of the traditional masculine role is a major factor in the continuation of these work activities. We believe that the traditional masculine role serves as the infrastructure for the rationalizations that most men give for their decision to continue to work. The vicissitudes of this construct will now be discussed.

The Importance of Work for Older Men

Work and Success. We have theorized that part of the older man's identity is maintained by the continuation of meaningful task-oriented behaviors, including those that help support a household. Even for those men who no longer have to work to financially support a family, the vicissitudes of traditional masculinity continue to push and define the need to continue task-oriented public behaviors. It is by these behaviors that success is measured. The intensity of the need to maintain work activities will be determined, in part, on how much the preoccupation with the work role is integrated into the older man's ego structure. Whether or not the man's identity is synonymous with his occupational role, or if success manifested through his occupational activities is only a part of his ego identity, will partially determine the importance of work and identity in old age.

Success has both psychological components and external manifestations. The latter attributes are frequently used to specify how men adhere to the traditional masculine gender role. David and Brannon's (1976) conception of this is that men pursue and perhaps even become preoccupied with the external manifestations of success. Solomon (1982a) discussed the need to maintain these external trappings as an important aspect of the feedback loop that perpetuates work-related behaviors. The inner and more egocentric aspects of success may be less likely to lead to potentially negative consequences. The man, regardless of age, feels pride, a sense of accomplishment, and a sense of success with the completion of task-oriented behaviors. Men who are somewhat "liberated" from the traditional gender expectations usually experience as much of this aspect of success from the process of reaching a goal or completing a task as from the actual completion of the task.

Success and Power. Adler (1927/1965) believed that healthy masculinity included a pursuit of power over oneself but that maladaptive masculinity included the relentless pursuit of power over others. It is this preoccupation with power and control over others that has had major psychological and biological consequences for men as well as sociological consequences for the world.

For older men, it is frequently not the pursuit of power but the maintenance of power that becomes important. Most societies invest power in individual men, and this power may be used jointly for community good and personal gain. For example, in many African tribes, the elderly men maintain exceedingly powerful roles in their roles as chieftains, judges, and religious leaders, and they may have the power to decide on marriages, land transfers, and other vital aspects of community life (Gutmann, 1991). Preoccupation with the maintenance of power can prove to be devastating for older men. Mandatory retirement or health-induced retirement is a fact of life for many men. Men who are focused on power may perceive these life changes as a loss of power. This loss of power may be based in reality, for example, if caused by illness, which may cause some men to lose their position as "head of the household," except in name only. We believe that the consequences of an inability to maintain power are many, including but not limited to depression, suicide, and alcohol and drug use (Solomon, 1982b).

On the other hand, an inner power is maintained from the feelings of being able to control one's own destiny within reasonable existential limits. Thus power and success do not have to be pathological. Although power is the direct result of success, and power also breeds further success, Adler (1927/1965) also noted that power and success can be inner qualities that give pride, define self-worth, and even help shape the identity of men and women without leading to pathology. The results of inner power and success may be associated with adaptation, alloplasticity of personality, personal growth, and increased intimacy, as well as with mental health and happiness.

From an internal, psychological perspective, the maintenance of success and power requires certain complex psychological processes and the successful resolution of several developmental tasks (Wong, 1982). For Freud (who did not pay particular attention to his own psychological aging or the psychological aging of others), the key to successful living was *"lieben und arbeiten,"* "to love and to work." Freud clearly articulated his belief that the traditional masculine gender role and psychological health were synonymous at all ages (Freud, 1905/1953, 1925/1961; Wong,

1982). In addition, Freud considered the personality structure of the older individual to be highly rigid, perhaps too rigid to change.

Jung (1950, 1960; Wong, 1982) and Sullivan (1953; Mullahy, 1970; Wong, 1982) were the first theorists to disagree with the notion of a rigid, lifelong masculinity. Erikson (1950, 1980; Wong, 1982) further expanded on these ideas in his model of eight psychosocial stages of human development. For Erikson, the major developmental task old men faced was "ego integrity versus despair." As with Freud, he did not consider old age to be a time of growth or even continued task-oriented activities. Rather it was a time of review and reflection and the reintegration of one's past activities.

Based on the work of Whitbourne (1985; Whitbourne & Weinstock, 1979), Vaillant (1977; Vaillant & Milofsky, 1980), Levinson et al. (1978), Gutmann (1976, 1987), and others, one can rephrase stage theory to include the work and success-oriented activities of older men. Based on our clinical experiences and a life span perspective, it has become apparent to us that the actual developmental task of old age is continued generativity versus despair, not ego integrity. Generativity has been defined as personal growth, an increase in knowledge, and an increase in successful activities and continued creativity (Erikson, 1950). Certainly, these activities continue in old age. The key for the older man is to be able to find ways of maintaining generativity and opportunities to create and use options for continued successful behaviors.

Older Men's Developmental Tasks

Peck (1968) has developed these concepts even further. He defined three psychological tasks of older age. The first task is ego differentiation versus work role preoccupation. For Peck, it is imperative that the older man differentiate his work-related identity from other aspects of his self. Our society conspires against this, in that men's success is frequently measured in occupational terms and the external trappings of these occupational terms. For men, the mirroring process (Kohut, 1971) and the process of consensual validation of one's identity (Mullahy, 1970; Sullivan, 1953) are often based in the work environment and related work roles. We believe that the loss of work—paid, volunteer, and underground—can lead to ego dedifferentiation in old age, with subsequent psychopathology (Solomon, 1982b). To maintain feelings of inner success, the older man must find other task-oriented behaviors that are important enough to be integrated into his ego structure so that feelings of success and subsequent ego strength can be maximized. Ekerdt and DeViney (1993) suggest that many men begin this process by devaluing their jobs shortly before retirement, providing them a means of preserving feelings of success at a time when the men must separate from a life of behaviors that have defined their identities. It is our impression that for many an older man, meaningless task-oriented behaviors only enhance the older man's sense of helplessness, despair, and powerlessness, all of which may trigger psychopathology, alienation, or anomie.

Peck also discussed the tasks of body transcendence versus body preoccupation and ego transcendence versus ego preoccupation. Although the former is a developmental task for all aging individuals, perhaps it is not a task related to the maintenance of success of many men. Two major groups might be an exception to this comment. The first group consists of those older men who have invested in their bodies. Although these men are less common than younger athletes and so-called fitness freaks, there are many older men who pride themselves in continued achievements through the use of a healthy body. Although senior athletics or retaining one's good looks can be important sources of self-esteem, it is important for the older man to differentiate the maintenance of these physical virtues as one of the foci of his ego activities from an obsessive need to preserve "youth." For the older man who continues to associate success with the physical accoutrements of youth, the actions necessary for the maintenance of these physical attributes and athletic successes become obsessively connected with any feelings of inner success. One of our patients was a 67-year-old former professional athlete who continued a rigorous athletic training schedule combined with a Spartan diet. His insistence that he would not let himself get "old and flabby" led to a series of devastating athletic injuries, including a broken ankle, several episodes of hospitalization for dehydration, and several torn muscles. After a surgical procedure to repair a torn muscle, he began to exercise extensively, against his physician's advice. He literally undid the surgical procedure and required extensive surgery and rehabilitation. He became severely depressed and contemplated suicide as he considered himself "an old creep" who was "washed up and useless." He believed that none of his friends (all age peers) would want to have any social interaction with him because he no longer had his "youthful good looks."

The second group of older men for whom this task becomes particularly important is composed of individuals who have always had to work via physical labor. As physical strength declines with aging, it may be more difficult for these men to complete their occupational tasks. Should this force retirement or diminish work responsibilities, the older man may see this as a sign of failure or as "terminal aging." This may trigger either depressive symptoms or counterphobic behaviors that may have disastrous consequences. A 72-year-old retired construction worker remained physically active as a neighborhood handyman. He mowed lawns in hot weather without paying attention to his hydration. He suffered a near-fatal heart attack after attempting to shovel the snow off his lengthy driveway following a blizzard, ignoring his increased difficulty with breathing, palpitations, and chest pain.

The same is true for the last of Peck's developmental tasks: Ego preoccupation can occur when the older man thinks solely of what he has done, what he could have done, or what he should have done. In ego transcendence, the older man is able to use past experiences, strengths, and feelings of success as sources of ideas for continued task-oriented behaviors that are consistent with his physical, psychological, and sociological station in life. A 74-year-old man requested psychotherapy for his depressive symptoms. He became depressed after his job was terminated because the company he worked for went out of business. He spent his therapy sessions whining and bemoaning his fate as "an old man" and reminiscing about the "glorious days" of his past work. In the past, the patient was a highly respected and very knowledgeable member of his profession, but he believed that his colleagues had lost their respect for him because he was no longer working. While the therapist was away on vacation for several weeks, the patient was given the "homework" task of finding a new job. When the therapist returned from vacation, the patient canceled his next appointment, citing work responsibilities and a remission of symptoms.

Life span development theorists disagree on the continuity or discontinuity of change in the elderly. Solomon (1982b) conceptualizes the process as one of a relatively continuous series of new "crises" that force change and result in differentials in older men's generativity, mastery (and remastery), and well-being. From a slightly different perspective, Havighurst (Cavan, Burgess, Havighurst, & Goldhamer, 1949; Havighurst & Albrecht, 1953), like Peck and others, views this process as a continuous process punctuated by a series of large and small crises.

Several of Havighurst's developmental tasks include age-related changes and thus elderly men's need to face the effects of declining strength and health. More important, Havighurst points out the need to establish intimate relationships within one's own age group and to continue to maintain social and family obligations and roles. For contemporary elderly men, both of these tasks were once fulfilled in their work roles. Work provided a community of others and breadwinning opportunities. Thus, without work, it may become more difficult for the older man to feel successful, to experience mastery, or, in general, to engage in generativity tasks. The majority of men's friendships and intimate relationships generally occurred in the workplace. These are no longer available to him, and he is now being called on to use intimacy-seeking behaviors that he may no longer have, if indeed he ever had them. Most men ignored the task of developing intimate family relationships when younger because the pursuit of the breadwinner role was the primary focus of their activities. The results of this type of behavior are poignantly expressed in Harry Chapin's ballad, "Cats in the Cradle." In addition, if the man's family and social connections were defined by the breadwinner role, other problems may develop as this role becomes no longer available.

Developmental Stresses

Older men are faced with many stresses and many may involve anticipated or fantasized or threatened loss. In a work-oriented society, these include actual retirement, whether voluntary or forced, and a diminished ability to perform work-related tasks because of physical limitations or changes in the technology of the tasks. Other work-related stresses include financial insecurity. After retirement, the need to find meaningful goal-oriented tasks to replace "work" becomes a chronic stressor for many men. One can often hear an older man report that he "just cannot sit still."

Havighurst and Solomon have noted that one of the tasks facing men as they get older is that they no longer have the physical or sociological means to complete tasks that were valued when they were younger. Because success in American society is often defined by the external products of actions (material and symbolic), older men are less able to demonstrate these actions to any significant degree. The limitations on dominance and success serve as the focus for one of the major life crises facing older men.

Foremost of the role-limiting changes are the physical changes that occur with aging. There is the gradual aging process of declining physical strength, stamina, and physiologic reserve. This may affect older men's ability to express the task-oriented aspects of the traditional masculine role. For the man who has viewed success in physical terms, whether it be physique, speed, or strength, this may be particularly stressful. Even for ordinary men, these changes require adaptation. It may no longer be possible for the man to climb onto the roof of his home and clean out the gutters, which may affect his self-image as a successful homeowner. For men who do no physical labor, a slower gait or a tremor may represent growing weakness and in turn be seen as a loss of power.

For many older men, earlier success options are less likely to be available because of the natural decline in physical strength and endurance, even in the absence of health problems. If a man is unable to adapt to these changes and find another source of task fulfillment more in keeping with his physical limitations and changes, psychopathology may occur (this will be discussed shortly).

Many older men seem to start new task-oriented behaviors associated with the traditional feminine role, such as housekeeping, cooking, shopping, etc. Some authors (Gould, 1978; Gutmann, 1976, 1987, 1991; Levinson et al., 1978; Sinnott, 1977) suggest that these behaviors are evidence of an increased role flexibility and can lead to feelings of internal success among men. However, others (Silverman, 1977; Solomon, 1982b) suggest that older men do not integrate these behaviors as part of their ego structure and that they do not feel successful in the adoption of these behaviors.

This process may be punctuated by the onset of an acute physical illness. Although some illnesses, such as a myocardial infarction or a peptic ulcer, may actually be viewed as a badge of success, more often than not they force the older man to put his life and goals into perspective.[1] Our observations suggest that some men blame the illness on weakness and strive even harder to find an outlet for power. The sense of powerlessness is exacerbated by the belief—one might even say, the ur-delusion (a primitive and often magical false belief, held by the large majority of people in a society, that allows an individual to function psychologically in the face of a countervailing reality; Werner, 1948)—of many men that they are invulnerable. Few men actually link their lifestyle and a lack of preventive health care to their catastrophic illnesses in old age (Nathanson, 1977). We will use the example of one of our patients to graphically illustrate this point: A 69-year-old, hard-driving salesman suffered his third myocardial infarction in 2 years. In spite of warnings from his physicians, he continued to smoke more than three packs of cigarettes daily, to work up to 18 hours a day, to eat rich foods (and often eat "on the run"), and to try to control all aspects of his and his family's life. He denied that any of his behaviors were related to his illness. He blamed his heart disease on "bad luck," and insisted that his heart would heal just as rapidly at home (and at work) as in the hospital. He signed out of the Coronary Care Unit of the hospital against medical advice, returned to work 2 days after his heart attack, and had a fatal heart attack later that week.

Changes in the social support system may be equally devastating to the older man. The death, either in reality or symbolically (such as through dementia), of a spouse makes it very clear to the older man that he is not in control of his external environment, and that he cannot control the forces of nature or even the forces that act on the lives of other human beings. If the man, as husband, was in reality overcontrolling and "ruled the roost" with unchallenged authoritative power through personality, threat, or violence, this loss may be particularly devastating, because it then becomes the loss of a part of self. If the elder husband was less traditional than his contemporaries and loses his soulmate and partner, the loss may be equally devastating.

Older Men's Well-Being

Goldfarb (1968, 1974) and Solomon (1981a, 1981b, 1981c, 1982b, 1982c, 1984a, 1984b, 1985a, 1985b, 1989, 1990a, 1990b, 1993; Solomon & Szwabo, 1992) have written extensively on the response to developmental stresses in older people, particularly older men. Stressors, individually or in a slow build-up, can trigger a diminished sense of mastery of the older man's internal and/or external environment. Ironically, successfully mastering one's environment could be considered the epitome of external success, whereas mastering one's inner psyche could be the epitome of internal success. However, these stressors directly threaten the older man's sense of mastery over self or others. As a result, feelings of helplessness and ambivalent feelings regarding dependency are triggered for some.

Just as the traditional masculine role puts a premium on mastery and power, it puts an equal premium on the avoidance of dependency and helplessness. The older man who has internalized traditional masculinity creates stress for himself by his inability to acknowledge dependency on the help of others. This may then trigger more feelings of diminished mastery and even more helplessness and dependency. The external environment and other people in the social system do not respond to his increased dependency in a way that increases his feelings of mastery but, rather, create an interpersonal, family, or institutional system that leads to development and reinforcement of learned helplessness (Maire & Seligman, 1976; Seligman, 1975; Solomon, 1979, 1982c, 1990b). The older man may get stuck in a cycle of continual reinforcement of learned helplessness and dependency.

Some men maladaptively respond by becoming increasingly socially withdrawn so that others do not see them in an "unsuccessful" mode. Others try to maintain the external accoutrements of their past success, even as their domestic situation deteriorates. One of our patients, a 78-year-old retired business executive, suffered a series of severe financial setbacks. Although he continued to belong to exclusive clubs, remain active in community affairs, dress impeccably by buying new and stylish clothes, and eat at the community's finest dining establishments, his 150-year-old mansion was literally falling apart. Part of the roof had caved in and a porch had collapsed (both were in the back of the home and could not be seen from the road). He could no longer afford a housekeeper and caregiver for his demented wife, whose medical condition was deteriorating. Garbage accumulated in the home because he was too proud to throw out the garbage himself; he felt that such an activity was beneath his station. He bought new clothes (which he could not afford) rather than do any laundry. Both he and his wife began to drink heavily. Only the intervention of an astute attorney saved him from bankruptcy.

Because some older men hold a staunch adherence to the traditional masculine role, they may not be able to successfully navigate themselves out of this maze of learned helplessness and dependency. They then experience the stress effects of anger, fear, and sadness. These feelings are uncomfortable and may trigger a "search for aid" (Goldfarb, 1968, 1974). Unfortunately for the men who staunchly adhere to the traditional masculine role, successful coping at this stage frequently requires the verbalization of feelings. Alexithymia, or the inability to label and express feelings, is noticeable among some contemporary elderly men, because it is a concomitant of traditional masculinity.

Adaptive coping has been described in part by Reichard, Livson, and Peterson (1962) for these older men to include an ability to allow oneself temporary dependency and the verbalization of feelings, thereby expressing concerns with weakness and failure. A willingness to rethink and reconceptualize one's position and seek alternatives also aid successful coping. Unfortunately, nonadaptive coping is the result of becoming stuck in one aspect of the psychodynamic process or overconforming to specific aspects of the traditional masculine role. Reacting with hostility or defensiveness, for example, can be disastrous. An inability to express weakness and to become dependent on others, or an inability to express feelings, will lead to increased anxiety, which, in turn, as we have witnessed in our patients, will inhibit successful coping.

It is our belief that using "work" as an alternative to work can be particularly harmful because this mechanism will only reinforce the negative aspects of the traditional masculine role. Lawton (1985) along with Nahemow (Lawton & Nahemow, 1973) and Csikszentmihalyi (1975), would likely concur. They have discussed the need for elders to balance their activity levels with a need to create challenge and comfort and to avoid boredom and overactivation. However, many elderly men use task-oriented activities, not as a means of creating challenge and meaning in their lives, but as substitutes for a lack of leisure interests and as a means to avoid boredom; the usual result is either profound ennui or overstimulation. The existential hollowness rapidly becomes apparent to the older man who attempts to use work as a means of maintaining external success and power rather than as a means of guaranteeing inner satisfaction.

Conclusion

This chapter has examined the importance of the interdependent issues of work, success, and power in elderly men's lives. We have theorized from a continuity model that contemporary elderly men who were born and grew up before the Great Depression or before World War I have adapted to a model of manhood consistent with the masculine mystique and traditional masculine role that O'Neil (1982) and Solomon (1982a, 1982b) outlined. From this perspective, the traditional masculinities that were present in older men's youth continue to be significant in their Third Age. What we have written may not be true for all older men, because there are differing masculinities in different age cohorts of the elderly. For example, many middle-class young-old (Neugarten, 1979) men (aged 65 to 75) are more psychologically sophisticated than men in the previous generation. They may be more sensitive to their own feelings and roles, and may be more willing to change not only their behaviors but their core self-perceptions in the face of changing sociological forces in contemporary society. As younger cohorts, with an even greater variation in their masculinities, age in the decades to come, we would expect that both the changes from the traditional masculine gender role and from the increased variability of behavior and role will lead to a diminished importance of work and success and to an increased importance of interpersonal experiences and intimacy in their lives. Thus what we have discussed in this chapter may no longer be valid and is likely to need reexamination.

Note

1. How two famous men coped with this life crisis is illustrated by the attempts by the composers Franz Josef Haydn and Johann Sebastian Bach to complete their last works in the face of illness. Haydn, at age 71, had been retired from active composition for several years when he agreed to compose a series of six string quartets, in spite of his awareness of the early effects of a dementing illness (probably Alzheimer's disease). After completing the first two movements of the first quartet (Op. 103), he realized that his creativity was completely gone (indeed, this music is quite simplistic and more characteristic of the adolescent Haydn rather than the mature Haydn). Rather than face this insurmountable task, Haydn simply stopped writing and proceeded to rest on his laurels. Bach, on the other hand, was 65 years old and had almost completed "Die Kunst der Fuge" ("The Art of the Fugue"), when he suffered a severe stroke. Realizing that his life was at an end, he furiously dictated as much of the final fugue as he could. He died 5 days later, leaving behind an incomplete masterpiece, which curiously ends with the notes that spell out his last name!

References

Adler, A. (1927/1965). *Understanding human nature* (W. B. Wolfe, Trans.). New York: Fawcett.

Ames, L. B. (1975). Are Rorschach responses influenced by society's change? *Journal of Personality Assessment, 39,* 439-452.

Astrachan, A. (1986). *How men feel: Their response to women's demands for equality and power.* Garden City, NY: Anchor.

Atchley, R. C. (1982a). The aging self. *Psychotherapy: Theory, Research, and Practice, 19,* 388-396.

Atchley, R. C. (1982b). The process of retirement. In M. Szinovacz (Ed.), *Women's retirement: Policy implications of recent research* (pp. 153-168). Beverly Hills, CA: Sage.

Atchley, R. C. (1988). A continuity theory of normal aging. *The Gerontologist, 29,* 183-190.

Avolio, B. J. (1991). A levels-of-analysis perspective of aging and work research. *Annual Review of Gerontology and Geriatrics, 11,* 239-260.

Avolio, B. J., Waldman, D. A., & McDaniels, M. A. (1990). Age and work performance in non-managerial jobs: The effects of experience and occupational type. *Academy of Management Journal, 33,* 407-422.

Barrows, G., & Zuckerman, M. (1976). Construct validity of three masculinity-femininity tests. *Journal of Counseling and Clinical Psychology, 34,* 1-7.

Brenton, M. (1966/1976). The breadwinner. In D. S. David & R. Brannon (Eds.), *The forty-nine percent majority: The male sex role* (pp. 92-98). Reading, MA: Addison-Wesley.

Bucher, G. R. (1976). *Straight, white, male.* Philadelphia: Fortress.

Cavan, R. S., Burgess, E. W., Havighurst, R. J., & Goldhamer, H. (1949). *Personal adjustment in old age.* Chicago: Science Research Associates.

Crites, J. O., & Fitzgerald, L. F. (1978). The competent male. *Counseling Psychology, 7,* 10-14.

Csikszentmihalyi, M. (1975). *Beyond boredom and anxiety.* San Francisco: Jossey-Bass.

David, D. S., & Brannon, R. (1976). The male sex role: Our culture's blueprint of manhood and what it's done for us lately. In D. S. David & R. Brannon (Eds.), *The forty-nine percent majority: The male sex role* (pp. 1-45). Reading, MA: Addison-Wesley.

Douglas, K., & Arenberg, D. (1978). Age changes, cohort differences, and cultural change on the Guilford-Zimmerman Temperament Survey. *Journal of Gerontology, 33,* 737-747.

Eisler, R. M., & Skidmore, J. R. (1987). Masculine gender role stress: Scale development and component factors in the appraisal of stressful situations. *Behavior Modification, 11,* 123-136.

Ekerdt, D. J., & DeViney, S. (1993). Evidence for a preretirement process among older male workers. *Journals of Gerontology: Social Sciences, 48,* S35-S43.

Emerson, G. (1985). *Some American men.* New York: Simon & Shuster.

Erikson, E. (1950). *Childhood and society.* New York: Norton.

Erikson, E. (1980). *Identity and the life cycle.* New York: Norton.

Fasteau, M. F. (1974). *The male machine.* New York: McGraw-Hill.

Franklin, C. W. II. (1984). *The changing definition of masculinity.* New York: Plenum.

Freud, S. (1905/1953). Three essays on the theory of sexuality. In J. Strachey (Ed. & Trans.), *Complete psychological works of Sigmund Freud* (Vol. 7, pp. 136-243). London: Hogarth.

Freud, S. (1925/1961). Some psychical consequences of the anatomical distinction between the sexes. In J. Strachey (Ed. & Trans.), *Complete psychological works of Sigmund Freud* (Vol. 19, pp. 248-258). London: Hogarth.

Gaylin, W. (1992). *The male ego.* New York: Viking.

Goldberg, H. (1977). *The hazards of being male.* New York: New American Library.

Goldberg, H. (1979). *The new male: From self-destruction to self-care.* New York: William Morrow.

Goldfarb, A. I. (1968). Clinical perspectives. In A. Simon & L. J. Epstein (Eds.), *Aging in modern society* (Psychiatric Research Rep. No. 23, pp. 170-178). Washington, DC: American Psychiatric Association.

Goldfarb, A. I. (1974). Minor maladjustments of the aged. In S. Arieti & E. B. Brody (Eds.), *American handbook of psychiatry* (Vol. III, 2nd ed., pp. 820-860). New York: Basic Books.

Goldmeier, J., & Fandetti, D. V. (1992). Self psychology in clinical intervention with the elderly. *Families in Society, 73,* 214-221.

Gould, R. (1973/1976). Measuring masculinity by the size of a paycheck. In D. S. David & R. Brannon (Eds.), *The forty-nine percent majority: The male sex role* (pp. 113-118). Reading, MA: Addison-Wesley.

Gould, R. (1978). *Transformations.* New York: Simon & Shuster.

Gutmann, D. (1969). The country of old men: Cross cultural studies in the psychology of later life. In *Occasional papers in gerontology* (No. 5). Ann Arbor, MI: Institute of Gerontology.

Gutmann, D. (1970). Female ego styles and generational conflict. In J. M. Bardwick, E. Donuvan, & M. S. Horner (Eds.), *Feminine personality and conflict.* Belmont, CA: Brooks/Cole.

Gutmann, D. (1976). Individual adaptation in the middle years: Developmental issues in the masculine mid-life crisis. *Journal of Geriatric Psychiatry, 9,* 41-77.

Gutmann, D. (1987). *Reclaimed powers: Toward a new psychology of men and women in later life.* New York: Basic Books.

Gutmann, D. (1991). The cross-cultural perspective: Notes toward a comparative psychology of aging. In J. E. Birren & K. W. Schaie (Eds.), *Handbook of the psychology of aging* (3rd ed.). New York: Academic Press.

Gutmann, D. (1991). Individual adaptation in the middle years. Development issues in the masculine mid-life crisis. *Journal of Geriatric Psychiatry, 9,* 41-77.

Harris, L., & Associates (1981). *Aging in the eighties: America in transition.* Washington, DC: National Council on the Aging.

Havighurst, R. J., & Albrecht, R. (1953). *Older people.* New York: Longmans, Green.

Hayward, M. D., Grady, W. R., & McLaughlin, S. D. (1988). Recent changes in mortality and labor force behavior among older Americans: Consequences for nonworking life expectancy. *Journals of Gerontology: Social Sciences, 43,* S194-S199.

Herzog, A. R., & Morgan, J. N. (1992). Age and gender differences in the value of productive activities. Four different approaches. *Research on Aging, 14,* 169-198.

Hochschild, L. (1973). *The unexpected community.* Englewood Cliffs, NJ: Prentice Hall.

Howard, M. I. (1986). Employment of retired-worker women. *Social Security Bulletin, 49*(3), 4-18.

Jackson, D. W. (1974). Advanced aged adults' reflection of middle age. *The Gerontologist, 14,* 255-257.

Jung, C. G. (1950). Concerning the archetypes, with special reference to the anima concept. In *Collected works* (Vol. 9, Part 1). Princeton, NJ: Princeton University Press.

Jung, C. G. (1960). The structure and dynamics of the psyche. In *Collected works* (Vol. 8). Princeton, NJ: Princeton University Press.

Keith, P. M., & Brubaker, T. H. (1979). Male household roles in later life: A look at masculinity and marital relationships. *Family Coordinator, 28,* 497-502.

Kohut, H. (1971). *The analysis of the self.* New York: International Universities Press.

Lawton, M. P. (1985). Activities and leisure. *Annual Review of Gerontology and Geriatrics, 5,* 127-164.

Lawton, M. P., & Nahemow, L. (1973). Ecology and the aging process. In C. Eisdorfer & M. P. Lawton (Eds.), *Psychology of adult development and aging.* Washington, DC: American Psychological Association.

Levinson, D. J., Darrow, C. N., Klein, E. B., Levinson, M. H., & McKee, B. (1978). *The seasons of a man's life.* New York: Knopf.

Lowenthal, M. F., Thurnher, M., & Chiraboda, D. (1977). *Four stages of life.* San Francisco: Jossey-Bass.

Maire, S. F., & Seligman, M. E. P. (1976). Learned helplessness: Theory and evidence. *Journal of Experimental Psychology, 105,* 3-46.

McEvoy, G. M., & Cascio, W. F. (1989). Cumulative evidence of the relationship between age and job performance. *Journal of Applied Psychology, 74,* 11-17.

Mor-Barak, M. E., & Tynan, M. (1993). Older workers and the workplace: A new challenge for occupational social work. *Social Work, 38,* 45-55.

Morgan, J. I., Skovholt, T. M., & Orr, J. M. (1979). Career counseling with men: The shifting focus. In S. G. Weinroch (Ed.), *Career counseling: Theoretical and practical perspectives* (pp. 260-266). New York: McGraw-Hill.

Morse, N. C., & Weiss, R. S. (1955). The function and meaning of work and the job. *American Sociological Review, 20,* 191-198.

Mullahy, P. (1970). *Psychoanalysis and interpersonal psychiatry: The contributions of Harry Stack Sullivan.* New York: Science House.

Nathanson, C. A. (1977). Sex roles as variables in preventive health behavior. *Journal of Community Health, 3,* 142-155.

Neugarten, B. L. (1976). Adaptation and the life cycle. *Counseling Psychology, 6,* 16-20.

Neugarten, B. L. (1979). Time, age, and the life cycle. *American Journal of Psychiatry, 136,* 887-894.

Neugarten, B. L., & Gutmann, D. (1968). Age-sex roles and personality in middle age. A thematic apperception study. In B. L. Neugarten (Ed.), *Middle age and aging* (pp. 58-71). Chicago: University of Chicago Press.

Nichols, J. (1975). *Men's liberation: A new definition of masculinity.* New York: Penguin.

Ochberg, R. L. (1987). The male career code and the ideology of role. In H. Brod (Ed.), *The making of masculinities: The new men's studies* (pp. 173-191). Boston: Allen & Unwin.

Olson, K. (1978). *Hey man! Open up and live.* New York: Fawcett.

O'Neil, J. M. (1981). Male sex role conflicts, sexism, and masculinity: Psychological implications for men, women and the counseling psychologist. *Journal of Counseling Psychology, 9,* 61-80.

O'Neil, J. M. (1982). Gender-role conflict and strain in men's lives. Implications for psychiatrists, psychologists, and other human-service providers. In K. Solomon & N. B. Levy (Eds.), *Men in transition: Theory and therapy* (pp. 5-44). New York: Plenum.

O'Neil, J. M., Helms, B. J., Gable, R. K., David, L., & Wrightsman, L. S. (1986). Gender-role conflict scale: College men's fear of femininity. *Sex Roles, 14,* 335-350.

Pasick, R. (1990). Raised to work. In R. L. Meth, R. S. Pasick, B. Gordon, J. A. Allen, L. B. Feldman, & S. Gordon (Eds.), *Men in therapy: The challenge of change* (pp. 35-53). New York: Guilford.

Peck, R. C. (1968). Psychological development in the second half of life. In B. L. Neugarten (Ed.), *Middle age and aging.* Chicago: University of Chicago Press.

Pleck, J. H., & Sawyer, J. (1974). *Men and masculinity.* Englewood Cliffs, NJ: Prentice Hall.

Reichard, S., Livson, F., & Peterson, P. G. (1962). *Aging and personality: A study of 87 older men.* New York: John Wiley.

Rix, S. E. (1990). *Older workers: Choices and challenges.* Santa Barbara, CA: ABC-CLIO.

Rosow, I. (1967). *Social integration of the aged.* New York: Free Press.

Rosow, I. (1973). The social context of the aging self. *The Gerontologist, 13,* 82-87.

Rosow, I. (1974). *Socialization to old age.* Berkeley: University of California Press.

Rosow, I. (1976). Status and role change through the life span. In R. H. Binstock & E. Shanas (Eds.), *Handbook of aging and the social sciences* (pp. 457-482). New York: Van Nostrand Reinhold.

Rubinstein, R. L. (1986). *Singular paths: Old men living alone.* New York: Columbia University Press.

Ryff, C. D., & Baltes, P. B. (1976). Value transition and adult development in women: The instrumentality-terminality sequence hypothesis. *Developmental Psychology, 12,* 567-568.

Seligman, M. E. P. (1975). *Helplessness.* San Francisco: Freeman.

Shostak, A. B. (1969/1976). Blue-collar work. In D. S. David & R. Brannon (Eds.), *The forty-nine percent majority: The male sex role* (pp. 98-106). Reading, MA: Addison-Wesley.

Silverman, M. (1977). The old man as woman: Detecting stereotypes of aged men with a femininity scale. *Perceptual and Motor Skills, 44,* 336-338.

Singer, M. T. (1963). Personality measurements in the aged. In J. E. Birren, R. N. Butler, & S. W. Greenhouse (Eds.), *Human aging: A biological and behavioral study.* Washington, DC: U.S. Government Printing Office.

Sinnott, J. D. (1977). Sex-role inconstancy, biology, and successful aging. A dialectical model. *The Gerontologist, 17,* 459-463.

Solomon, K. (1979). Social antecedents of learned helplessness in the elderly in the health care setting. In E. P. Lewis, L. D. Nelson, D. H. Scully, & J. S. Williams (Eds.), *Sociological research symposium proceedings* (Vol. IX, pp. 188-192). Richmond: Virginia Commonwealth University.

Solomon, K. (1981a). The elderly patient. In J. A. Spittell, Jr., & E. B. Brody (Eds.), *Clinical medicine: Vol. XII. Psychiatry* (pp. 1-14). Hagerstown, MD: Harper & Row.

Solomon, K. (1981b). The masculine gender role and its implications for the life expectancy of older men. *Journal of the American Geriatrics Society, 29,* 14-18.

Solomon, K. (1981c). Personality disorders in the elderly. In J. R. Lion (Ed.), *Personality disorders: Diagnosis and management* (2nd ed., pp. 310-338). Baltimore: Williams & Wilkins.

Solomon, K. (1982a). The masculine role: Description. In K. Solomon & N. B. Levy (Eds.), *Men in transition: Theory and therapy* (pp. 45-76). New York: Plenum.

Solomon, K. (1982b). The older man. In K. Solomon & N. B. Levy (Eds.), *Men in transition: Theory and therapy* (pp. 205-240). New York: Plenum.

Solomon, K. (1982c). Social antecedents of learned helplessness in the health care setting. *The Gerontologist, 22,* 282-287.

Solomon, K. (1984a). The geriatric patient with cognitive dysfunction. In L. Robinson (Ed.), *Psychological aspects of the care of hospitalized patients* (4th ed., pp. 105-124). Philadelphia: F. A. Davis.

Solomon, K. (1984b). Psychosocial crises of older men. *Hillside Journal of Clinical Psychiatry, 6,* 123-134.

Solomon K. (1985a). Mental health and the elderly. In A. Monk (Ed.), *Handbook of gerontological services* (pp. 79-106). New York: Van Nostrand Reinhold.

Solomon, K. (1985b). Psychodynamic psychotherapy with the elderly. In M. Bright, E. Stilwell, & M. Tayback (Eds.), *Proceedings of the second annual meeting and scientific conference of the Maryland Gerontological Association* (pp. 17-21). Baltimore: Maryland Gerontological Association.

Solomon, K. (1989). Psychosocial dysfunction in the aged: Assessment and intervention. In O. L. Jackson (Ed.), *Physical therapy of the geriatric patient* (2nd ed., pp. 95-127). New York: Churchill Livingstone.

Solomon, K. (1990a). Learned helplessness in the elderly: Theoretic and clinical implications. *Occupational Therapy in Mental Health, 10*(3), 31-51.

Solomon, K. (1990b). Mental health and the elderly. In A. Monk (Ed.), *Handbook of gerontological services* (2nd ed., pp. 228-267). New York: Columbia University Press.

Solomon, K. (1991). The psychodynamics of male chauvinism in an elderly man. *The Clinical Gerontologist, 10*(3), 23-28.

Solomon, K. (1993). Behavioral and psychotherapeutic interventions in the nursing home. In P. A. Szwabo & G. T. Grossberg (Eds.), *Problem behaviors in long-term care: Recognition, diagnosis, and treatment* (pp. 147-162). New York: Springer.

Solomon, K., & Szwabo P. (1992). Psychotherapy for patients with dementia. In J. E. Morley, R. Coe, R. M. Strong, & G. T. Grossberg (Eds.), *Memory functioning and aging related disorders* (pp. 295-319). New York: Springer.

Strong, E. K. (1943). *Vocational interests of men and women.* Stanford, CA: Stanford University Press.

Sullivan, H. S. (1953). *The interpersonal theory of psychiatry.* New York: Norton.

Tausky, C. (1969). Meaning of work among blue collar men. *Pacific Sociological Review, 12*, 49-55.

Tolson, A. (1977). *The limits of masculinity: Male identity and women's liberation.* New York: Harper & Row.

U.S. Senate Select Committee on Aging. (1988). *Aging America: Trends and projections.* Washington, DC: U.S. Department of Health and Human Services.

Vaillant, G. E. (1977). *Adaptation to life.* Boston: Little, Brown.

Vaillant, G. E. (1988). Attachment, loss and rediscovery. *Hillside Journal of Clinical Psychiatry, 10*, 148-164.

Vaillant, G. E., & Milofsky, E. (1980). Natural history of male psychological health: Vol. IX. Empirical evidence for Erikson's model of the life cycle. *American Journal of Psychiatry, 137*, 1348-1359.

Waldman, D. A., & Avolio, B. J. (1986). A meta-analysis of age differences in job performance. *Journal of Applied Psychology, 71*, 33-38.

Weiss, R. S. (1990). *Staying the course: The emotional and social lives of men who do well at work.* New York: Free Press.

Werner, H. (1948). *Comparative psychology of mental development* (rev. ed.). New York: International Universities Press.

Wesley, F., & Wesley, C. (1977). *Sex role psychology.* New York: Human Sciences Press.

Whitbourne, S. K. (1985). The psychological construction of the life span. In J. E. Birren & K. W. Schaie (Eds.), *Handbook of the psychology of aging* (2nd ed., pp. 594-618). New York: Van Nostand Reinhold.

Whitbourne, S. K., & Weinstock, C. S. (1979). *Adult development: The differentiation of experience.* New York: Holt, Rinehart & Winston.

Williams, R. M., Jr. (1951/1976). Achievement and success. In D. S. David & R. Brannon (Eds.), *The forty-nine percent majority: The male sex role* (pp. 106-113). Reading, MA: Addison-Wesley.

Wong, M. R. (1982). Psychoanalytic-developmental theory and the development of male gender identity. In K. Solomon & N. B. Levy (Eds.), *Men in transition: Theory and therapy* (pp. 77-98). New York: Plenum.

4

Development and Pathology in Postparental Men

A Community Study

DAVID GUTMANN
MARGARET HELLIE HUYCK

This chapter takes up the unfinished task (Gutmann, 1990) of extending a developmental geropsychology into the field and practice of clinical geropsychology. Gutmann's earlier studies (1964, 1987, 1990; Huyck & Gutmann, 1992) have indicated that older men experience reorganization of their sexual nature[1] in the transition to postparental life, and that some older men's lives are marked by strains of adapting to changing versions of manhood. As it is in adolescence, so can it be in adulthood: The sources of development and growth for one man may drive another man's desperate psychopathology.

But before we consider its possible derailments, we will first briefly review the main sequence, the course of normal development in late adulthood. Gutmann has argued (1964, 1987) that the developmental trajectory is not completed for males or females in early life. Thus, although the condition of being parented is necessary for human development to go forward in childhood, the state of being parental is a condition of equal force and dignity, powerful enough to drive psychosocial development in adulthood, and even in the postreproductive years. The parental and postparental periods are the second and third ages of human development.

Gutmann's developmental model (1964, 1987) holds that, although societies have different ideas as to the developmental end points, men and women in all cultures experience a profound psychic reorganization in early adulthood and again in later life. Across traditional and modernizing societies, the requirements of parenting and the later emptying of the parental nest are preemptive enough to orchestrate normal psychosocial development. As a primary experience, the chronic emergency of parenthood drives the reorganization of the human psyche, and parental responsibilities define the developmental trajectory of early and late adulthood. Finally, it is the parental and postparental stages, rather than ad hoc adaptations to the losses and insults of aging, that drive and direct normal development in later life.

In the postparental stanza of men's lives, the gender constructions that had underwritten the active parenting years are revised. No longer are the realities for men and women located in separate parental orbits and activities. Instead, the psychic and social worlds of older men and women converge. As emeritus parents, older men and older women are freed to move jointly toward the late-life conditions of gender expansion, sometimes referred to as *androgyny*. Older men leave behind the sexual and role masculinity that parenthood enforces to experience a broadened gender style. They are unshackled from the parental restraints that require them to be stereotypically masculine fathers. Exempted now, they can reclaim some of their blunted "feminine" component and experience new potentials as resources of an expanded self. Rekindling such qualities of self, they move out to a spiritual (rather than a physical) perimeter, participate in culture tending, engage in noninstrumental relationships, and, in doing so, reveal an understructure of hitherto hidden affectional and cognitive potentials (La Bouvie-Vief & Hakim-Larson, 1989). Men begin to live out directly, to own as part of themselves the accommodative qualities of sensuality, affiliation, and nurturance.

Across societies, we see a similar process of women expanding their core sense of gender; women generally become more independent, unsentimental, and confident in asserting their own desires. The consequences of this internal revolution, this shift in the politics of self, are that the sharp gender distinctions of earlier, actively parental adulthood break down and that each sex incorporates qualities and behaviors previously associated with the other.[2]

The Stressful Passage to Postparental Androgyny

The tendency for older men and women to become more androgynous, to take on appetites, attitudes, and even behaviors characteristic of the opposite sex, has been studied as it affects the personality and behavior of normal individuals in this and other cultures. This phenomenon was first identified by Carl Jung (1933) on the basis of clinical evidence, and it was first studied empirically in the United States and other cultures by Gutmann (1964).

Despite his informal study methods, Jung quite accurately described the healthy as well as the pathological outcomes of the gender shifts that mark later life. He observed that the "sharpness of mind" of the older wife as well as the unexpected "softness" of the aging husband could lead to marital troubles for the couple and to neurotic difficulties for the individuals who experience such change in themselves. Starting with Neugarten and Gutmann (1958), many investigators (Atchley, 1976; Benedek, 1952; Brenneis, 1975; Brown, 1985; Feldman, Biringen, & Nash, 1981; Galler, 1977; Gold, 1969; Hurlbert, 1962; Huyck, 1989, 1991, 1992; Jacobowitz, 1984; Jaslow, 1976; Leonard, 1961; Levinson, Darrow, Klein, Levinson, & McKee, 1978; Lewis, 1965; Lowenthal, Thurnher, & Chiriboga, 1975; Ripley, 1984; Shanan, 1978; Streib, 1968; Tachibana, 1962; Van Arsdale, 1981) have since studied and confirmed this bimodality of the later years in community-dwelling, nonclinical populations. However, they have not followed up on Jung's clinical intuition: They have not studied the contributions of this normal, developmental stage to late-onset psychopathology. Although speculation about these matters is sometimes found in the literature, no investigator has attempted careful empirical studies of those individuals who convert an expectable and often desirable transformation into a vexing stressor, the precipitant of symptoms and psychopathology. Gutmann's clinical studies of the postparental period (see Gutmann, 1987, 1990; Gutmann, Grunes, & Griffin, 1982) confirm Jung's original insight into the clinical risks of late androgyny: He predicted that pathology would sometimes result from this development, and his insight appears to be as correct today as when it was first put forward.

Senior Androgyny and Severe Clinical Conditions

The next task seemed clear: To extend the reach and power of the "developmental" insights by applying them to the clinical pictures presented by older victims of late-onset psychopathology. Thus, for the past 15 years, colleagues in clinical geropsychology at Northwestern University Medical School have approached appropriate older adults with an implicit question: Is this patient reacting catastrophically to growth potentials rather than the usual suspects—the losses that have been end-lessly enumerated by conventional geriatricians? In other words, are these late-onset patients reacting with a kind of anaphylactic shock to their own growth potentials, construing—like many adolescents—new develop-ment as though it were a grievous loss?

The Northwestern group has found that, although the "contrasexual" shift is universal, it is by no means reacted to as "normal" by all adults. Instead, it is all too frequently a cause of late-onset (often first-onset) affective disorders in middle-aged and young-old patients. Thus we find that a significant number of men and women, without prior history of psychiatric symptoms, appear to have specific sensitivities, particularly to later life changes that enhance their bimodality. In many cases, these same patients have shrugged off, without pathological consequences, threats and pressures that loom much larger on any objective register of stress: They have survived combat in war, widowhood, or lethal illness with grace and even good humor, but they are devastated by the normal changes of the postparental years, those that attack their sense of being unequivocally "feminine" or "masculine."

It is not simply the loss of gender clarity within the self that proves to be traumatic, but also the corresponding changes within the spouse. This pathogenic linkage between the anxieties of the aging husband and the changing psychology of the wife became evident to Gutmann et al. (1982) when their group studied, via diagnostic interviews and projective tests, a sample of 82 older veterans hospitalized for the first time with severe affective disorders (e.g., depression, acute anxiety, paranoia). Contrary to the conventional geropsychiatric wisdom, which holds that such late-onset dis-orders are almost always precipitated by clear catastrophes, in more than half of the cases there was no drastic loss of health, income, kin, or employment. Instead, these aging veterans, who once faced mortal enemies, now fear their own emerging passivity and their consequent vulnerability to newly assertive wives: As one man put it, "My wife is like a Sherman tank!"

It was only when our Northwestern group investigated the predisposing aspects of patient personality, including developmental history, covert per-sonal myths, and major ego defenses, that we came to understand the subjectivity of their stress as well as the predisposing personality constella-tions that rendered such stressors particularly traumatic for these patients. We came to recognize two major classes of predisposed individuals: dystonic dependent men and syntonic dependent men. The dystonic dependent men produce fewer but more severe casualties; they will be presented first.

The Dystonic Dependent Older Men

In their impressionable, formative years, these men had known weak or psychologically absent fathers and powerful, sometimes destructively aggressive mothers. They denied their own sense of Oedipal complicity in the father's weakness or absence by blaming the overpowering mother: She (and not themselves) had gutted the father; she had driven him from the home.

In reaction, swearing that they would never suffer their father's shameful fate, these men typically married kindly, biddable, even adoring women—the perceived opposites of their intimidating mothers. But as the gender shift of their own postparental years renders them milder and toughens their wives, these men become disturbed. For them, a traumatic history is being repeated. Their father's fate at the hands of a powerful, demasculinizing wife has finally caught up with them. Thus it is not some undifferentiated barrage of unspecified "losses" that brings about the male patients' symptoms and affective disorders, but a quite specific sequence of interactions between predisposing vulnerabilities in themselves and specific dangers represented to them by their wives.

These proud but at-risk men had preserved a tenuous sense of masculinity by taking risks, by demonstrating that they were not like their cowardly fathers, that others rather than themselves were the fearful "Mama's boys," and that their wives (again, rather than themselves) were clearly the women. But in their later years, it is too late for them to be in the forefront of the battle; and their wives, who were supposed to be their "little women," had also changed and now refuse to be the holders of the husband's feminine side. Predictably, these men are shocked, and their unconscious reactions of shame and rage can fuel paranoid sensitivities— "Why do those guys say that I'm gay?"—as well as suicidal attempts to kill off the corrupted "female" part of themselves.

It is important to remember that we are describing the husband's perceptions of his wife's behavioral changes. This does not necessarily mean that the wife would be evaluated by anyone else as "aggressive" or highly assertive, nor does it mean that she has necessarily taken over the domineering stance that was previously exclusive to her husband. Vulnerable men may be sensitive to very subtle shifts in patterns of deference from their wives. Thus, because of their prior, long-established vulnerabilities, when they become aware of the gender shifts in themselves and their wives, the dystonic dependent men feel castrated.

The Dystonic Assertive Women

In similar fashion, although most older women accommodate and even enjoy their new postparental aggressiveness, a minority—often wives of dystonic dependent men—do become clinical casualties of their own developmental potentials. Just as the dystonic male patients devote themselves during the parental years to demonstrating that they are not replicas of their weak fathers, some female patients devote themselves, as "super-moms," to their children and husbands. Thus they demonstrate that they are not replicas of their destructive mothers. However, when their own nests emptied, these women lost the special niche in which they enacted their defense against the hidden taint of their witch-mother. In the deep fantasies of these patients, they could destroy the age-weakened husband, just as their mother once seemingly destroyed their father. Furthermore, like the witch-mother, they would be hated. In revulsion against this possible fate, some women spare their vulnerable husbands by becoming preemptively depressed *for* the husband. By damaging themselves, they protect their husband against the distress he would feel if his wife came out of the feminine closet in a more aggressive guise. Their illness maintains the status quo ante: the disparity between an overadequate husband and an underadequate wife. These women—like the counterpart male casualties—have reacted catastrophically against normal changes within themselves and their husbands. They have been, for their own private reasons, devastated by the expectable passage toward the androgyny of later life.

The Syntonic Dependent Older Men

As they become aware of their contrasexual shifts, dystonic dependent men are likely to feel covertly castrated and consciously ashamed. In their turn, syntonic dependent men are likely to suffer masked feelings of abandonment. Their catastrophic reactions are more likely to lead to depression and psychosomatic symptoms than the shame-avoiding paranoia shown by the dystonic dependent men. Thus they frequently complain of somatic symptoms that can have a psychogenic basis; they show acute vulnerability to frustration and much need for external direction and reassurance. Work difficulties are often precipitating, particularly when they find themselves unable or unwilling to meet the requirements of their employment. But with great unanimity, they maintain that their troubles began at about the time that their children were launched or showed imminent signs of launching: "Everything changed when the kids grew up and got married. My wife got a job and we began to have all our troubles."

Typically, the patient's complaints increasingly focus on his wife. He laments her lack of interest in domestic activities and her growing interest in extradomestic, often career-related pursuits. The wife's developmental moves toward greater independence and self-fulfillment seem to pose a notable threat to his security, often expressed as fear of "desertion" or "abandonment." Predictably, the wives in their turn complain of their husband's extreme dependency and burdensome, self-centered demands. In this respect, the wives appear to be excellent diagnosticians: "My husband is a dependent baby," or "He doesn't want a wife, he wants a mother," or "In his mind, he didn't marry a wife, he married a mother image."

In these clinical cases, the developmental history is fully consistent with the presenting picture. Seventy-five percent of the hospitalized syntonic dependent men were the youngest sons of aging parents. In their early memories they report a lost Eden—a blissful, almost symbiotic union with a mother who was omnipresent and indulging, while the father is seen as having been absent, relatively unimportant, and unavailable in the emotional if not the physical sense. The contrasting sense of almost seamless maternal union was often ratified by the mother, who turned to the son as compensation for the absent husband. Thus these men did not have a strong but benign father to provide a way station or transitional object in their migration away from the mother and toward greater self-reliance. Nor did they strive against a stern father and thereby gain the superego that controls but also enlivens the psyche. They did not accomplish the usual transition of the young male, from being the "mother's child" in the home to being the "father's child" in some version of the outer world. Put simply, they did not finally detach from the maternal symbiosis, and they did not develop the reliable internal structures that underwrite the drive toward independence and that are finally confirmed as independence is achieved. As they saw it, the ultimate resource was not in themselves but belonged to the strong maternal persons on whom they continued to rely.

In young adulthood, these patients managed to compensate for their lack of internal substance—the "internal good parent"—by maintaining the maternal bond in its outward form, through dependent liaisons with mothering persons. Usually, these were their nurturing, yet managerial wives: "My wife always made the decisions since the day we were married," or "I've always been the type to lean on others, especially my wife." These men accept their own dependency: It is syntonic. They are content so long as they can retain, via their wives, some version of the unrelinquished maternal bond. During the period of peak parental emergency, they work hard to please her, and—because they can identify with the mothering that their children receive from "Mom"—they are generally stabilized through their young to midadult years. In their postparental years, satisfied that they have done their duty as good providers, they say, in effect, "It's my turn," and they move to occupy the filial niche that their launched children have emptied. That is, because they can no longer identify with the mothering that their children had once received, they have to reestablish a more direct tie to the wife-mother: They become her postlaunch "child."

However, developmental tides have surged through both partners, wife as well as husband: Just as the husband has recaptured his covert dependency, the wife has recaptured the strivings toward autonomy and self-assertion that she had kept on hold during the emergency years of parenthood. The syntonic dependent husband may want to be mothered, but many postlaunch wives are no longer interested in being motherly. The heightened postparental dependency of the husband collides with eruptive strivings in the wife: Now she is more apt to be interested in her own growth, rather than in the growth and nurturance of others. However, she does not actually desert her domestic post. Although she may be employed, she is still present in the home, usually cooking the meals and sharing the conjugal bed. An objective, behavioral checklist questionnaire would not pick up any significant change in her established modus operandi. The true change is internal: While her body remains in place, a subjective shift has taken place in her psyche. Her concerns and appetites have begun to migrate elsewhere. It is these subjective shifts, not captured by our usual psychometric barometers, that trouble the syntonic dependent husband: The wife is still present in the flesh, but her mothering part has gone away. In our clinical population, this insult, intangible but nonetheless real, can bring about depressions, sometimes of suicidal and psychotic proportions. We suspect that the same kind of shift, based on reciprocal developments in the husband and wife, will also account for subclinical yet distressed reactions in those community-dwelling men who show the stigmata of syntonic dependency.

Male Syntonic Dependency in the Community

Having identified the pathogenic personality orientations in the clinical population, we asked if equivalent men would be found in Margaret Huyck's "Parkville" sample of middle-aged and older community-dwelling men and whether such men would show an abnormal degree of psychogenic symptoms. One hundred and seven parental and postparental Parkville men participated in a larger study as parents of young adults. Participants were recruited by initially selecting a random sample of young adults who were in the Parkville public high school graduating classes of 1970-1971, 1973, and 1979. The parents of these young adults were recruited if they lived close by and were still married to each other. "Parkville" is a middle-sized Midwestern suburb with strong settlement from Western European immigrants. Until the past two decades, the community was almost entirely white, and the sample is all-white. Half the sample is Catholic; most of the rest is Protestant. The mean of 2.65 on the Hollingshead Two-Factor Index of Social Status (1957) indicates the sample as a whole is somewhat above middle class. The majority (79%) of the couples married between 1946-1959; they were postwar baby boom parents.

The question asked of the Parkville sample was this: Would men of the syntonic dependency type in a nonclinical population react like the hospitalized veterans—that is, with abnormal (if subclinical) degrees of pain—to the normal contrasexual shift of the postparental period? Besides signs of pathology, we were also interested in the older males' adaptation—the psychological and marital conditions that sponsor "successful" outcomes of this potentially troubling transition.

To explore the personal characteristics and psychosocial circumstances of men who show psychogenic distress in the transition away from active parenthood, we adopted the following strategies. First, we would identify those men in the Parkville sample—known as "vulnerables"—who show significant evidence of the contrasexual shift. These are men with low masculinity scores and high femininity scores on the PRF-Andro Scale (Berzins, Welling, & Wetter, 1978) or with Thematic Apperception Test (TAT) stories tilted toward passive mastery (Gutmann, 1987).

The sample of men who were postparental and who met these criteria for heightened passivity and gender bimodality ($N = 55$) were divided into two subgroups. The first ($N = 21$) consisted of the "vulnerable and challenged" men. They either evidenced psychosomatic symptom distress on the SCL-90 (Derogatis, Rickles, & Rock, 1976) of more than one standard deviation above the mean for the entire male sample, or their TAT protocols revealed two or more "magical mastery" (e.g., disordered thinking) indications.

The "vulnerable but unchallenged" group ($N = 34$) consisted of all those clearly passive, potentially vulnerable men whose SCL-90 scores were at or below the mean for the male sample as a whole. These men show the typical postparental pattern of gender bimodality: Their masculinity quotient is lower than their femininity quotient, their TAT stories are of the passive-mastery variety, but they are at the same time "feeling no pain," and even enjoying their relaxed condition. Judging from their histories, this latter group included some men who had always been passive, as well as those men who had successfully completed the postparental transition toward heightened—and, in their case, welcomed—passivity.

We then explored factors that can account for a stressful transition toward bimodality in the case of the vulnerable and challenged men, and for the relatively benign passage toward bimodality in the case of the potentially vulnerable but seemingly unchallenged men. Our experience with the Northwestern Hospital and VA clinical samples had taught us where to look for answers. These earlier clinical investigations showed that late-onset pathology in overtly dependent patients was stimulated by the crescent assertiveness of the middle-aged wife. We expected that the wife's heightened aggressiveness would have the same drastic effect on the vulnerable Parkville husbands as it had on the hospitalized veterans of the Northwestern clinical sample. Accordingly, we generated a 2×2 table in which symptom level for the vulnerable men was cross-tabulated against the self-declared "marital politics" of their wives. Our prediction was that vulnerable men with high symptom levels would have wives who acknowledged their own assertiveness, while vulnerable men with low symptom levels would have wives who declared themselves to be uncomplicatedly benign toward their husbands (or, at worst, inhibited in expressing any opposition toward them).

As the distribution in Table 4.1 indicates, this prediction was borne out, at a statistically significant level ($\chi^2 = 8.04$, $df = 1$, $p < .005$). The vulnerable men who show relatively high degrees of psychological and psychosomatic distress tend to have wives who, although they may be ambivalent and guilty about their aggression, will nevertheless vent it bluntly, in the form of directives, criticism, or nagging. Again, despite their rancor these wives stay true to their marriage vows, but they are less likely to idealize the husband, withhold criticism, or serve his career by

Table 4.1   Vulnerable Parkville Men (*N* = 55): Husband's Symptoms
and Wife's Aggression

	Wife Benign or Unaggressive Toward Husband	Wife Openly Assertive Toward Husband
Vulnerable men—syntonic-dependent, asymptomatic	23 (68%)	11 (32%)
Vulnerable men—syntonic-dependent, symptomatic	6 (29%)	15 (71%)

giving up their own. Men who have always been passive or men whose quotient of passivity has been heightened by the postparental transition appear to be particularly vulnerable to this newfound sharpness of the wife.

By comparison, equally passive postparental men whose wives remain tenderly disposed seem to be particularly advantaged in later life. These are the men who sink blissfully into the condition of marital symbiosis that we have called "Mommy and I are one." These are the men who tell interviewers that "She and I think the same way about everything. We try to do everything together. I can't conceive of life without her." For these men, two physically distinct individuals have fused into a single psychological organism. Of interest is that this sense of fusion does not require the actual physical coupling of sexual intercourse: Many of the "Mommy and I are one" types report diminution of phallic sexuality; and sometimes, usually because of health problems, a complete cessation of actual intercourse.[3]

It is the vulnerable and challenged men, those with an abnormally high level of psychic or psychosomatic distress, who have wives who have refused the symbiosis: Although remaining physically close to their husbands, they also maintain or even thicken their personal boundaries. As we found in our clinical samples, the wives of the vulnerable and distressed postparental men avoid the kind of fusion that their husbands seek. They may well protect their boundaries with anger: If the husband expects too much, if he challenges some prerogative, they are not shy about telling him where to get off. In short, wives of the vulnerable and challenged men do not match the covert fantasy of their dependent post-parental husbands, which is that the wife he inherited from his children will be like the indulging "Mom" that he inherited from his father. In his young adulthood, this man—perhaps reluctantly—left the special romance with his mother to become a "father's son" in the world of work. Becoming a father in his own right, he acquired his own wife but again had to give her up—at least, in her mothering aspect—to the children. However, when we meet him in later life, he believes that he has paid his dues to the paternal ideal: His kids are raised, and he can—with honor, without shame—turn back to claim the wife-mother that he had given up to be a father, breadwinner, and proper man. But the wife that he now encounters has also moved on. She too has paid her dues and raised her children; now she is more interested in her own development. She is not ready to take on a new child in the person of the husband. She puts limits on the merger that he seeks, and she sometimes guards her personal boundaries with prickly anger as though they were fortified frontiers. The husband feels rebuffed, and his unrequited dependency, thrown in his face, can make him feel ashamed and quietly angry in his own right.

Often, as we see clinically, these husbands seek new ways to justify the dependent needs that their wives have not legitimated: They develop symptoms, usually depressions masked as psychosomatic ailments. Through these, the men turn the anger that would further alienate their wives back on themselves. But such a husband is also using his discontent to pass on a quiet rebuke to the wife: "If I cannot be your child, then I will be your patient." In so doing, they shift the blame for their dependency from their psyche, for which they do feel responsible, to the soma, for which they bear no responsibility. It is as if their troubled organs speak for them: "It is not I, a person, who asks for your help and concern: It is my weak heart, my stomach, my liver." The psychosomatic symptoms, being overdetermined, may send other messages that have the effect of subtly controlling the wife, of keeping her in the "prelaunch" posture of benign tenderness toward the damaged husband. Sometimes it works: Many Parkville wives transfer the sense of parental emergency away from their separating children to the damaged husband; he replaces the now self-reliant kids as an object of concern.[4] And as we saw in the clinical sample, some women go so far as to become depressed on the husband's behalf: They preempt the pathology that he would suffer were they to become aggressive toward him.

Early History and Late Androgyny

Further support for the psychodynamic interpretation of our findings is provided when we extend our exploration along the lines dictated by this particular theoretical approach. Besides investigating the husband's relationship to the wife in the family of procreation, we examined the relationship, as remembered by the husband, to his parents—and particularly, to his mother—in the family of orientation. We theorized that older men whose passive dependency is above the sample norm have memorialized a common history in regard to the mother. Generalizing from our clinical experience, we suspected that the vulnerable Parkville men had a particularly close tie to the mother and that the golden cord was never really broken: These men are still "mother's sons." Moved by shame and social prompting, they had separated from their mothers in the physical and social sense—they left home, they married and formed their own families—but not in the psychological sense: The tie to the mother forged in the family of orientation was reproduced with the wife in the family of procreation.

The question then arose: Do the dependent Parkville men report, as predicted, an early history centered on vivid memories of a maternal Eden? Conversely, do the more independent, nonvulnerable men report a childhood history that is substantially different from their vulnerable peers? Our hypothesis was that the less androgynous, more independent older men would be less likely to report an intense tie to the mother. In their case, both parents would be seen as strong and valued, though in different ways; and their memories of the formative years would be marked by important ties to the father as well as to the mother.

Our assumptions were again tested by comparing groups of postparental men in the Parkville sample. Basically, the childhood memories of the most vulnerable men were contrasted to those from the least vulnerable men. In this comparison, three types of men were considered. As before, the vulnerable men were subdivided: One group contained the vulnerable men who suffer symptoms; the contrast group is composed of equally dependent, vulnerable men who are symptom-free. The third group is composed of the small subsample of low-vulnerability men—those less androgynous subjects whose TAT scores are in the active mastery range and whose PRF-Andro masculinity scores are higher than their femininity scores. Although these postparental men have access—on schedule—to both masculine and feminine modes of experience, their masculine orientation is still primary and consistent with their biological sex.

The early parental memories of all the Parkville men were subjected to content analysis, and we focused on the qualities reported for the father, the mother, the parents' relation to each other, and their relation to the subject. Three distinct types of personal histories were identified. Type I contains those subjects who portray the father as being psychologically

Table 4.2 Parkville Men: Parental Memories (*N* = 33)

	Type I Father Distant or Weak, Mother Strong and Cherished	Type II Father Strong but Feared, Mother Weak but Cherished	Type III Both Parents Strong in Distinctive Ways
Vulnerable men— challenged, symptomatic	14 (78%)	3 (17%)	1 (5%)
Vulnerable men— unchallenged, asymptomatic	4 (66%)	1 (17%)	1 (17%)
Nonvulnerable men— unchallenged, asymptomatic	0 (0%)	3 (33%)	6 (67%)

remote or weak, while the same subject remembers an intense although sometimes ambivalent tie to the mother. Included here are the "mother's sons," as well as the "Oedipal victors," those favored by dominant mothers over a disparaged father. Type II identifies the men who portray the father as powerful but harsh, the mother as nurturing but ineffectual, and the subject as closer to the mother than to the father. Type III groups men who present both parents as strong and admirable, yet different from each other, and effective in ways that fit the conventional gender definitions of their youth. The father is presented as being stern but also just and approachable: He is the disciplinarian who would also take his son to the ballpark. The mother is seen as nurturing but devoted to social standards as well as to her children's welfare. Her kids could expect love from her but not automatic approval: She expected proper performance from them at school and in the home. These mothers were loving, but their kids had to earn their respect.

The three groupings that resulted from the content analysis of "memorialized parent imagery" were cross-tabulated against the three already established groups of paradigm vulnerable and nonvulnerable men. As shown in Table 4.2, our hypothesis was borne out: Thus 78% of the vulnerable and challenged (symptomatic) men gave memorialized parental reports that fall under Type I, featuring a weak or absent father coupled with a strong, unrelinquished tie to the mother. Similarly, two thirds of the vulnerable but unchallenged (asymptomatic) men also group under this first type. However, none of the reports from the men who are both low-vulnerable and asymptomatic fall into this father-absent, omnipresent-

Table 4.3 Parkville Men: Parental Memories (*N* = 33)

	Type I Father Distant or Weak, Strong Tie to Mother	Type II Father Strong, Mother Weak or Strong
Vulnerable men—symptomatic and asymptomatic	18 (75%)	6 (25%)
Nonvulnerable men—asymptomatic	0 (0%)	9 (100%)

mother category. Instead, two thirds of their reports meet the criteria for parental Type III: both parents strong and available, though in different ways. The remainder of their parental images fit the criteria for parental Type II: The father was powerful but feared, and there was some identification with—or protection of—a loving but ineffectual mother.

These distributions permit us to combine cells for computational purposes. As shown in Table 4.3, when we condense men's memorialized parental descriptions to two categories—(a) father as weak or absent and (b) father as significant in the home, although possibly autocratic—and compare these to subjects' degree of psychological vulnerability, the resulting pattern is statistically significant ($\chi^2 = 14.84$, $df = 1$, $p < .001$). The nonvulnerable men recalled relationships with and between parents that are strikingly different from those reported by their vulnerable peers: Their parents were affectionate to each other and—each in his or her own way—to their children; but they were at the same time emotionally self-sufficient, not entangled with each other. These accounts of the memorialized parents parallel the current psychological and marital arrangements of their nonvulnerable, now grown-up sons. Like their parents, these Parkville men are congenial with their wives, but they are quite capable of surviving, psychologically speaking, on their own.

Discussion and Conclusions

The typical text on life-span development begins with a chapter about infancy and ends with a chapter titled "Aging and Death." According to conventional gerontology, psychological development is in no way a feature of late adulthood. The aged are not thought of as facing new challenges, nor are they deemed capable of managing them. Instead, in the bulk of the geropsychology literature, the aged are presented as terminating: Aging equals death, and elders can barely adapt to or compensate for the avalanching losses of this terminal period. By contrast, this chapter argues for a new and more hopeful recognition—that late-adult development is linked to the parental cycle; and that the surge of postparental development can lead to pathology as well as to growth. Unlike the irreversible losses catalogued in our literature, disorders of developmental origin are reversible and treatable. With the help of psychotherapy, the developmental energies that have been derailed into symptoms can be put back on track to drive new executive capacities of the aging personality.

Although based on small samples, these preliminary results support the syntonic dependency model of late-onset pathogenesis. As predicted by that model, we found that men who show an abnormally high passive and feminine profile in the later years are precisely those whose early years were characterized—according to them—by a powerful and still unrelinquished tie to a devoted mother. If the aging wife is willing to replicate the mother's attention and concern, then these men appear to be soothed, often immensely content, and symptom-free.[5] But if the older wife refuses to be hypermaternal and does not match the husband's internally imprinted magna mater, then the dependent man either becomes depressed or uses somatic symptoms as a cry for help.

These results indicate that older men who did not separate psychologically from their mothers during the formative years are particularly at risk in the later years. Rendered particularly vulnerable by the normal developmental shift toward postparental androgyny, their own well-being is chronically hostage to their wives' shifting moods.

But there are good outcomes as well: Those men who rounded out the transition from childhood to adulthood by separating from the mother enter the postparental stage relatively unscathed by the psychic reorganization of that time. Better yet, they are invigorated by the new affectional and cognitive potentials that can be reclaimed in the passage to emeritus parenthood. Having long ago faced the necessary terrors and separations of childhood, they are not, as elders, terribly daunted by their encounter with alien parts of the psyche, nor by the final separation, the final loss, the final passage into death.

Finally, these provocative results also indicate that fathers of young sons are important in their own right, and are necessarily different from mothers. Contrary to much current belief, which insists on gender equality in parenting roles—fathers are required to be essentially indistinguishable from mothers in the home—these results suggest that boys need fathers who are admirable in their own right. The bimodal, even androgynous parent is a feature of the postparental rather than the actively parenting "parental emergency" family. A strong father—even if he is autocratic, even if the son has to rebel against him—nevertheless provides an alternative to the mother. He is a way station on the boyhood voyage away from the mother. Lacking a distinctive father, lacking the "transitional object" that he provides, a son, as indicated by our data, is much less likely to undertake the risky journey toward early self-reliance and independence. The last stanzas of the life story are drafted at its beginning, and so the bill for some older men's developmental failure in early life finally comes due in their later years.

Notes

1. Concerning the ultimate sources of male-female differences, there are two major doctrines, one stressing nature, the other stressing social conditioning, or nurture. Those who hold that the seeming differences (with the exception of those bearing on reproduction) between men and women are mutable social constructions prefer to group masculine or feminine characteristics under the term *gender.* Theoretically, there can be as many genders as there are societies to conceive of and nurture them; but when it comes to nature, to the requirements of human procreation, there are and can only be two sexes. Accordingly, those who are more interested in the contributions of immutable nature to masculinity and femininity prefer the term *sex* to gender. In this chapter, we will apply both terms, depending on the context. When we refer to those aspects of masculinity and femininity that express our biopsychological or species nature, and to deep developmental shifts unfolding outside of awareness, we will use terms such as *sex* and *sexual.* When we refer to the largely conscious social and personal reactions to these tectonic shifts and to the socially sculpted aspects of maleness and femaleness, we will use the *gender* terminology.

2. In much of the literature, this shift has been described as a move toward androgyny, or even, in an early formulation by Gutmann, as "The unisex of later life." However, as Huyck (1992, in press) has pointed out, this imprecise phrase implies that adults become "degendered" or uncharacterized by qualities associated with their sex. Huyck argues that persons persist in viewing themselves in gender terms, and whatever characteristics and behaviors they show are evaluated by themselves and by others in terms of gender-linked expectations. In short, we need a vocabulary to discuss changes in gender identity style that takes account of the fact that men and women, regardless of age, are never regarded as genderless. So guided, we would know that using a single term such as *androgyny* to acknowledge shifts in gender-congruent style is often misleading. Lacking such a rich vocabulary, we will proceed with the convention and use the term *androgyny* as a cryptic term to describe complex outcomes of change.

3. There appear to be "seasons of Eros" that continually change across the life span. The act of intercourse can lose its primacy in the pleasure diet of the marriage, to be replaced by more diffuse and less spasmodic excitements—touching, cuddling, looking, and eating, for example. It is as though the natural condition of the erotic life is multimodal, dispersed across all the receptive zones of skin, genitalia, mouth, and eyes. Thus the concentration of the pleasure principle in the genitalia is temporary, seemingly a transient interference in the natural order. In the life of Eros, diffusion rather than concentration seems to be the rule; and the gratified, unchallenged men of our passive sample are those who have managed to reopen—with the help of a willing wife—the multiple passages to pleasure that were available to them in their earliest years.

4. At this point a critical reader might object to our model of pathogenesis because it views the husband's psychopathology as reactive to the characteristics of his wife. We have proposed a causal line that starts with the qualities of the postparental wife and that has as a dependent outcome the presence or absence of symptoms in the vulnerable husband. But a critic could use these same data and findings to reverse the flow of causality, starting with the husband's symptoms or lack thereof, back to the wife's mood and bearing toward him. In this alternative scenario, when the husband is symptom-free and uncomplaining, the wife feels well-disposed toward him. But when he burdens her with his ailment, she is prone to become—quite understandably—angry and withholding. Rather than the converse, her anger is reactive to his symptoms.

This nondynamic interpretation is disarmingly uncomplicated—which adds to its plausibility. It is also politically correct to propose that the wife is potentially "burdened" or victimized by the demanding husband. But despite the attractions of the alternate hypothesis, we should remember that the observed findings of a relationship between the husband's symptoms the wife's affections had been predicted a priori from our theory. The parental emergency model suggested that, following the postparental transitions, the flow of causation would proceed from the perceived affective qualities of the wife to the response, whether symptomatic or contented, of the aging and now dependent husband. A more adequate test of the model must wait for a longitudinal study of these same respondents, the prediction being that assertion on the part of the wife will precede the onset of symptoms in the husband.

5. These passive-dependent men require a "maternal" wife for at least two reasons: She confirms their core illusion, namely, that they are still at one with the mother; and she enacts for them—and thus extracts from them—the potentially troublesome maternal identification. When the internal mother is "out there," in the wife, she does not present a troubling, contramasculine presence within the husband's psyche. Accordingly, when this postparental wife is benign and nurturing, these men feel that they have restored the blissful connection to the mother in all respects—physical, social, and psychological. Second, because the "mother" has been restored as an external but constant presence, and she is again safely "outside," these men do not have to preserve the maternal tie via the potentially shameful tactic of "becoming" the mother—they do not have to "mother" themselves. But when the older wife closes out her maternal career and refuses to be a mother to her husband, these vulnerable men feel that the long-avoided separation has finally been forced on them and without consultation. Depression or psychosomatic symptoms are likely outcomes. However, if they try to preserve the linkage internally, through identification, through becoming like the mother, they may suffer feelings of emasculation and shame. Either way, they lose.

References

Atchley, R. (1976). Selected social and psychological differences between men and women in later life. *Journal of Gerontology, 31,* 204-212.

Benedek, T. (1952). *Psychosexual functions in women.* New York: Ronald Press.

Berzins, J., Welling, M., & Wetter, R. (1978). A new measure of psychological androgyny based on the personality research form. *Journal of Clinical and Consulting Psychology, 46,* 126-138.

Brenneis, C. R. (1975). Developmental aspects of aging in women. *Archives of General Psychiatry, 32,* 429-435.

Brown, I. (1985). *In her prime: A new view of middle-aged women.* South Hadley, MA: Bergin & Garvey.

Derogatis, L., Rickles, K., & Rock, A. (1976). The SCL-90 and the MMPI: A step in the validation of a new self-report scale. *British Journal of Psychiatry, 128,* 280-289.

Feldman, S., Biringen, C., & Nash, S. (1981). Fluctuations of sexual-related self-attributions as a function of stage of family life cycle. *Developmental Psychology, 17,* 24-25.

Galler, S. (1977). *Women graduate student returnees and their husbands: A study of the effects of the professional and academic graduate school experience on sex-role perceptions, marital relationships, and family concepts.* Unpublished doctoral dissertation, Northwestern University, Evanston, IL.

Gold, S. (1969). Cross-cultural comparisons of role change with aging. *Student Journal of Human Development, 1,* 1-15.

Gutmann, D. (1964). An exploration of ego configurations in middle and later life. In B. Neugarten (Ed.), *Personality in middle and later life* (pp. 114-148). New York: Atherton.

Gutmann, D. (1987). *Reclaimed powers: Toward a new psychology of men and women in later life.* New York: Basic Books.

Gutmann, D. (1990). Psychological development and pathology in later adulthood. In R. A. Nemiroff & C. A. Colarusso (Eds.), *New dimensions in adult development* (pp. 170-185). New York: Basic Books.

Gutmann, D., Grunes, J., & Griffin, B. (1982). Developmental contributions to the late-onset disorders. In O. Brim & P. Baltes (Eds.), *Life-span development and behavior* (Vol. 4). San Diego, CA: Academic Press.

Hollingshead, A. B. (1957). *The two factor index of social position.* Unpublished manuscript. New Haven, CT: Yale University.

Hurlbert, J. (1962). *Age as a factor in the social organization of the Hare Indians of Fort Good Hope, Northwest Territories.* Ottawa, Canada: Northern Coordination and Research Centre, Department of Northern Affairs and National Resources.

Huyck, M. H. (1989). Mid-life parental imperatives. In R. Kalish (Ed.), *Midlife loss* (pp. 115-148). Newbury Park, CA: Sage.

Huyck, M. H. (1991). Gender-linked self-attributions and mental health among middle-aged parents. *Journal of Aging Studies, 5,* 111-123.

Huyck, M. H. (1992). *Evaluating the parental imperative in Parkville.* Paper presented at annual meetings of the Gerontological Society of America, Washington, DC.

Huyck, M. H. (in press). Marriage and close relationships of the marital kind. In R. Blieszner & V. Bedford (Eds.), *Handbook on aging and the family.* Westport, CT: Greenwood Press.

Huyck, M. H., & Gutmann, D. (1992). Thirtysomething years of marriage: Understanding experiences of women and men in enduring family relationships. *Family Perspective, 26*, 249-265.

Jacobowitz, J. (1984). *Stability and change of coping patterns during the middle years as a function of personality style.* Unpublished doctoral dissertation, Hebrew University of Jerusalem.

Jaslow, P. (1976). Employment, retirement and morale among older women. *Journal of Gerontology, 31*, 212-218.

Jung, C. (1933). *Modern man in search of a soul.* New York: Harcourt, Brace.

La Bouvie-Vief, G., & Hakim-Larson, J. (1989). Developmental shifts in adult thought. In S. Hunter & M. Sundel (Eds.), *Mid-life myths: Issues, findings, and practice implications* (pp. 69-96). Newbury Park, CA: Sage

Leonard, O. (1961). The older Spanish-speaking people of the Southwest. In E. Youmans (Ed.), *The older rural Americans* (pp. 239-261). Lexington: University of Kentucky Press.

Levinson, D. J., Darrow, C. N., Klein, E. B., Levinson, M. H., & McKee, B. (1978). *The seasons of a man's life.* New York: Knopf.

Lewis, O. (1965). *Life in a Mexican village: Tepoztlan restudied.* Urbana-Champaign: University of Illinois Press.

Lowenthal, M., Thurnher, M., & Chiriboga, O. (1975). *Four stages of life.* San Francisco: Jossey-Bass.

Neugarten, B., & Gutmann, D. (1958). Age-sex roles and personality in middle life: A thematic apperception study. *Psychological Monographs, 470*, 1-33.

Ripley, D. (1984). *Parental status, sex roles, and gender mastery style in working class fathers.* Unpublished doctoral dissertation, Illinois Institute of Technology, Chicago.

Shanan, J. (1978). The Jerusalem study of mid-adulthood and aging (JESTEA): Effects of ecology and culture on stability and change of psychological functions and structures in the transition from middle to later adulthood. *Israel Journal of Gerontology, 2*, 44-59.

Streib, G. (1968). Family patterns in retirement. In M. Sussman (Ed.), *Sourcebook of marriage and the family* (pp. 405-414). Boston: Houghton Mifflin.

Tachibana, K. (1962). A study of introversion-extroversion in the aged. In C. Tibbitts & D. W. Donahue (Eds.), *Social and psychological aspects of aging: Aging around the world* (pp. 655-656). New York: Columbia University Press.

Van Arsdale, P. (1981). The elderly Asmat of New Guinea. In T. Amoss & S. Harrel (Eds.), *Other ways of growing old: Anthropological perspectives* (pp. 111-124). Stanford, CA: Stanford University Press.

5

Faith Development in Older Men

BARBARA PITTARD PAYNE

Do not think that at my age one becomes a fully serene, mature, believing and regenerated human being. The inner struggle is going on to the last day no matter how old one becomes.

Martin Kahler, "Justification by Faith" (1967)

Men do not inevitably mature in their faith as they grow older. They do not, as Kahler observed, become fully serene, mature, believing human beings because they are 65, 75, 85, 95, or 100-plus years old. Men enter later life at different stages of faith development based on wide variations in their life experiences, including but not limited to their education, family careers, life experiences, and religious involvement. The inner struggle in a man's faith goes on "to the last day no matter how old one becomes" (Kahler, 1967). What happens to stimulate or stagnate faith development in older men is the subject of this investigation.[1]

Men begin very early to seek the meaning of their lives. By the time they are teenagers they are raising very fundamental questions such as, "What is the meaning of my life?" and "Is there really a God?" (Gallup, 1993). This interest endures and expands until, as elders, men review the meaning of their own lives and of long life in general. About the need of a man to find a meaning to his long life, Carl Jung (1933) observed, "A human being would certainly not want to grow to be seventy or eighty years old if this longevity had no meaning for the species to which he belongs. The afternoon of human life must have a significance of its own and cannot be merely a pitiful appendage to life's morning."

Theologian Kahler and psychologist Jung alert us to the dynamics of faith in the lives of men—and women—as they become older. The insights Kahler and Jung provide serve as a point of departure for understanding faith development in older men, reminding us that faith is a continuous, never-ending developmental process and that the search for the meaning of life is even more important in later life.

Faith as a Social Construct

Observations about religious life across the life cycle have suggested that adults become more religious as they grow older and that women are more religious than men at every age. Early studies of the religious practices of older people did show that religion becomes more important and private practices increase with age, but that church attendance and participation declines (Blazer & Palmore, 1976; Hall, 1922; Moberg, 1965; Orbach, 1961; Starbuck, 1911). Change in these long-held patterns occurred in the late 1980s.

According to National Opinion Research Center surveys, people attend church more regularly as they grow older "until by the age of 70 six in ten adults (60 percent) say they go to religious services weekly" (Gallup, 1991). Although attendance drops by the age of 80 to 49%, it is still much higher than for adults younger than 60. Interest in church membership also now increases steadily with age to 75% by age 50 and older and to 80% among those older than 65 (Gallup, 1993).

For older women, church attendance decreases less and religion participation seems to become more important (Gallup, 1991). Women continue to be reported as more religious than men. For example, Gallup (1987) noted that twice as many women than men 50 and older rate themselves as "very religious." The more recent faith development research is finding similar gender differences in religious experiences (Faracasin, 1992; Thompson, 1991). Although these studies indicate higher religiosity among women, it does not mean, as we will show, that men do not experience increases in religiosity as they get older. It may be that men and women with similar life experiences have similar faith development (Stokes, 1990b). It may be that men experience faith in different ways than women (Levin & Taylor, 1993). The point is that men and women do not experience faith development in a uniform or consistent way in older adulthood; such development occurs in varying ways that are not necessarily related to chronological age.

As we will see, religion and religiousness are important parts of life for men at all ages, and faith development occurs across their life cycle. It is not always linear. In fact, it is more likely to be curvilinear, punctuated by highs and lows. The growth occurs in different dimensions and areas of faith and at different ages. Overall, however, as men become older the depth of their faith increases (Benson & Elkin, 1990). The greatest faith maturity comes in men's late 70s and continues to grow (Faracasin, 1992). Like the "Energizer Bunny," it just keeps going and going.

Prior religiosity studies about the beliefs, religious participation, and faith behaviors of older men and women tell more about the aggregate of men compared to women or about the continuation of one's experiences and social roles. Little information is imparted about shifts in one's spiritual or faith life (Agostino, 1987). By comparison, faith development investigators examine the dynamics by which a person finds and makes meaning of life's significant questions and issues, adheres to this meaning, and acts it out. Currently, the continued increase in life expectancy and the growing number of centenarians are bringing additional attention to faith development in late adulthood.

In this chapter we will examine the forces influencing faith development in older men, including gender, the aging process, and social forces. At the beginning of our discussion it is important to recognize that all faith is not religious faith. There are secular forms and objects of faith, such as humanism, materialism, and narcotization. But for this chapter we are limiting the discussion to religious faith. It is also important to understand the relationship between the dynamic physical and social-psychological changes in adult development and the dynamics of development in individual faith.

Adult Development and Faith Development

Development is not a new concept. Developmental theory is "based on the principle that human beings move through life according to regular and known principles of stability and change" (Gallup, 1985, p. vi). The developmental tasks or stages in the developmental process are sequential and usually relate to age or the stage in the life cycle.

During the first part of this century, psychologists studying human development focused primarily on children and youth. Jung (1933) was one of the first pioneers to include adults in his developmental work. However, it was Havighurst's work in the 1940s (1948) that attracted attention to the patterns of adult change and development. He looked at the entire life cycle and the related developmental tasks.

Of interest is that this occurred during the same period of a noticeable increase in life expectancy. It was also during this period that the passage of Social Security (1935) marked the beginning of retirement as a new experience for all adults in the United States. For the first time in history, all workers, including professionals, would be expected to live to retirement and retire. A new stage in the adult life cycle was begun.

In 1950, Erikson introduced his major formulation relating developmental theory to adulthood. He delineated eight stages or periods of psychosocial development (see Table 5.1), and all contribute to an understanding of adult development. These stages are not age-specific but sequential and operative throughout life. Each produces a "personal crisis" or is a transition period with conflicting, polar alternatives of positive or negative solutions. The positive or negative resolution of earlier tasks build the foundation for the resolution of the tasks of late adulthood.

Although all eight of Erikson's stages contribute to an understanding of elders' late-life experiences, including their faith needs and responses, only the last two have particular relevance for understanding older men's faith development. Stage 7 proposes a tension during middle adulthood between generativity and stagnation. Generativity is the interest and commitment to make this a better world for the next generation and actively working to contribute to this improvement. Stagnation represents the absence of this kind of interest, involvement, and caring, and this leads to a sense of purposelessness. In Stage 8, the late adulthood strains concern the maintenance of ego integrity versus sinking into despair. Ego integrity (or what Erikson called "integration") involves a review of one's life and feeling satisfied that it has had meaning. Erikson's developmental model has influenced gerontological research, particularly on the psychology of older adulthood. The stages are widely used by gerontologists in interpreting the social psychological processes of aging, as well as by Fowler (1981, 1987) in interpreting adult faith development.

The contribution to adult developmental theory for the study of faith development in men was made by Levinson (1978). His theory of the "seasons" of a man's life was derived from a study of men between ages 35 and 50. One of Levinson's more significant contributions for our discussion is his view that life structure for males "evolves through a relatively orderly sequence of alternating stable and transitional periods"

Table 5.1   Erikson's Eight Stages and Positive and Negative
Polarities

Stage	Period	Favorable Resolution	Unfavorable Resolution
1.	Early infancy	Trust	Mistrust
2.	Late infancy	Autonomy	Shame and doubt
3.	Early childhood	Initiative	Guilt
4.	Middle childhood	Industry	Inferiority
5.	Adolescence	Identity	Identity confusion
6.	Young adulthood	Intimacy	Isolation
7.	Middle adulthood	Generativity	Stagnation
8.	Older adulthood	Ego integrity	Despair

SOURCE: Derived from Erikson (1950).

(Levinson, 1978, p. 42). The stable periods are ones of firm choices and the enhancement of one's life. The transitional period is the time "to question and reappraise existing structure . . . and . . . explore the possibilities for change in self and the world" (p. 42). It is in these periods of reappraisal that men are most likely to experience changes and maturing in their faith.

From his analysis of the midlife period, Levinson documents those changes that enable a man to enrich his life. He argues that a modest decline in youthful drives of passion, in capacity for anger and moral indignation, in self-assertiveness and ambition, and in the wish to be cared for and supported contributes to a freedom to develop the quality of man's deeper relationships. "He may develop a greater capacity for intimacy by integrating the feminine aspects of his self. He may become a more responsive friend, facilitating parent, to his adolescent children and young adult sons [and] daughters, become a more caring son of aging parents and a more compassionate authority in his work" (Levinson, 1978, p. 25). Levinson likened these changes in men to Neugarten's (1964; Neugarten & Datan, 1973) work on personality changes beginning in midlife. She found that an interiority develops, especially in older men, along with changes in role performances that reflect more of the "feminine" aspects of male behavior.

In the 1980s, James Fowler applied the concept of development directly to faith. He understood faith as something one does not have, but as a process of becoming, as movement. Faith is more than a doctrine or a set of beliefs or creeds. Faith is active. It is thus more than something received from God, possessed or confessed. Fowler proposed that *faith* is a verb that captures the dynamic and changing quality of one's religiousness. In the faith development process, we are faithing.

In Fowler's theory of faith development, stages are hierarchical and build on one another. There is no right or wrong faith or the assumption that some persons have more or less faith or are more or less faithful than others. As Stokes (1990a) explains, the doctrines and traditions of the many religions help define those beliefs most commonly held and acted on. They are but a means to the end of individuals discovering a personal faith that speaks to needs. "Each [developmental] stage is a point in our faith and aging journey and experience. It represents the dimension of faith appropriate for our needs" (Stokes, 1990a, p. 23).

Fowler's stages are briefly summarized in Table 5.2 and fully developed in *Stages of Faith* (1981). The table does not do justice to the stages. It needs to be supplemented by reference to Fowler's works (1981, 1987) and interpretations of Stokes (1982, 1990a, 1990b) and Faracasin (1992). However, it summarizes the principle that faith development is hierarchical, moving from ritualistic faith to expressions of connectedness.

This sketchy review of Erikson's developmental theory, Levinson's analysis of men's lives, and Fowler's work on faith development provides a logical framework for understanding and interpreting faith development in older men. First, the framework promotes attention to men's experiences as men, and it brings into focus older men as individuals. It also recognizes that there are varieties of religious experiences (James, 1902) and varieties of aging (Maddox, 1987). We faith and age differently. When we combine the faithing differences and the aging differences, we have an even more heterogeneous experience.

Age and Faith Stages

Data on variations in older men's faith development are currently available. Grounded in the theories of Erikson, Levinson, and Fowler, two major national research projects explore the relationship between the dynamics of adult aging and personal faith development. The first is the 1981-1987 *Faith Development in the Life Cycle* study sponsored by the Religions Education Association of the United States and Canada (Stokes, 1990a). Second is Benson and Elkin's (1990) national study of 11,122

Table 5.2 Fowler's Stages of Faith Development

Stage 1: Intuitive-Projective Faith

Almost totally limited to children (to age 6), individuals in Stage 1 reflect the faith attributes of parents and family as perceived by the individual. Typically, at this time of life, the preschool child accepts parental faith attitudes without question.

Stage 2: Mythic-Literal Faith

In later childhood, the person becomes aware of and begins to internalize the faith attitudes and views of persons, primarily adults, other than family members. There is an increasing awareness of different faith attitudes in society, but the individual still tends to hold to those of family and religious traditions. Some adults remain in this stage through much of their lives.

Stage 3: Synthetic-Conventional Faith

The attitudes and values of peers (or the "gang") are major determinants of one's values at this stage, including those related to faith. Adherence to the "norm" is paramount as life's increasing complexities are perceived as necessitating the set of values held in common by the others close to the individual. This affiliation with a community continues for many into adulthood, where a large percentage of people find a faith, or security, in their relationship with a church, synagogue, or religious body.

Stage 4: Individuative-Reflective Faith

As adolescents move into adulthood and assume adult responsibilities—marriage and family, vocation, financial interdependency—they often again question some of the fundamental faith assumptions of their parents or religious tradition. For many, the need to doubt, question, and even reject elements of one's faith traditions is necessary for further faith development. This phenomenon is not restricted to young adulthood; an increasing number of persons in the middle and later years are faced with the need to rethink their faith.

Stage 5: Conjunctive Faith

Usually no earlier than the middle years, some adults are able to bring into meaningful reconciliation the variety of faith dynamics that have played important roles in previous stages of their faith development; their faith roots of family and church, the beliefs of others, and the answers they have found in their own questions are all tempered with the maturity that comes only with the experiencing of life. Individuals are able to identify beyond boundaries of race, class, or ideology to understand and integrate the views of others into their own expression of faith, arrived at individually as a mature expression of a faith that is wholly their own.

Stage 6: Universalizing Faith

Persons in Stage 6 are rare. They are, however, those whose lives are so attuned to the ultimate meaning of life that their faith expression is beyond self-interest, taking on a universalizing quality. Fowler theorizes that this stage "represents the culmination of growth in faith, brought about by human fidelity and Divine grace and revelation."

SOURCE: From Bruning and Stokes (1982, pp. 35-37). Used with permission.

churchgoers across six Protestant denominations. In addition, the dissertations of Faracasin (1992) and Shulik (1979) investigate how gender and age jointly affect the faith development among older men (midlife and beyond). And qualitative data on the faith development in older men are derived from biographical case histories and interviews with elders (Payne, 1990, 1993). Together, the survey data and inquiries into men's faith development can be used to review the way faithing differences and aging differences intersect to affect men's lives.

Shulik's (1979) dissertation examined faith development in older men and women using Fowler's conceptualization and semistructured faith interview. At the time of Shulik's study, only 4% of Fowler's interviews had been with older persons. Shulik interviewed 20 men aged 53 to 87 in lengthy, two-session discussions to determine the faith stage of each older man. Most of the men were in Stage 3 or 4. Two scored in Stage 2, and three were in Stage 5. The relationships to age showed that faith stage and age were not directly connected. Some chronically older men were at an earlier faith stage than other younger male elders.

Two of the older men interviews Shulik conducted were reported in enough detail to illustrate stage placement for faith Stages 3 and 4. My own research illustrates Stage 5:

Dr. Blain was a retired professor who invested authority in others, especially academicians, rather than himself. He was concerned with other people's approval of him. His sense of community identity and approval was very important and was derived from his colleagues. This is the "gang" and peer identity of the Stage 3 person.

Mr. Greely, a retired insurance executive, was highly achievement-oriented, individualistic in his lifestyle. For him, work and achievement in work defines the person. He was concerned about how he would be remembered and wanted to be remembered for good works. He was very ecumenical and appreciated other religions and religious views, consistent with faith Stage 4.

Dr. Lindsey (Payne, 1993) is a retired New Testament Professor who continues to lecture, write, and conduct study tours to the Holy Land. We asked him to describe change of movements in his personal faith since he retired [five] years ago. As he carefully outlined his perceived changes, I recognized a better summary of a Stage 5 person would be hard to find:

He noted, most significantly, a greater appreciation of the centrality of God rather than Christ. This represents a broadening of horizons to take seriously non-Christian religious insights. Second, a greater appreciation of the relativity of all things and the erasure from his vocabulary of the word "absolute." Third, a greater awareness of the importance of culture in influencing our beliefs and customs, social anthropology studies the chief cause. And, fourth, a keener sense of individuality.

These stage cases tell us where men are, the varieties in their faith development. Not all men, not even those in a specific stage, are in the same place in their development. Stages are a tool for understanding and appreciating variations.

Absent from the faith development and religiosity studies are samples of the oldest-old, especially centenarians. The Georgia Centenarian Study is filling this gap. The study investigates the ways in which religiosity factors into the adaptability of centenarians and how their faithing compares with younger elders. Courtenay and his colleagues (1992) reported that religious practice is used as a coping devise for the oldest-old: They rely on religion more when faced with health problems. The centenarians are not as likely to participate in organized religious activity; rather, they rely more on their beliefs, prayer, and faith. The Georgia researchers conclude that a significant number of the centenarians interviewed would agree with 101-year-old Charles C.: "I represent a father in heaven who owns everything. That's one reason I've gotten along so well. I haven't worried about where the next dollar was coming from. . . . I don't worry about the future; it's in God's hands."

Factors Influencing Faith Development in Older Men

Gender

As a graduate research assistant in a theological seminary, I was responsible for grading students' research papers on local church membership characteristics. One male student, puzzled by the higher attendance and involvement of women in all church functions, concluded that women were born more religious than men. Although there are gender differences in faith practice and experience, such popular beliefs about biological differences in male versus female behavior are not supported by social or biological research. In the area of faith, there appear to be no major difference between men and women in terms of the content of their faith development—for example, the amount and nature of faith changes (Cornwall, 1989; Stokes, 1990b).

What is different is the way in which they experience faith (for example, see Gilligan, 1986; Moberg, 1990; Stokes, 1982, 1990a). Men make noticeable changes and grow in the maturity of their faith well into their 70s and beyond. Quite likely, the greatest level of development occurs after age 70. However, the provinces of faith change. Benson and Elkin (1990) divide faith development into horizontal and vertical faith maturity. The horizontal includes a prochurch involvement and translating faith into acts of love, mercy, and justice. Vertical faith includes devotionalism, a deep personal relationship with God; having a faith that shapes thinking, moral action, and a life filled with meaning and purpose.

Throughout their adult life, men develop the horizontal dimension of their faith in a rising and falling pattern. Faracasin (1992) suggests that the reason for the uneven development and decline is that men have traditionally held the organizational leadership positions, are very prochurch and involved in the decision making about the functioning of their church. It is only in their mid-60s that there is a decrease in men's horizontal faithing. Thus it is in their early years that men tend to develop the horizontal dimension of their faith by helping people who have problems or need, promoting world peace, and expressing concern about social issues. Their horizontal faith constitutes giving organizational leadership within a church or synagogue.

Beginning in their mid-50s, men tend to experience a shift in their faith development to a vertical or more relational area of faithing. That is, they shift to a deeper personal relationship with God that shapes thinking, moral action, and purpose. These changes of decline and increase seem to represent a balancing of horizontal and vertical faith, which represents an overall maturing of faith in men's late life (Faracasin, 1992). These changes also seem to correspond to the period of pre- and postretirement—the time when occupancy of the "good" provider role and thus the relationship between work and self is no longer dominant. Ralph N. is an example of this balancing:

> When Ralph retired as an executive from a *Fortune* 500 company, he had been a "good" churchman. He had served as chair of all the major church boards, particularly those related to budget and finance; he attended regularly and supported the social policies of his church, even when he did not always agree with them. And, he reported, he endured many social issues sermons when he was more deeply concerned about his company or the workforce.
>
> He thought when he retired, he would continue to be active by serving on boards of voluntary organizations that helped people with a variety of problems. Instead, he found himself a member of an older men's prayer group.

They read religious literature, studied prayer, and focused on their individual spiritual needs and what other older people in their parish community needed. Out of this prayer group was born the Shepherd's Center in Kansas City, now a national and international organization of local Shepherd's Centers responding to the needs of older persons.

Ralph organized the Meals on Wheels program and was one of the volunteers to deliver meals. He organized a group of men to staff this program. What happened to Ralph was a profound religious experience that changed his faithing. As he said, "I learned what my faith was all about. I learned the meaning of ministry to those who were physically, socially, and spiritually hungry." Ralph N. experienced a balancing of his horizontal and vertical faith development.

Retirement

Aging as a social event appears to regulate men's faith development. The alternating periods of stability and transition that occur throughout the adult life cycle are useful in understanding men's faith changes. From his research, Levinson found that in periods of relative stability men work on improving existing areas of their lives—family, work, friendship, and so on. In periods of transition, these life patterns either change or need restructuring. Those transitions that affect adult men the most are at midlife, preretirement, and retirement.

Levinson brought attention to midlife as a crisis time for men. He suggests that midlife is a meaning crisis when men ask, "What have I done with my life? What do I really get from and give to my wife, children, friends, work, community and self? What is it I truly want for myself and others? What are my central values and how are they reflected in my life?" Stokes (1982, 1990a) theorized that the midlife crisis may be the most critical period of adult male faith development. Those personal meaning questions raised by Levinson are also religious questions, signaling a man's concerns with the vertical dimension. That is, if the questions are faced in the context of faith, they can be expected to stimulate faith changes.

I believe that shifting from the preretirement years into retirement is an important transition period for faith development and a time of reflection on priorities and values. Faith development does not occur in a uniform way throughout adulthood, but rather in varying patterns of activity (Stokes, 1990b). Anticipating retirement during the preretirement years and soon thereafter leaving the workforce might mean loss of identity and power, a loss of the community of co-workers. The experience of retirement is an emptying out of a persons's work life, his or her most sturdy crutch stripped away. It is death to a former lifestyle. The transition from paid work to unpaid or no work can be troublesome; although it frequently begins with a vacationlike excitement, this gives away to underload, and for some men feelings of uselessness, a sense of loss, and depression. Adjustment to the new life and the search for new meanings is a must. Stokes (1990a) and Gallup (1992) reveal that it is at this time that men are most likely to be interested in their faith development. Some, like Bill S., may intentionally seek a new relationship with their church.

> Soon after his retirement as an insurance company executive, Bill S. attended a meeting of retirees at his church. They were discussing what they wanted or expected from the church in their retirement. After much discussion Bill said he wanted to be in the church during the week, not just on Sunday. He wanted to be there when he did not have to rush to get away to attend to business. He did not want to hold any offices in the church organization; he wanted to discover things that need to be done, to have time to talk to other members. He has done that, and discovered a need he could meet. He used his knowledge of insurance to study and interpret plans for members who were confused about or needed counseling about coverage. This filled a need among his fellow members and . . . he gets to talk with them. This has become his new one-on-one ministry and a part of his vertical faith development.

During the stable period of retirement, men's faithing may be more directly affected when they respond to organized religion and educational opportunities, rather than just reflection. One educational setting Stokes (1982) observed was a Bible study group offered in a United Methodist Church. Participants make a 24-week commitment to read the assignments daily, make notes, and attend a weekly 2-hour study-discussion session. The classes are small and open to all ages of adults. In that 24 weeks the entire Bible is covered. After conducting more that 36 of those classes, one minister reported that more than half of the participants were elders, equally represented by older men and older women. It was the first time that most of these older men had read the entire Bible and discussed the meanings and history. An additional value of men seeking out educational classes is that men were with women, who are more social and relational in their faithing, whereas men are more reserved in their faith expression and tend to keep faith experiences more to themselves (Stokes, 1990b).

Prior research has shown that men usually avoid discussion groups and hold their beliefs and faith experiences very close. The question becomes,

Do older men have opportunities to engage in vertical faith development? Without opportunity, older men are restricted to addressing their "meaning questions" outside the boundaries of the ministry. When they want or need guidance, they are limited to sharing with a close friend or family member or to certain issues with their clergy (Stokes, 1990a).

Health

Changes in men's health or that of their wives are events that alter lifelong lifestyle patterns and relationships. If it is a life-threatening disease such as cancer or the more recently dreaded Alzheimer's, then the older man becomes either a caregiver or a care receiver. He faces the loss of a wife or self. The significance of the changes involved are described to be factors in faith development (Levin, 1988).

When men become caregivers, they report changes in their faithing. They assume nurturing roles and homemaker roles usually performed by and expected of women (see Kaye & Applegate, Chapter 12 in this volume). Studies of men, and older men in particular, who become caregivers for wives who are victims of Alzheimer's disease often suggest that the men act out of an ethic of duty (Gilligan, 1982; Miller, 1987, 1990). By comparison, other researchers have found that husband caregivers are motivated by an ethic of caring, love, and commitment (Harris, 1993; Kaye & Applegate, 1990; Montenko, 1988). In her qualitative research of the older male caregiver, Harris (1993) identified not just two, but four types of older male caregivers.

Some of the men reported that the experience with their wives made them better people, more compassionate and more thoughtful, and some reported that they relied on the clergy for social support. Two older husband caregivers I interviewed credit caregiving with their most recent faith development. These two cases are not systematic, but they serve as examples of the positive stimulus the caregiver experience can be for personal growth and faith development in older men:

> Bill, a retired political science professor, cared for his Alzheimer's wife for [more than 10] years. He was experiencing his own aging as he undertook the sole care of his wife. He easily recounted his experiences of anger, frustration, humor, tender moments, and his own difficulties with severe arthritis. Out of all this he grew in patience and appreciation for the life he had shared with his wife. His vertical faith experience and caregiving experience motivated him to further share what it was like to be a male caregiver. Bill is now 93 and his book is being promoted by the Alzheimer's Association for other older men.

Bert C. is a retired minister whose wife developed Alzheimer's disease during his [preretirement] years. He cared for her for [more than 15] years. He found a new (vertical) experience of love from the congregation, which accepted her and supported his efforts to keep her a part of the life they had shared. He took her with him to church meetings and on his travels, and he found new ways to communicate and receive love from her. He also developed the ability to mainstream an Alzheimer's victim and to help countless hundreds learn to respond to the afflicted. When she died there was a special article of appreciation for both of them in the city paper.

When the health changes are one's own and are life-threatening, an older man is faced not only with the meaning of his life but also with his death and the meaning and beliefs he holds about death. Most older men have experienced the death of significant people in their lives. These deaths cause reflection and affect faithing, but not like that of his own impending end. For example, Paul Maves (1986) was in his 70s when he wrote *Faith for the Older Years*. In it he recounts his experience with the death of a close friend and colleague and his own experience in "living in the shadow of death" with prostate cancer. It was through these two health and death experiences that his faith was changed by integrating the meaning of hope into his faithing. Hope was not wishful thinking about his life-threatening illness. Hope, Maves (1986) writes, "allows me to make plans and take on projects that stretch several years ahead. Hope lets me rejoice in each day as it comes. It lets me anticipate the days to come." Hope is found in the possibility of making good use of the time still available, bearing witness to what devotion and commitment can do even then.

Maves's journey is more than about coping with death. It is about faithing and struggling with the meaning of life in the older years. Faithing involves its own struggles and can ameliorate the strains of physiological aging (Morse & Wisocki, 1987), the difficulty of postsurgical recovery (McSherry, Salisberg, Ciulla, & Tsuang, 1987), and the loss of a spouse (Rosik, 1989; Siegel & Kuykendall, 1990), yet faithing has proved to be a varied experience (Chatters, Levin, & Taylor, 1992; Nelson, 1989; Thomas, 1991). It differs for older men of different faiths, ethnicity, culture, and life stage.

Developmentally, these varied faithing experiences among older men are triggered by personal crises of aging, hospitalization, loss of a loved one, or chronic illness. Levinson's and Stokes's research suggest that the dealing with and resolution of psychosocial tensions lead to reevaluation and faith development. Goodwin (1982) argues that crisis does threaten the organization, structure, and meaning of one's life. One's self-concept and identity may no longer be viable, and the crisis happening requires a new way of envisioning one's life. Faith may develop and be more pronounced during and after a crisis because the circumstances force men to confront vertical faith issues of meaning and ultimacy. But crisis is not necessary for faith development (Goodwin, 1982). In fact, Goodwin advises that we should not be in a hurry to recommend crisis as a pathway for men's faith development: Health-related crises sometimes may destroy faith or result in a stalemate, leaving the individual stuck in an earlier level of integration.

As much as older men's health and death experiences influence their faith development, faith stages seem to have reciprocal effects on health and well-being. Shulik (1979) observed that the older men who had achieved a higher faith stage continued to enjoy the richness of life despite physical limitations and restrictions on mobility. It seems that faith stage, independently of devotionalism or other content dimensions of religiosity, may have a positive, independent effect on how older men experience aging.

Involvement in Organized Religion

Lifelong membership in a church, which began with strong family involvement in the church, is a major factor in the pace and stage of faith development in men (Stokes, 1990a). As in the case of Ralph N., some men continue to attend church and provide leadership for programs, but in a more personal, hands-on way. Generally, however, prochurch and leadership activities decline as men age and approach their mid-60s. This may result from declining health and not men's lessening or diminishing faith (Ainlay, Singleton, & Swigert, 1992). As the health of each cohort of older men continues to improve in these later years, we can expect current and future cohorts to increase their prochurch and leadership involvement and therefore continue their horizontal faith along with the vertical development.

At the time that church involvement declines, devotionalism increases. It could be, as Faracasin (1992) suggests, that attending church is perceived as less useful by men for their faith development in their 70s and older. Or it is possible that some males redefine what they believe is important to their religious growth in such a manner that a church is not perceived by them as central to their faith and religious growth (Buhler, 1974).

Conclusion and Implications for Research and Practice

Although the research on faith development among older men is limited, there is sufficient evidence that older men do experience change and growth in their faith experiences after their mid-50s. These changes are more in relational, educational, devotional, and congregational care than in church organizational involvement.

The need for more research is obvious. Methods and focus are not as clear. Birren (1990) and Gallup (1992) believe that the focus should be on the "inner space" of older persons and men in particular. Birren recommends that the focus of future research should shift from the outer to the inner faith life of older persons. The most important data needed to understand faith development and aging is the internal testimony of the older person.

The differences between Birren and Gallup are in methods of studying inner space. The faith development researchers believe that an adaptation of the Fowler structured interview that focuses on older men is the best method. Birren (1990) recommends the autobiography. On the other hand, Gallup (1992, p. 5) believes that "carefully conceived and executed surveys that penetrate beneath the surface of lives can help build up the body of Christ and further the kingdom of God." He also argues that because the "majority of people of the world believe in God or a power outside ourselves, the most profound and worthy pursuit of scientific surveys is to probe the response of humanity to God, to the extent that this is possible" (p. 5).

They both may be right. Some combination of the two approaches would provide more information from a larger number of older men from more diverse backgrounds. It would also make it possible to begin to include younger cohorts and project future trends in faith development and the interaction of aging and faith development among men. Research that focuses on the oldest old men is needed to understand the faith continuities and changes occurring after 85 years of age and among centenarians. Furthermore, although I found research examining ethnic or racial religiosity, there was no research analyzing racial and ethnic variations in older men's faithing. This omission of subjects or analysis needs to be addressed.

Implications for practice are directed toward the major faith groups, theological schools, and adult education programmers. From the *Faith Development in the Adult Life Cycle* study, Stokes (1990a) recommends that religious communities need their faith. Instead of academics and theologians stating what should be believed, people need to be helped to identify for themselves which spiritual resources they can and do call upon. Stokes also believes that older men need to be helped to reflect on their lives as faithing experiences.

Drawing from the limited research that is available, more in-depth, short-term adult educational opportunities are needed that recognize the variety of faith stages and needs of men, and that will take men where they are and provide opportunities for growth. From the research findings, the programs need intentionally to include the transitional areas affecting older men and the questions such events raise. In addition, older men appear to want help in developing devotional life and opportunities to be involved in more service-related church or congregational programs.

Implications for seminaries include a curriculum emphasis on adult education that recognizes the unique needs of older adults and older men in particular. As Birren (1990) points out, we know much about biological, psychological, and social aging but little about how it interacts with theology and organized religion. As society and churches gray, it is increasingly important to meet the spiritual quests of older men and women and recognize the gender differences.

Note

1. For this discussion of faith and faith development, I am adopting the definitions used by Stokes (1982): Faith is the finding and making meaning of life's significant questions and issues, adhering to this meaning, and acting it out. Faith development is the dynamics by which a person finds and makes meaning of life's significant questions and issues and then acts it out.

References

Agostino, J. N. (1987). Religiosity and religious participation in the later years: A reflection of the spiritual needs of the elderly. *Journal of Religion and Aging, 4,* 75-82.

Ainlay, S. C., Singleton, R., & Swigert, V. L. (1992). Aging and religious participation: Reconsidering the effects of health. *Journal of the Scientific Study of Religion, 31,* 175-188.

Benson, P. L., & Elkin, C. H. (1990). *Effective Christian education: A national study of Protestant congregations. A summary report on faith, loyalty, and congregational life.* Minneapolis, MN: Research Institute.

Birren, J. E. (1990). Spiritual maturity in psychological development. In J. J. Seeber (Ed.), *Spiritual maturity in the later years* (pp. 41-53). New York: Haworth.

Blazer, D. G., & Palmore, E. (1976). Religion and aging in a longitudinal panel. *The Gerontologist, 16,* 82-85.

Bruning, C., & Stokes, K. (1982). In K. Stokes (Ed.), *Faith development in the adult life cycle.* New York: W. H. Sadlier.

Buhler, C. (1974). Theories of the life cycle. In D. C. Kimmel (Ed.), *Adulthood and aging.* New York: John Wiley.

Chatters, L. M., Levin, J. S., & Taylor, R. J. (1992). Antecedents and dimensions of religious involvement among older black adults. *Journal of Gerontology: Social Sciences, 47,* S269-S278.

Cornwall, M. (1989). Faith development of men and women over the life span. In S. Bahr & E. Peterson, *Aging and the family* (pp. 115-139). Lexington, MA: Lexington Books.

Courtenay, B. C., Poon, L. W., Martin, P., Clayton, G. M., & Johnson, M. A. (1992). Religiosity and adaptation in the oldest-old. *International Journal of Aging and Human Development, 34,* 47-56.

Erikson, E. (1950). *Childhood and society.* New York: Norton.

Faracasin, T. W. (1992). *The relationship of gender differences to adult religious development.* Unpublished doctoral dissertation, University of Minnesota, Minneapolis.

Fowler, J. (1981). *Stages of faith: The psychology of human development and the quest for meaning.* New York: HarperCollins.

Fowler, J. (1987). *Faith development in the adult life cycle: The report of a research project.* New Haven, CT: Religious Research Association.

Gallup, G. (1985). *Faith development and your ministry.* Princeton, NJ: Princeton Religion Research Center.

Gallup, G. (1987). Age a key factor in comparing religiousness of men and women. *Emerging Trends* (Princeton Religion Research Center), *9*(9).

Gallup, G. (1991). What every pastor should know about the average American. *Emerging Trends* (Princeton Religion Research Center), *13*(3).

Gallup, G. (1992). Surveys reveal religious "inner life." *Emerging Trends* (Princeton Religion Research Center), *14*(10).

Gallup, G. (1993). eens want answers to the hard questions of life. *Emerging Trends* (Princeton Religion Research Center), *15*(9).

Gilligan, C. (1982). *In a different voice: Psychological theory and women's development.* Cambridge, MA: Harvard University Press.

Gilligan, C. (1986). In a different voice: Visions of maturity. In J. W. Conn (Ed.), *Women's spirituality: Resources for Christian development* (pp. 63-87). New York: Paulist Press.

Goodwin, W. (1982). Responses from an adult development perspective. In K. Stokes (Ed.), *Faith development in the adult life cycle* (pp. 85-119). New York: W. H. Sadlier.

Hall, G. S. (1922). *Senescence, the second half of life.* New York: Appleton.

Harris, P. B. (1993). The misunderstood caregiver? A qualitative study of the male caregiver of Alzheimer's disease victims. *The Gerontologist, 33,* 551-556.

Havighurst, R. (1948). *Developmental tasks and education.* Chicago: University of Chicago Press.

James, W. (1902). *Varieties of religious experience.* New York: Longman, Green.

Jung, C. (1933). *Modern man in search of a soul.* New York: Harcourt, Brace & Wold.

Kahler, M. (1967). Justification by faith. Lecture in P. Tillich (Ed.), *Perspectives on 19th and 20th century Protestant theology.* New York: Harper & Row.

Kaye, L. W., & Applegate, J. S. (1990). *Men as caregivers to the elderly: Understanding and aiding unrecognized family systems.* Lexington, MA: Lexington Books.

Levin, J. S. (1988). Religious factors in aging, adjustment, and health: A theoretical overview. *Journal of Religion and Aging, 4,* 133-146.

Levin, J. S., & Taylor, R. J. (1993). Gender and age differences in religiosity among black Americans. *The Gerontologist, 33,* 16-23.

Levinson, D. J., Darrow, C. N., Klein, E. B., Levinson, M. H., & McKee, B. (1978). *The seasons of a man's life*. New York: Knopf.

Maddox, G. L. (1987). Aging differently. *The Gerontologist, 27,* 557-564.

Maves, P. B. (1986). *Faith for the older years: Making the most of life's second half.* Minneapolis, MN: Augsburg Press.

McSherry, E., Salisberg, S. R., Ciulla, M. R., & Tsuang, D. (1987). Spiritual resources in older hospitalized men. *Social Compass, 34,* 515-537.

Miller, B. (1987). Gender and control among spouses of the cognitively impaired: A research note. *The Gerontologist, 27,* 447-453.

Miller, B. (1990). Gender differences in spouse management of the caregiver role. In E. K. Abel & M. K. Nelson (Eds.), *Circles of care: Work and identity in women's lives* (pp. 92-104). Albany: New York State University Press.

Moberg, D. O. (1965). Religiosity in old age. *The Gerontologist, 5,* 78-87.

Moberg, D. O. (1990). Spiritual maturity and wholeness in the later years. *Journal of Religious Gerontology, 7,* 5-24.

Montenko, A. K. (1988). Respite care and pride in caregiving: The experience of older men caring for disabled wives. In S. Reinhatz & C. Rowles (Eds.), *Qualitative gerontology* (pp. 104-126). New York: Springer.

Morse, C. K., & Wisocki, P. A. (1988). Importance of religiosity to elderly adjustment. *Journal of Religion & Aging, 4,* 15-26.

Nelson, P. B. (1989). Ethnic differences in intrinsic/extrinsic religious orientation and depression in the elderly. *Archives of Psychiatric Nursing, 3,* 199-204.

Neugarten, B. L. (1964). *Personality in middle and late life*. New York: Atherton.

Neugarten, B. L., & Datan, N. (1973). Sociological perspectives on the life cycle. In P. B. Baltes & K. W. Schaie (Eds.), *Life-span developmental psychology: Personality and socialization* (pp. 53-69). San Diego, CA: Academic Press.

Orbach, H. L. (1961). Aging and religion: Church attendance in the Detroit metropolitan area. *Geriatrics, 16,* 530-540.

Payne, B. P. (1990). Spiritual maturity and meaning-filled relationships: A sociological perspective. *Journal of Religious Gerontology, 7,* 25-39.

Payne, B. P. (1993). *Faith development among older men: Case studies*. Unpublished papers.

Rosik, C. H. (1989). The impact of religious orientation in conjugal bereavement among older adults. *International Journal of Aging and Human Development, 28,* 251-260.

Shulik, R. N. (1979). *Faith development, moral development, and old age: An assessment of Fowler's faith development paradigm*. Unpublished doctoral dissertation, University of Chicago.

Siegel, J. M., & Kuykendall, D. H. (1990). Loss, widowhood, and psychological distress among the elderly. *Journal of Consulting and Clinical Psychology, 58,* 519-524.

Starbuck, E. D. (1911). *The psychology of religion: An empirical study of the growth of religious consciousness*. New York: Walter Scott.

Stokes, K. (1982). *Faith development in the adult life cycle*. New York: W. H. Sadlier.

Stokes, K. (1990a). *Faith is a verb*. Mystic, CT: Twenty-Third Publications.

Stokes, K. (1990b). Faith development in the adult life cycle. *Journal of Religious Gerontology, 7,* 167-184.

Thomas, L. E. (1991). Dialogues with three religious renunciates and reflections on wisdom and maturity. *International Journal of Aging and Human Development, 32,* 211-227.

Thompson, E. H. (1991). Beneath the status characteristic: Gender variations in religiousness. *Journal of the Scientific Study of Religion, 30,* 381-394.

6

Masculine Identity
From Work to Retirement

THEODORE J. GRADMAN

Work and career dominate a man's identity, leaving him unprepared for the realities of retirement. Retirement is often perceived as a vague and distant goal and a reward for years of hard labor. Men sometimes plan for its financial impact but rarely acknowledge its psychological impact. Retirement results in the loss of colleagues and social support (Ochberg, 1987), loss of opportunities to feel competitive and independent (Weiss, 1990), loss of an arena to risk failure and feel accomplished (Filene, 1981; Willing, 1989), and loss of income. In these ways, retirement threatens a man's sense of masculinity. Many men do not realize this until they decide to retire.

The perceived threat to masculine identity marks the beginning of adaptation to retirement (Gradman, 1990). A man must evaluate how he will retain his sense of masculinity when deciding when and how to retire. No overnight transformation occurs. Priorities, goals, and everyday activities need to be gradually reformulated.

AUTHOR'S NOTE: Many people and organizations made this chapter possible. Jackie Goodchilds of UCLA encouraged me to develop this project in conjunction with a larger study that she and Tora Bikson were conducting at the RAND Corporation (supported by a grant from the John and Mary R. Markle Foundation). Sy Feshbach expertly guided me and my UCLA dissertation committee. My thinking further developed at the Stanford Older Adult Center at the Palo Alto Veterans Administration Hospital, where I received excellent postdoctoral training. Many significant contributions came from friends in Los Angeles and the Bay Area and my colleagues at Mills Hospital in San Mateo. A more complete report of the research (Research Report No. P-7626) can be obtained from the RAND Corporation, 1700 Main Street, P.O. Box 2138, Santa Monica, CA 90406-2138.

The retirement transition is an ideal period to study late-life masculine identity. Although most subjects in retirement studies are men and most studies focus on traditionally male goals and life choices (Szinovacz, 1982; Szinovacz & Washo, 1992), the experience of retirement to men as men is rarely addressed. This chapter focuses on how men as men change from committed workers to well-established retirees.

Masculine Identity and Work

Historically, the prototype for American men was a single standard against which all men were measured: the white, heterosexual, middle-aged, married good provider (Bernard, 1981; Kimmel & Messner, 1992). Adult men were expected to be invested in their work as a source of status, stability, and identity. Retired men, unemployed men, and other men who departed from the normative standard were stereotyped adversely and thought to suffer psychologically (Ehrenreich, 1983; Rubin, 1976).

American culture of the first half of the 20th century stressed distinct roles for men and women (Doyle, 1983; Pleck, 1981). To be a man meant to work, to share the community of other working men, and to support a family. Recent studies reveal that work and its rewards remain prominent in men's conception of themselves today (Ochberg, 1987; Weiss, 1990).

Work supports a sense of masculinity both overtly and in ways that are not acknowledged consciously. Throughout adulthood, men work to obtain extrinsic (monetary and social) and intrinsic (self-expression and fulfillment) rewards. Work supports a man's perception of his status, ability, and worthiness (Kosloski, Ginsburg, & Backman, 1984). Work provides sustenance with productive activity, income, status, self-fulfillment, and social contact. Work creates multiple opportunities for a man to see himself as powerful, self-reliant, and competent. In general, work enables a man to meet the social norms for masculine attitudes and behavior.

The primacy of work is supported by research. Many studies show that most men identify foremost with their work (Elder, 1974; Miller, 1965; Veroff & Feld, 1970; Weiss, 1990). They use their occupational role in part to negotiate family, leisure, and community identities (Miller, 1965). Some men balance work and family identity, but most retain great emotional investment in work (Ochberg, 1987; Veroff, Douvan & Kulka, 1981).

The work ethic underlies many older men's beliefs about manhood. Most men believe that if a man works hard, uses time wisely, and makes self-sacrifices, he will achieve occupational success and acquire wealth (Benner, 1984; Gouldner, 1970). Historically, the Protestant work ethic equated career success with salvation (Benner, 1984). The modernized utilitarian tradition equates success with self-worth. Individuals who embrace the work ethic in their working years show a decrease in both activity and satisfaction in retirement (Hooker & Ventis, 1984). When work is perceived as a moral imperative, retirement instills feelings of uselessness and apathy.

Loss of work threatens a man's sense of identity (Weiss, 1990). Unemployed men report feelings of worthlessness and marginal social standing, regardless of previous status. As unemployment is painful, so the termination of work at retirement is no less painful. As retirement approaches, many men become anxious once they sense a lack of familiar masculine anchors (Ochberg, 1987; Weiss, 1990). They will lose their main arena for achievement, aggressive competition, status, power, and self-reliance. Because men maintain gender-appropriate attitudes and behaviors through work, retirement challenges a man's sense of masculinity.

Men often perceive retirement as an entry to the feminine turf of the household and family (Willing, 1989). A man's entry into his wife's domain, and loss of his own, can result in uncertainty about appropriate masculine behavior. Many married men express concern that they will be criticized by their wives once they can be observed more closely (Bikson & Goodchilds, 1989; Szinovacz, Ekerdt, & Vinick, 1992; Willing, 1989). Retired men perform more household tasks than before but view themselves as "helping" their wives through these domestic tasks (Vinick & Ekerdt, 1992). This view enables men to adhere to previously held conceptions of masculine behavior despite some behavioral change. However, most household tasks remain divided according to gender. Women continue to do most of the housework and men concentrate on yard work and appliance repair. Change in underlying attitudes about gender-appropriate household activities is unlikely (Keith, Wacker, & Schafer, 1992). Retired men also imagine that they will now socialize more with relatives and friends, but this rarely occurs (Kaye & Monk, 1984; Vinick & Ekerdt, 1992). They continue to engage in activities that utilize work skills and maintain the same (often low) level of social activity that characterized their working years (Kaye & Monk, 1984). Retired men appear to adhere to the code of behaviors and attitudes for the workplace even though retirement places them in new territory.

After retirement, men continue to emphasize the same masculine attributes as before. They demand of themselves continued strength, decisiveness, and power (Solomon, 1982). Many older men worry about feeling emasculated as their physical capabilities decline; they are concerned about obtaining respect from their family and community as opportunities for work achievement decrease (Rubinstein, 1986).

Masculine Identity and Retirement Adaptation

Changes in Masculinity During Later Adulthood

The importance of work to male identity might suggest that retirement generates a rupture or at least a marked discontinuity. But a man's sense of masculinity evolves throughout the adult life span as he grows older. There are three primary elements of this process. The first element is the maintenance of societal expectations for masculine behavior and attitudes (Sinnott, Rabin, & Windle, 1986). These prescriptions for behavior are strongly reinforced and remain relatively constant throughout adulthood (Rubinstein, 1986; Solomon, 1982). Gender-appropriate attitudes such as instrumental orientation (focus on getting the job done) and analytical orientation (reliance on step-by-step logic) are often emphasized by older men (Bem, 1974; Kaye & Monk, 1984; Solomon, 1982). Older men want to be vigorous despite physical decline, to suppress emotions even after loss, and to maintain control and authority despite lessened leadership responsibilities (Rubinstein, 1986). Men rely on their internal sense of how they are masculine to assist them in coping with the transitions and losses of aging. The process of maintaining a consistent view of oneself to cope with aging is known as *continuity* (Atchley, 1971, 1972, 1989).

The second element is the gradual emergence of feminine attributes to complement existing masculine attributes (Levinson, Darrow, Klein, Levinson, & McKee, 1978; Sinnott, Rabin, & Windle, 1986). Work environments restrict creative, affiliative, and emotional expression for the majority of younger and middle-aged men (Filene, 1981). Retirement often presents the first real opportunity to depart from the confines of the working world and cultivate these formerly unexpressed characteristics. Social pressures for emotional sensitivity and personal connection in later life reassure older men of the value of increased affiliation and self-expression (Levinson et al., 1978; Neugarten, 1968; Vaillant, 1977). Fletcher and Hansson (1991) noted that men demonstrating both instrumental-oriented masculine traits and affiliation-oriented feminine traits form and maintain new relations more successfully after retirement. This integration of feminine traits requires reconciliation of prohibitions stemming from the societal expectations for men reinforced during their working years. Underground feminine traits balance strong masculine qualities as a man matures and the yoke of work is removed.

The third element is the biological process of declining vigor. Androgens start to decrease in middle age, resulting in a loss of virility, muscle mass, energy output, and dominance (Brim, 1976; Vaillant, 1977). Together, biological slowing, the continuity of gender expectations, and the emergence of new modes of self-expression become the foundation of an older man's sense of himself as a man.

Theories of Retirement Adaption

Previously, various models of retirement adaptation emphasized discontinuities across the male life span. For example, the disengagement model posits a withdrawal from primary roles of early and middle adulthood. An individual disengages by adopting a more passive problem-solving style and becomes more self-centered during the transition to retirement (Cumming & Henry, 1961). The activity model proposes that a maintenance of activity levels after retirement is necessary for successful aging, and men substitute leisure and community-maintenance activities for work activities (Friedmann & Havighurst, 1954; Hochschild, 1978; Miller, 1965). By comparison, the continuity approach to masculine identity in later adulthood emphasized in this chapter stems from the more recent continuity model of aging and retirement adaptation. The continuity model (Atchley, 1971, 1972, 1989; Neugarten, Havighurst, & Tobin, 1968) links adaptation to a person's personal history and a stable self-perception (internal continuity) and an ongoing social support network and interactions in the community (external continuity). Continuity theory does not emphasize the maintenance of activity levels but postulates an evolution of an individual's personal characteristics to a different life situation. A reduction in expectations coupled with a broader definition of success permits continuity of perceived self-worth (Atchley, 1989).

Stages of Retirement

The psychological and social adaptations of retirement do not occur abruptly. Adaptation requires several years before and after retirement and includes several stages (Atchley, 1976; Willing, 1989). Retirement requires a decision (or mandate from an employer), varying amounts of preparation, a last day at work, initial adaptation to retirement conditions, and establishment of a long-term retirement lifestyle (Atchley, 1976). This lifestyle may include part-time or occasional work, which is often related to a man's former career, as an adaptive link to the past (Kaye & Monk, 1984). Men experience fluctuation in their satisfaction with life in retirement and may cope more effectively with some stages than others (Stokes & Maddox, 1967).

A Study of Masculine Identity and Retirement

One recent study uniquely examines successful men at different stages of retirement and isolates psychological determinants of retirement decisions from other factors such as health, finances, and age (Gradman, 1990). This study was part of a larger longitudinal study of the social-psychological process of the retirement transition (Bikson, Goodchilds, Huddy, Eveland, & Schneider, 1991). Work identification and masculine identity were measured in 76 men from one large company at different points in the retirement process (11 workers with no date set; 8 with one to three years to go; 7 with less than one year to go; 11 within 18 months after retirement; and 39 past two years of retirement) (Gradman, 1990). The three subgroups of working men may not completely simulate how a man progresses toward retirement. However, most men predict their retirement dates well and progress from no decision to deciding on a distant date to preparing for imminent retirement (Ekerdt, Vinick, & Bosse, 1989).

The subjects in this study were "successful men" because they had high status and stability in multiple areas, including career, finances, health, social networks, and intimate relationships (Bikson & Goodchilds, 1989). They were relatively healthy and could make a voluntary decision based on individual psychological needs more than on income or health concerns. The average age was 64.1. The age range was 57.4 to 74.1 for workers and 58.7 to 72.1 for retirees, showing great overlap. Analyses were essentially equivalent whether age was controlled or not. The minimal effect of age permitted focus on retirement stage.

Measures

Work identification and masculine identity were assessed during a follow-up to the larger longitudinal study (see Gradman, 1990, for details). *Work identification* is the degree to which a man identifies closely with his job and makes a commitment to work to the best of his ability.

Work identification is multidimensional. *Job involvement* refers to the importance of the specific job to a man's self-image; *career commitment* refers to the importance of work and a career in one's life; *organizational commitment* refers to an individual's identification with a particular organization and its goals. The empirically validated work commitment scales (Blau, 1985, 1988) were used to measure each of these concepts independently (e.g., "I consider my job to be central to my existence," or "I find that my values and my company's values are very similar"). A man's degree of liking or disliking of his job is also associated with work identification, and this was measured by the Job Satisfaction Scale (Hackman & Oldham, 1975). Finally, a man's adherence to work ethic attitudes is also closely related to work identification, and his work ideology was measured by five items from the Work Ethic Scale (Mirels & Garrett, 1971; e.g., "A distaste for hard work usually reflects a weakness of character").

Masculine identity is also multidimensional. Recognizing that retirement is a period in which a man's identity is vulnerable, Eisler and Skidmore's (1987) Masculine Gender-Role Stress (MGRS) scale was selected to measure retiring men's perceived distress in specific situations relating to traditional gender expectations (e.g., "being outperformed at work by a woman"; "getting passed over for a promotion"). Similar questions about situations requiring aggressiveness or competitiveness were added to reflect these expected masculine characteristics. In addition, a trait measure of self-reported masculinity, the M scale of the Personal Attributes Questionnaire (PAQ; see Spence, Helmreich, & Stapp, 1974), was included to complement the situation-specific MGRS with a global self-rating of decisiveness, competitiveness, confidence, and other stereotypically masculine traits.

Adjustment to retirement was assessed by a single-item measure (from the larger study) asking each subject how well he has adjusted (or will adjust) to retirement. Overall well-being was assessed by two scales that were repeated through the course of the study. The General Positive Affect Scale (Veit & Ware, 1983) measures happiness (e.g., "I generally enjoy the things I do"). A shortened version (Hays & DiMatteo, 1986) of the UCLA Loneliness Scale (Russell, Peplau, & Ferguson, 1978) measures distress (e.g., "I feel isolated from others").

Results and Interpretation

Examining work identification and masculine identity at different stages of retirement reveals several striking and counterintuitive findings.

First, retired men view their overall identification with job, career, and organization more strongly than workers ($t = 2.26$, $df = 74$, $p < .05$). As detailed fully in Gradman (1990), this difference holds for career commitment ($t = 2.33$, $df = 74$, $p < .05$), organizational commitment ($t = 2.45$, $df = 74$, $p < .05$), and job satisfaction ($t = 3.06$, $df = 74$, $p < .005$). These enduring elements of work may be sources of stability for retired men in line with continuity theory. Second, masculine identity fluctuates throughout the transition. Gender distress first appears when a man sets his retirement date. The men closest to the decision point, those with a date set of one to three years away, report more gender role stress than all other subjects (on the MGRS, $t = 2.19$, $df = 73$, $p < .05$; on the aggressiveness inadequacy scale, $t = 2.97$, $df = 73$, $p < .005$; on the competition difficulty scale, $t = 3.40$, $df = 73$, $p < .005$). They also show a trend toward a decreased sense of masculinity on the M scale of the PAQ ($t = 1.93$, $df = 73$, $p < .10$). Although the number of subjects is small, the study is cross-sectional, and the analysis is exploratory, these nonchance findings invite further research (see Gradman, 1990, for further details).

Setting a date for retirement, more than being retired, threatens a man's sense of masculinity and well-being (see Figure 6.1). The retirement decision heightens uncertainty about masculine identity. Working men see themselves as well-adjusted (low loneliness, high positive affect) only when gender role stress is low ($R = .54$, $df = 24$, $p < .005$). By contrast, men who have already retired show no correlation between well-being and gender role stress. Retirees may have completed the most intense part of the transition; they report greater well-being than workers. This is validated longitudinally with the 11 men retiring during the course of the larger longitudinal study.

Eight types of gender-related stress situations were measured by the expanded MGRS scale. Three types of situations were perceived as more stressful at the decision point than at other times: *aggressiveness inadequacy* (inability to respond to challenges from others), *competition difficulty* (lack of confidence in competing with others), and *subordination to women* (being outperformed by or needing help from a woman). A man may worry about his competitive edge when contemplating leaving the male-oriented workplace for the female-oriented world of retirement. A man may be concerned about the potential loss of authority and dominant status that took so many years to earn.

The three most stressful situations over the entire transition were *performance failure* (in both sexual performance and work competency), *personal life management conflicts* (difficulty in balancing work with

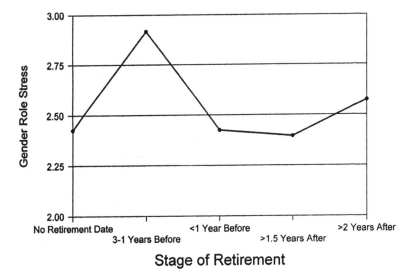

Figure 6.1. Gender Role Stress by Retirement Stage

family and health matters), and *aggressiveness inadequacy*. The retirement transition challenges a working man's aggressive and egocentric stance. Men may experience physical decline and increased concern with health and family matters, but the workplace demands continued commitment and competitive performance.

The perception of moderate to high stress in these situations contrasts with the highly positive ratings of well-being and overall adjustment to retirement. Violating expectations for masculine behavior leads to anxiety and self-devaluation for most men (Pleck, 1981). Societal expectations for masculinity are clearly salient and distressing at this time (Garnets & Pleck, 1979). However, the distress decreases as a man ages (Sinnott, Rabin, & Windle, 1986) and adjusts to the challenges of retirement.

Work identification also changes over the retirement transition. Work commitment is lowest among men who have decided to retire and highest among retirees ($t = 2.54$, $df = 63$, $p < .05$; see Figure 6.2). This pattern holds for career commitment ($t = 3.02$, $df = 63$, $p < .005$), organizational commitment ($t = 2.30$, $df = 63$, $p < .05$), job satisfaction ($t = 3.96$, $df = 63$, $p = .001$), and overall well-being ($t = 2.21$, $df = 62$, $p < .05$). It does not hold for adherence to work ethic values or job involvement.

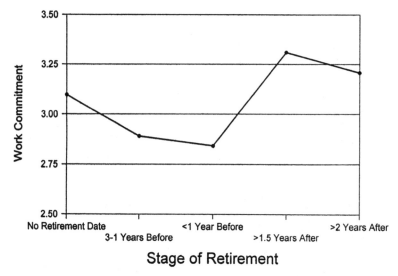

Figure 6.2. Work Commitment by Retirement Stage

Previously, strong identification with work was seen as an obstacle to constructive retirement adaptation (Dreyer, 1989; Simpson, Back, & McKinney, 1966). Several studies of postretirement adaptation show a negative correlation between work identification and well-being (Haug & Belgrave, 1988; Hooker & Ventis, 1984). By contrast, strong work identification correlates with good adjustment for retirees in this study ($R = .44$, $df = 47$, $p < .005$). A study of 2,794 representative American men also shows voluntary retirees identifying strongly with work and adjusting well to retirement (Crowley, 1985).

Some elements of work identification are vital to maintain, while others are less important. In the present study, retirees report high retrospective job satisfaction but low job involvement; the opposite is true of workers (Gradman, 1990). This suggests that postretirement work identification involves pleasurable memories of the job but no particular attachment to the everyday tasks. Belief in the value of hard work continues throughout the entire transition, dropping only among the men closest to the decision ($t = 3.19$, $df = 69$, $p < .005$, compared to other workers and retirees). Most importantly, successful men hold onto their work by regarding their careers as productive and complete and their companies as powerful and important to society. Fried (1949) also found that a sense of career completion was vital for adapting well to retirement.

The Stages of Continuity in the Retirement Transition

Increased work identification after retirement supports the continuity model of retirement and challenges discontinuity models. Success and competent performance are continued as the perception of a successfully completed career with a worthwhile organization. This realignment provides the foundation for masculine identity to remain intact.

The continuity model of retirement does not specify steps in the process. Bereavement theory suggests a progression of stages from shock, panic, and depression to acceptance (Parkes, 1986); retirement may require a similar kind of progression (Atchley, 1976; Kosloski, Ginsburg, & Backman, 1984). Retirement most closely parallels an anticipated type of bereavement because it is clearly foreseen by most men. Anticipatory coping behavior before such a loss includes rehearsing for a new role, following role models, and determining how one's current capabilities will fit the new role (Pearlin, 1980). Most men engage in increasingly frequent preparatory behavior before retirement (Evans, Ekerdt, & Bosse, 1985) to cope with the anticipated loss of career employment.

In the current study, men who have set a retirement date appear to be under the most stress. They disengage from work to rehearse for job loss and find that their sense of masculinity and well-being suffers. They sense elements in the connection between work and masculinity that were not acknowledged before. This temporary disengagement is followed by an acceptance of the loss, as in the bereavement model (Parkes, 1986), by maintaining a connection with the fulfilling and enduring elements of work. The relative stability of masculinity and work identification after retirement reflects integration of revised ways of fulfilling expectations for masculine behavior and attitudes without relying on actual work participation (Gradman, 1990). It is likely that subsequent losses will occur later in retirement. Work identification and other continuing elements of a man's sense of masculinity will assist him in coping with these losses (Atchley, 1976; Willing, 1989).

Diversity Among Men's Work Identification

Work identification is particularly strong when the intrinsic and extrinsic rewards of work are high. Access to rewards is dependent on one's status in the working world. Lower occupational status may lead to lower identification with work. Racial or ethnic differences and marital status also affect a man's perception of his place in the working world.

Occupational Status

Blue-collar workers view retirement more positively than white-collar workers and report greater initial retirement satisfaction (Kellams & Chronister, 1987). Blue-collar workers emphasize extrinsic rather than intrinsic work rewards and are thus less emotionally involved in work (Dreyer, 1989; Filene, 1981). Middle-level workers (clerical, sales, foremen, and skilled workers) find somewhat more intrinsic meaning in work and have a higher level of commitment than unskilled workers, but they generally hold similar retirement attitudes as blue-collar workers and report similar satisfaction (Simpson, Back, & McKinney, 1966). Professionals and executives demonstrate the greatest negative attitude to retirement, stemming perhaps from higher work commitment and higher intrinsic rewards derived from work. Despite greater difficulty with initial adjustment, later satisfaction is often better for the white-collar worker (Loether, 1964; Stokes & Maddox, 1967).

Proposed reasons for these differences in adjustment include greater role flexibility, social facility, communication ability, and general skill levels that accompany a higher occupational status (Loether, 1964; Seccombe & Lee, 1986). Men of higher status have more control over their working environments (Friedmann & Orbach, 1974). They feel the general control over their lives that predicts successful adaptation to retirement (Walker, Kimmel, & Price, 1981). Mandatory and health-related retirees are less satisfied than those who retire by volition (Crowley, 1985). However, increased access to income and medical and social resources may be the prime determinant of the impact of occupational status on retirement adjustment (Seccombe & Lee, 1986).

Race and Ethnicity

Most research on racial and ethnic differences in retirement addresses differences between blacks and whites. Although blacks appear to show the same retirement satisfaction, they have considerably less income, lower longevity expectations, and less preparation for retirement (Palmore, Burchett, Fillenbaum, George, & Wallman, 1985). Blacks and other minorities also have less access to formal preretirement plans (Ferraro, 1990). Blacks are more likely to need to work after retirement and are less likely to regard themselves as "retired" (Gibson, 1993). This appears to be true even among professionals (Richardson & Kilty, 1992). Black professionals who socialize primarily with co-workers and have high work commitment avoid planning for retirement—similar to white professionals (Richardson & Kilty, 1992). There is little evidence to suggest that black men experience work commitment differently than white men. Their more limited access to resources and previous occupational status appear to be the prime determinants of differences in retirement satisfaction.

Marital Status

Marital status further modifies adjustment to retirement. Work may be especially important to the unmarried man, purportedly compensating for the lack of gratification from marriage (Ward, 1979). Unmarried individuals seek more social validity from work than married peers and so are more sensitive to their reputation as workers (Veroff, Douvan, & Kulka, 1981). Work provides a major connection to the community and opportunity for social contact. Single men with increased work commitment may find the decision to retire more difficult and continued employment more desirable (Rubinstein, 1986; Ward, 1979). A longitudinal study of 1,398 unmarried individuals did not substantiate this, but there was no control married group (Keith, 1985). Another study found that single men focus on leisure more than married men as retirement approaches (Veroff, Douvan, & Kulka, 1981), perhaps to find a substitute for fulfillment of work and to maintain social relations. Among unmarried men, attitude toward work and retirement is independent of socioeconomic status and race (Keith, 1985, 1989). Lacking the ability to meet certain expectations for masculine behavior (marriage and providing for family), unmarried men appear to focus on work and leisure activities to garner self-worth. They may experience particular distress near the time of retirement but gain security from their greater repertoire of leisure pursuits.

Cohort

Until now, retirement studies have examined subjects who were young adults before the sexual revolution and feminist movements. Many changes in expectations for commitment to work and appropriate masculine behavior at work and home have occurred in the intervening years. Younger cohorts of men may have an entirely different pattern of work identification during their adulthood. The nature of this pattern will be determined only when these cohorts are old enough for a life span study.

Summary of Group Differences

Social scientists have begun to address systematically the impact of occupational status, ethnicity, and marital status on the retirement transition from preretirement attitudes to postretirement satisfaction. The most visible effect occurs in preretirement planning options and postretirement monetary, medical, and social resources.

Work identification may be less intense at lower occupational levels and with individuals further from the core of power in the working world. This reduced focus on one's job as the primary source of a man's identity may abate the initial shift to retirement status. When the lessened identification is linked with lessened opportunities and different types of skills, a man may be constrained in his ability to create a retirement life that enriches his sense of self.

Conclusion

Success in the workplace parallels success in meeting societal expectations for masculine behavior. As rewards are obtained from work, a man invests psychologically in the work that creates these rewards. At every step, masculine identity is cultivated.

As a man grows older, aging and maturation processes lead to reformation of masculinity and gender-appropriate behavior. Masculine qualities that decrease with biological changes include aggression, vigor, and dominance (Brim, 1968; Vaillant, 1977). Masculine qualities that remain stable or increase as a function of psychological continuity include attitudes such as instrumental orientation and analytical orientation (Kaye & Monk, 1984). Feminine qualities that emerge with maturation and social pressures include self-expression and affiliation (Levinson et al., 1978; Neugarten, 1968; Vaillant, 1977). This progression of changes is not unsettling until a man decides to retire. He then realizes how much his sense of masculinity has been supported by work.

After a man decides to retire, he may question the sense of authority, self-reliance, and competence that he has earned from years at work. He disengages from work to prepare for retirement, but the workplace still expects competitive drive and productivity. He feels anxious about leaving the traditionally masculine turf of the workplace for the traditionally feminine realm of the household. He may yearn for freedom from everyday work constraints, but he worries about maintaining respect in his new role.

Retirement intensifies the threat of physical and psychological disintegration that comes with aging (Antonovsky & Sagy, 1990). A new integration of strengths is necessary to maintain vitality after retirement. A man's entire career and professional affiliations must be internalized securely in order to renew and stabilize his sense of masculinity.

References

Antonovsky, A., & Sagy, S. (1990). Confronting developmental tasks in the retirement transition. *The Gerontologist, 30,* 362-368.

Atchley, R. C. (1971). Retirement and leisure participation: Continuity or crisis. *The Gerontologist, 11,* 29-32.

Atchley, R. C. (1972). *The social forces in later life.* Belmont, CA: Wadsworth.

Atchley, R. C. (1976). *The sociology of retirement.* New York: John Wiley.

Atchley, R. C. (1989). A continuity theory of normal aging. *The Gerontologist, 29,* 183-190.

Bem, S. L. (1974). The measurement of psychological androgyny. *Journal of Consulting and Clinical Psychology, 42,* 155-162.

Benner, P. E. (1984). *Stress and satisfaction on the job: Work meanings and coping of mid-career men.* New York: Praeger.

Bernard, J. (1981). The good provider role. *American Psychologist, 36,* 1-12.

Bikson, T. K., & Goodchilds, J. D. (1989). Experiencing the retirement transition: Managerial and professional men before and after. In S. Spacapan & S. Oskamp (Eds.), *The social psychology of aging* (pp. 81-108). Newbury Park, CA: Sage.

Bikson, T. K., Goodchilds, J. D., Huddy, L., Eveland, J. D., & Schneider, S. (1991). *Networked information technology and the transition to retirement: A field experiment* (Research Report No. R-3690-MF). Santa Monica, CA: RAND.

Blau, G. J. (1985). A multiple study investigation of the dimensionality of job involvement. *Journal of Vocational Behavior, 27,* 19-36.

Blau, G. J. (1988). Further exploring the meaning and measurement of career commitment. *Journal of Vocational Behavior, 32,* 284-297.

Brim, O. G. (1968). Adult socialization. In J. Clausen (Ed.), *Socialization in society* (pp. 182-226). Boston: Little, Brown.

Brim, O. G. (1976). Theories of the male mid-life crisis. *Counseling Psychologist, 6,* 2-9.

Crowley, J. E. (1985). Longitudinal effects of retirement on men's psychological and physical well-being. In H. S. Parnes, J. E. Crowley, R. J. Haurin, L. J. Less, W. R. Morgan, F. L. Mott, & G. Nestel (Eds.), *Retirement among American men* (pp. 147-173). Lexington, MA: D. C. Heath.

Cumming, E., & Henry, W. E. (1961). *Growing old: The process of disengagement.* New York: Basic Books.

Doyle, J. A. (1983). *The male experience.* Dubuque, IA: William C. Brown.

Dreyer, P. H. (1989). Postretirement life satisfaction. In S. Spacapan & S. Oskamp (Eds.), *The social psychology of aging* (pp. 109-133). Newbury Park, CA: Sage.

Ehrenreich, B. (1983). *The hearts of men* (2nd ed.). Garden City, NY: Doubleday.

Eisler, R. M., & Skidmore, J. R. (1987). Masculine gender-role stress: Scale development and component factors in the appraisal of stressful situations. *Behavior Modification, 11*, 123-136.

Ekerdt, D. J., Vinick, B. H., & Bosse, R. (1989). Orderly endings: Do men know when they will retire? *Journal of Gerontology: Social Sciences, 44*, S28-S35.

Elder, G. H. (1974). *Children of the Great Depression: Social change in life experience.* Chicago: University of Chicago Press.

Evans, L., Ekerdt, D. J., & Bosse, R. (1985). Proximity to retirement and anticipatory involvement: Findings from the normative aging study. *Journal of Gerontology, 40*, 368-374.

Ferraro, K. F. (1990). Cohort analysis of retirement preparation, 1974-1981. *Journal of Gerontology: Social Sciences, 45*, S21-S31.

Filene, P. G. (1981). *Men in the middle: Coping with the problems of work and family in the lives of middle-aged men.* Englewood Cliffs, NJ: Prentice-Hall.

Fletcher, W. L., & Hansson, R. O. (1991). Assessing the social components of retirement anxiety. *Psychology and Aging, 6*, 76-85.

Fried, E. G. (1949). Attitudes of the older population groups toward activity and inactivity. *Journal of Gerontology, 4*, 141-151.

Friedmann, E. A., & Havighurst, R. J. (1954). *The meaning of work and retirement.* Chicago: University of Chicago Press.

Friedmann, E. A., & Orbach, H. L. (1974). Adjustment to retirement. In A. Silvana (Ed.), *American handbook of psychiatry* (Vol. 1, pp. 609-645). New York: Basic Books.

Garnets, L., & Pleck, J. H. (1979). Sex role identity, androgyny, and sex role transcendence: A sex role strain analysis. *Psychology of Women Quarterly, 3*, 270-283.

Gibson, R. C. (1993). The black American retirement experience. In J. S. Jackson, L. M. Chatters, & R. J. Taylor (Eds.), *Aging in black America* (pp. 277-297). Newbury Park, CA: Sage.

Gouldner, A. W. (1970). *The coming crisis of Western sociology.* New York: Basic Books.

Gradman, T. J. (1990). *Does work make the man: Masculine identity and work identity during the transition to retirement* (Research Report No. P-7626; based on unpublished doctoral thesis, University of California at Los Angeles, 1989). Santa Monica, CA: RAND.

Hays, R. D., & DiMatteo, M. R. (1986). *A short-form measure of loneliness.* Unpublished manuscript.

Hackman, J., & Oldham, G. (1975). Development of the Job Diagnostic Survey. *Journal of Applied Psychology, 60*, 159-170.

Haug, M., & Belgrave, L. (1988, November). *Gender differences in the effects of work commitment and health on retirement adaptation.* Paper presented at annual meeting of the Gerontological Society of America, San Francisco.

Hochschild, A. (1978). *The unexpected community.* Berkeley: University of California Press.

Hooker, K., & Ventis, D. G. (1984). Work ethic, daily activities, and retirement satisfaction. *Journal of Gerontology, 39*, 478-484.

Kaye, L. W., & Monk, A. (1984). Sex role traditions and retirement from academe. *The Gerontologist, 24*, 420-426.

Keith, P. M. (1985). Work, retirement, and well-being among unmarried men and women. *The Gerontologist, 25*, 410-416.

Keith, P. M. (1989). *The unmarried in later life.* New York: Praeger.

Keith, P. M., Wacker, R. R., & Schafer, R. B. (1992). Equity in older families. In M. Szinovacz, D. J. Ekerdt, & B. H. Vinick (Eds.), *Families and retirement* (pp. 189-201). Newbury Park, CA: Sage.

Kellams, S. E., & Chronister, J. L. (1987, November). *Life after early retirement.* Paper presented at meeting of the Association for the Study of Higher Education, Baltimore, MD.

Kimmel, M. S., & Messner, M. A. (1992). *Men's lives* (2nd ed.). New York: Macmillan.

Kosloski, K., Ginsburg, G., & Backman, C. W. (1984). Retirement as a process of active role transition. In V. L. Allen & E. van de Vliert (Eds.), *Role transitions: Explorations and explanations* (pp. 331-341). New York: Plenum.

Levinson, D. J., Darrow, C. N., Klein, E. B., Levinson, M. H., & McKee, B. (1978). *The seasons of a man's life.* New York: Knopf.

Loether, H. J. (1964). The meaning of work and adjustment to retirement. In A. B. Shostak & W. Gomberg (Eds.), *Blue-collar world* (pp. 517-525). Englewood Cliffs, NJ: Prentice Hall.

Miller, S. J. (1965). The social dilemma of the aging leisure participant. In A. M. Rose & W. A. Peterson (Eds.), *Older people and their social world* (77-92). Philadelphia: F. A. Davis.

Mirels, H. L., & Garrett, J. P. (1971). The Protestant ethic as a personality variable. *Journal of Consulting and Clinical Psychology, 36,* 40-44.

Neugarten, B. L. (1968). Adult personality. In B. Neugarten (Ed.), *Middle age and aging* (pp. 137-147). Chicago: University of Chicago Press.

Neugarten, B. L., Havighurst, R. J., & Tobin, S. S. (1968). Personality and patterns of aging. In B. Neugarten (Ed.), *Middle age and aging* (pp. 173-177). Chicago: University of Chicago Press.

Ochberg, R. L. (1987). *Middle-aged sons and the meaning of work.* Ann Arbor, MI: UMI Research Press.

Palmore, E. B., Burchett, B. M., Fillenbaum, G. G., George, L. K., & Wallman, L. M. (1985). *Retirement: Causes and consequences.* New York: Springer.

Parkes, C. M. (1986). *Bereavement: Studies of grief in adult life* (2nd ed.). London: Tavistock.

Pearlin, L. I. (1980). Life strains and psychological distress among adults. In J. J. Smelser & E. H. Erikson (Eds.), *Themes of work and love in adulthood* (pp. 174-192). Cambridge, MA: Harvard University Press.

Pleck, J. H. (1981). *The myth of masculinity.* Cambridge: MIT Press.

Richardson, V., & Kilty, K. M. (1992). Retirement intentions among black professionals: Implications for practice with older black adults. *The Gerontologist, 32,* 7-16.

Rubin, L. B. (1976). *Worlds of pain.* New York: Basic Books.

Rubinstein, R. L. (1986). *Singular paths: Older men living alone.* New York: Columbia.

Russell, D., Peplau, L. A., & Ferguson, M. L. (1978). Developing a measure of loneliness. *Journal of Personality Assessment, 42,* 290-294.

Seccombe, K., & Lee, G. R.. (1986). Gender differences in retirement satisfaction and its antecedents. *Research on Aging, 8,* 426-440.

Simpson, I. H., Back, K. W., & McKinney, J. C. (1966). Orientation toward work and retirement, and self-evaluation in retirement. In I. H. Simpson & J. C. McKinney (Eds.), *Social aspects of aging* (pp. 75-84). Durham, NC: Duke University Press.

Sinnott, J. D., Rabin, J. S., & Windle, M. T. (1986). *Sex roles and aging: Theory and research from a systems perspective.* Basel, Switzerland: Karger.

Solomon, K. (1982). The older man. In K. Solomon & N. Levy (Eds.), *Men in transition* (pp. 205-240). New York: Plenum.

Spence, J. T., Helmreich, R. L., & Stapp, J. (1974). The personal attributes questionnaire: A measure of sex role stereotypes and masculinity-femininity. *Selected Documents in Psychology, 4,* 43 (MS No. 617).

Stokes, R. G., & Maddox, G. L. (1967). Some social factors on retirement adaptation. *Journal of Gerontology, 28,* 339-344.

Szinovacz, M. (1982). Introduction: Research on women's retirement. In M. Szinovacz (Ed.), *Women's retirement: Policy implications of recent research* (pp. 13-21). Beverly Hills, CA: Sage.

Szinovacz, M., Ekerdt, D. J., & Vinick, B. H. (1992). Families and retirement: Conceptual and methodological issues. In M. Szinovacz, D. J. Ekerdt, & B. H. Vinick (Eds.), *Families and retirement* (pp. 1-19). Newbury Park, CA: Sage.

Szinovacz, M., & Washo, C. (1992). Gender differences in exposure to life events and adaptation to retirement. *Journals of Gerontology: Social Sciences, 47,* S191-S196.

Vaillant, G. E. (1977). *Adaptation to life.* Boston: Little, Brown.

Veit, C. T., & Ware, J. E. (1983). The structure of psychological distress and well-being in general populations. *Journal of Consulting and Clinical Psychology, 51,* 730-742.

Veroff, J., Douvan, E., & Kulka, C. (1981). *The inner American.* New York: Basic Books.

Veroff, J., & Feld, S. (1970). *Marriage and work in America: A study of motives and roles.* New York: Van Nostrand Reinhold.

Vinick, B. H., & Ekerdt, D. J. (1992). Couples view retirement activities: Expectation versus experience. In M. Szinovacz, D. J. Ekerdt, & B. H. Vinick (Eds.), *Families and retirement* (pp. 129-144). Newbury Park, CA: Sage.

Walker, J. W., Kimmel, D. C., & Price, K. F. (1981). Retirement style and retirement satisfaction: Retirees aren't all alike. *International Journal of Aging and Human Development, 12,* 267-281.

Ward, R. A. (1979). The never married in later life. *Journal of Gerontology, 34,* 861-869.

Weiss, R. S. (1990). *Staying the course.* New York: Free Press.

Willing, J. Z. (1989). *The reality of retirement* (2nd ed.). Chapel Hill, NC: Lively Mind.

7

A Gender Analysis
of Older Men's Sexuality

Social, Psychological, and Biological Dimensions

WILLIAM MARSIGLIO
RICHARD A. GREER

Older men's[1] self-perceptions and lived experience are affected by several transitions associated with the physiological aging process and the social rhythms of the life career (e.g., retirement, grandfatherhood, widowhood). Because sexuality represents one of the key life domains typically affected by the aging process, we examine aspects of heterosexual men's sexuality during their later years of life.[2]

Our analysis of the transitional nature and significance of sexuality for older men is informed by social constructionist, symbolic interactionist, and life span perspectives (Gagnon & Simon, 1973; Plummer, 1982; Simon & Gagnon, 1986; Tiefer, 1987; Weeks, 1986). We organize our discussion around the conceptual model displayed in Figure 7.1. This model illustrates our position that older men's sexual self-concept and sexual behavior tend to be affected primarily by cultural and sexual scenarios, previous sexual experiences and attitudes, contextual factors (e.g., partner's availability, health status, and sexual expectations, as well as the quality of relationship with the partner), and physiological factors. For growing numbers of older men, modern forms of medical treatment also may represent an important factor. The central focus of our conceptualization is the relationship among the aging process, the larger cultural and sexual scenarios (related to gender and age), and physiological changes associated with aging. Our

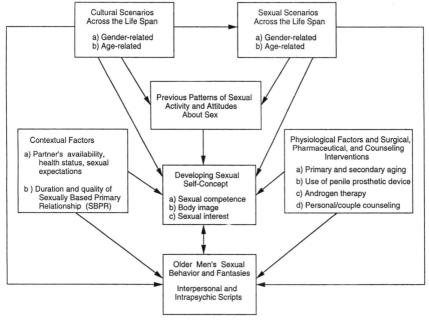

Figure 7.1. Conceptual Model of Older Men's Sexuality

discussion also underscores how the typical masculine style of sexuality learned in early adolescence can have lifelong implications for many older men. Consistent with our social-psychological orientation, we consider the mediating role that older men's sexual self-concept has in shaping their sexual expression. We conclude by highlighting several strategies for improving the social and interpersonal context within which older men experience their sexuality. We also identify key areas for future research.

A Social Constructionist View of Male Sexuality

A social constructionist perspective on human sexuality emphasizes the important role that culture plays in providing individuals with a framework to structure their perceptions and experiences in the sexual realm (Gagnon & Simon, 1973; Plummer, 1982; Tieffer, 1987; Weeks, 1986). Simon and Gagnon's (1986) scripting theory is consistent with this tradition and depicts social behavior as a set of scripts. This theoretical framework synthesizes three interrelated levels of scripting: cultural scenarios, interpersonal scripts, and intrapsychic scripts. At the most general level, cultural scenarios provide individuals with information and normative guidelines about behavior. Sexual cultural scenarios present social guidelines in the form of meanings and norms that instruct individuals on the conditions under which they should be aroused erotically, as well as on what feelings they and their partner should have. These sexual scenarios are quite broad in scope and are shaped by cultural scenarios dealing with gender- and age-related activities. Other factors—for example, race, ethnicity, and religious background—also may be important. The cultural and sexual scenarios that men experience in their later years of life will probably be the most relevant to their sexual self-concept and their current sexual activity; however, our model attempts to convey the image that scenarios across the life span can have both an immediate and long-term effect on men's developing sexual self-concept (including perceptions of sexual competence, body image, and sexual interest).

Because sexual scenarios are quite broad in scope, individuals rely on interpersonal scripting as a means to interpret, modify, and apply the general norms to their own specific circumstances. Thus individuals are seen as active agents as they shape their behavior to reflect their desires and to respond to the contingencies at hand (Turner, 1962). The behavioral concept, *sexual script,* refers to the interaction strategies (behaviors) individuals use to enact or attempt to enact specific social guidelines regarding sexuality.

Finally, individuals' intrapsychic activities are shaped by sexual scenarios and scripts as well as their own idiosyncratic interests and experiences. This third level of scripting enables individuals to develop images about their actual and ideal sexual self through their sexual fantasies and internal rehearsals of specific sexual episodes. As a dynamic process, intrapsychic scripting affords people an opportunity to play an active role in constructing and modifying their own perceptions about their sexuality by working with various cultural messages. Individuals will internalize these modified messages to one extent or another. This process will in turn influence how individuals engage in interpersonal scripting. Moreover, and as depicted in Figure 7.1, men's interpersonal and intrapsychic activities are likely to be related in a reciprocal manner to their sexual self-concept.

When this scripting perspective is applied to older men's sexuality, it is instructive to consider how traditional images of heterosexuality and masculinity may affect older men. For example, social scientists consistently have found gender differences in younger men's and women's sexual fantasies (Ellis & Symons, 1990; Follingstad & Kimbrell, 1986; Kimmel & Plante, 1992) and preferred sexual scripts. Men are more likely than women to be active and visual in their intrapsychic scripting and fantasize about explicit sexual activities. These differences are thought to stem largely from gender role socialization. It is not surprising, then, that men's perceptions about their masculinity play a fundamental role in shaping their sexual behavior, and that their behavior in turn reinforces their sense of masculinity (Gross, 1978; Herek, 1986).

Masculinity themes usually begin to shape males' sexuality at an early age and may continue to affect male sexuality throughout the life span. Marsiglio (1988) noted that traditional gender socialization during males' formative years encourages boys to develop characteristics such as an appetite for success, status, toughness, independence, aggressiveness, and dominance as well as a desire to avoid things associated with femininity. If adopted, these characteristics can be applied to various aspects of males' lives, including their sexuality. For example, masculinity norms that encourage men to be competent, assertive, and willing to assume the initiator role with women may contribute to older men's (especially single men's) performance anxiety, especially if they are experiencing physiological changes in their sexual response capabilities. The importance of these gender norms should not be underestimated despite changing images of female sexuality in recent years. These norms still affect how sexual episodes evolve. Studies conducted in the late 1970s and early 1980s of young and older married and cohabiting couples have found that men are much more likely than their female partners to initiate sex (Blumstein & Schwartz, 1983; Brecher, 1984; Starr & Weiner, 1981).

For many boys and young men, developing and sustaining a masculine identity entails the notion that they must be successful in their sexual relationships with women (Herek, 1986; Pleck, 1981). In short, prevailing cultural scenarios encourage young men to see their sexuality as a means to reaffirm their masculine role identity and their maturation toward adulthood (Gross, 1978). Among older men, positive views about their sexual prowess can also represent a self-affirming process that enables them to retain the masculine sense of self that probably has been a central feature of their self-concept throughout their lives. This point is particularly important because a large percentage of older men living today were socialized to accept traditional ideas about sex and gender issues. They were adolescents in the 1920s, 1930s, and 1940s. Although the dynamic, ongoing process of self-development may lead some males to develop novel intrapsychic scripting patterns as adults, it is likely that early socialization experiences may have a lasting effect on the way many men experience their sexuality.

One important aspect of older men's sexuality is that although older men are unlikely to experiment with intrapsychic scripts that involve impotency (defined as the inability to maintain an erection sufficient to complete coitus), they may have to deal with moments of impotency in their interpersonal sexual episodes. Tiefer (1986, p. 579) observes from a social constructionist perspective that the increased use of the stigmatizing "impotence" label "reflects a significant moment in the social construction of male sexuality." The factors that have produced this moment, as Tiefer correctly observes, include the "increasing importance of lifelong sexual activity in personal life, the insatiability of mass media for appropriate sexual topics, the expansionist needs of specialty medicine and new medical technology, and the highly demanding male sexual script."

In addition to personal experiences with impotency, older men will be confronted with stereotypical images of older persons' sexuality or lack thereof. Although there may be a greater awareness of older persons' sexuality in recent years (e.g., the recent popular television show *The Golden Girls* portrays older women as having strong sexual desires), the general public's perception of older persons still assumes that older persons are largely asexual beings (Dagon, 1983), even though data indicate that many older persons are sexually active.

Cultural Images, Male Physiology, and Male Social Psychology

Throughout history, the erect phallic symbol has been a cultural icon representing sexual virility and powerful masculinity (Rathus, Nevid, & Fichner-Rathus, 1993). It has in some respects symbolized the ultimate and most basic image of masculinity in many cultures. Consequently, any discussion of older men's sexuality must address the interrelationships among these public images of male sexuality and masculinity, the physiological changes that accompany the aging process for men, and the social-psychological processes affecting men's varied responses to these physiological changes. It also is important to recognize that older men's sexuality may be influenced by both the gradual process of primary aging as well as secondary aging—the results of abuse, disuse, and disease (Libman, 1989).

During the past 30 years or so, an important shift in cultural images of male sexuality has occurred. The women's movement and sex researchers (e.g., Masters & Johnson, 1966) have been instrumental in redefining female sexuality. One consequence of this redefinition has been women's heightened sensitivity to their own sexual needs. Adult women today probably possess higher expectations for achieving an orgasm regularly, although many of the women most affected by societal changes during the 1960s have not yet joined the cohort of elderly persons in our society. These changes in female sexuality have in turn prompted changes in the image and expression of male sexuality. For instance, Gross (1978) argued that the United States has been experiencing a transition in the popular cultural view of men as "sexual animals" to "competent lovers" or sexual technicians. This modern image of male sexuality places greater pressure on men to be highly skilled lovers and to satisfy their partners sexually. To the extent that men expect themselves or are expected by their partners to satisfy women through vaginal intercourse, older men may more readily experience problems associated with performance anxiety. However, for those older men who are still able to achieve and maintain an erection with relative ease, the ability to satisfy their partner through vaginal intercourse may actually increase because they typically will need a longer period of time to ejaculate. Moreover, male erectile dysfunction may be less disruptive for those couples when the woman can achieve orgasm or sensual pleasure through manual or oral sex.

Men's erectile function and ejaculation abilities are affected by hormonal developments and associated physiological changes that represent normal aspects of the aging process (Brecher, 1984; Thienhaus, Conter, & Bosmann, 1986). It is clear that with advancing age a majority of men experience a decrease in their circulating testosterone levels and bioavailable (amount available that can affect tissue) testosterone (Morley & Kaiser, 1989). It is not well understood, though, how men's sexuality is affected by the diminishing levels of bioavailable testosterone associated with aging (for a general discussion of the relationship between testosterone and men's sexuality, see Kemper, 1990; Knussman, Christiansen, & Couwenbergs, 1986). On the one hand, Davidson et al. (1983) found that high doses of testosterone given to hypogonadal males (those with significantly diminished levels of testosterone) clearly increases the frequency of both erections and libido. Meanwhile, Bancroft (1980) observed that men given antiandrogens continued to maintain their erectile capacity, although they had a decreased libido. He also found that the frequency of erections in response to erotic films did not increase in hypogonadal men receiving androgen replacements.

Although the significance of these hormonal developments for older men's sexuality is unclear, it is known that aging is associated with a general loss of muscle tone throughout the somatic musculature and a decrease in the skin's elasticity. Vasculature in general becomes less pliable and blood circulation is reduced. As a result, men notice changes in erectile function as their ability to have an erection tends to diminish during their middle and later years of life. For example, the typical 18-year-old male requires approximately 3 seconds to achieve a maximum erection, while it is likely to take a 45-year-old man 18-20 seconds and a 75-year-old man as long as 5-6 minutes (Thienhaus, Conter, & Bosmann, 1986). In addition, young males usually can retain their erections after ejaculation for a longer period of time than older men, and young men also can more readily regain an erection within a shorter period of time (Kaplan & Sager, 1971). A young male may need only a minute or so to regain an erection, but an 80-year-old man may need a week or more. Thus older men take longer to achieve an erect state, their erection is less turgid, detumescence occurs more quickly without continued stimulation, and the refractory period between erections (the time when achieving erection is physiologically impossible) increases.

Although older men tend to have lower confidence in their erectile ability (Libman, 1989; Starr & Weiner, 1981), the manner in which these changes affect older men's sexual self-concept and sexual behavior depends in part on the type of relationships they have with their sexual partners. Experiencing these gradual changes within the context of a loving, committed relationship is likely to be much less problematic than dealing with them in a context in which partners have little rapport with one another. In fact, some couples may even develop a stronger appreciation for their sexuality and each other through their cooperative efforts to sustain the quality of their sexual relationship despite the physiological changes associated with the aging process.

Many men may be able to manage the gradual changes described above, but these changes may portend an even more serious problem. Most older men experience partial or total impotence at some point in their lives (Fleming, 1985). Episodic impotency often leads to self-recrimination and a cycle of "spectatoring," whereby men watch themselves perform and consequently have a more difficult time obtaining and maintaining an erection (Williams, 1987). The psychological and emotional significance of impotence is accentuated not only by the pervasive stigmatic labeling associated with it, but also because throughout their lives men have encountered an experiential sense of virility and a taken-for-granted form of achievement when their flaccid penis became turgid. Although men who experience at least partial impotence are likely to express some concern, research has shown that some older men are basically free from performance anxiety (Martin, 1981). Masters and Johnson (1966) did find that more-educated men tended to have more trouble than their less-educated counterparts in dealing with erectile difficulties.

Some research indicates that male sexual dysfunction is highly correlated with impairment in physical health and alcohol-abusive behavior (Roy, 1983). A common pattern seems to begin with physiological changes that precede some degree of male sexual decline, which often then leads to self-imposed anxiety and pressure resulting in further erectile difficulties and finally an unwillingness to seek outside assistance. Men's resistance to pursue health care is not surprising in that men, unlike women, tend not to establish an ongoing relationship with a particular reproductive health care professional or even develop a regular visitation schedule. One earlier study showed that approximately 50% of men who experienced erectile dysfunction were unwilling to address this sensitive issue associated with their masculinity (Cooper, 1972). However, it appears that increasing numbers of men are willing to talk about their sexual problems with their physician (Bancroft, 1982).

One consequence of the patterns described above is that some males respond to their difficulties by adopting maladaptive coping strategies, such as further alcohol abuse, increasing their workload, having sex with prostitutes, or social withdrawal. These coping strategies tend to increase the rift between older males and their sexual partners and may themselves be deleterious to sexual function. For example, alcohol abuse may cause peripheral neuropathy (diminished sensation), increasing workloads may lead to general fatigue and boredom, and the use of surrogate sex partners may increase the risk of contracting sexually transmitted diseases.

Older Men's Sexual Experiences

There is considerable public and scholarly interest in the extent to which older persons remain sexually active. Unfortunately, research on older men's sexuality is limited. In general, studies based on nationally representative data deal with sexuality in a very narrow context (Marsiglio & Donnelly, 1991), and studies that do inquire about a range of sexuality topics are based on small or nonrepresentative samples with low response rates, or both (Brecher, 1984; George & Weiler, 1981; Starr & Weiner, 1981). Studying men's sexuality or sexual response is complicated by the fact that they are multidimensional with behavioral, cognitive, and affective dimensions (Libman, 1989). Because researchers have used a variety of strategies for measuring these dimensions and delineating age categories, it is often difficult to compare results. Another concern is that researchers' ability to explain the overall decline in older men's sexuality (at the individual and aggregate level) is complicated by the fact that men's sexual self-concept and interest in sex are shaped not only by the physiological aging process but also by interpersonal and intrapsychic scripting processes (see Figure 7.1). Thus it is important to consider how men's sexual activity during the latter years of life is conditioned in significant ways by previous patterns of sexual activity and social-psychological factors. With these caveats in mind we present a brief overview of the empirical research on different aspects of older men's sexuality.

Perhaps the most prominent research question relevant to older men's sexuality involves the frequency with which these men engage in sexual activity. Popular myths notwithstanding, available data indicate that many older persons remain sexually active, albeit with decreasing frequency. Marsiglio and Donnelly's (1991) study of married persons 60 and older, based on the National Survey of Families and Households (NSFH), indicated that 54% of men (51% of women) interviewed in 1988 reported being sexually active when they were asked: "About how often did you and your husband/wife have sex during the past month?" Among the subsample of male respondents who reported being sexually active within the past month, the mean rate of frequency was 4.15 times per month. Meanwhile, Starr and Weiner (1981) found, based on their study of 282 older men (60-91 years old, 64% married), that those who reported a specific frequency engaged in sex an average of 1.44 times per week. The most comprehensive information about older men's sexuality is based on Brecher's survey of 1,366 married and unmarried men aged 60 and older. These respondents were participants in a larger study of persons 50 and older who answered a research announcement in the November 1977 issue of *Consumer Reports*. Brecher found that among those who were at least 60 years old, 89% of married men and approximately 80% of unmarried men reported being sexually active (not defined by the author, but presumably including masturbation). In addition, 67% of older men (married and unmarried combined) who were sexually active reported having sex at least once a week.

Brecher (1984) and Marsiglio and Donnelly (1991) have documented that older men's sexual activity and interest levels are lower than those of younger men (see also George & Weiler, 1981; Hegeler & Mortensen, 1978). In Brecher's study, 73% of sexually active men in their 60s reported having sex at least once a week (married and unmarried combined), whereas only 58% of men 70 and older gave a similar reply. Husbands in their 60s reported having sex with their wives exactly once per week, while husbands aged 70 and older reported a rate of .6 per week. Brecher also found that among men in their 50s, 60s, and 70s and older, 24%, 40%, and 52%, respectively, reported having a weaker level of interest in sex than they did when they were about 40 years of age. A similar pattern was found in the declining rate of masturbation (66%, 50%, 43%) among men in these three age categories.

NSFH data also documented a decline in the frequency of sexual relations among older cohorts. Although patterns controlling for respondent's age were not reported for married men and women separately, other analyses with these data suggest that gender differences in sexual activity were not significant, so the overall figures are basically representative of males as a group (Marsiglio & Donnelly, 1991). With this in mind, the percentage of respondents (men and women) who reported being sexually active with their spouse at least once within the past month declined steadily (65%, 55%, 45%, to 24%) for older persons categorized in the following manner, 60-65, 66-70, 71-75, and 76 and older. Among the sexually active, the overall mean frequencies per month for persons in these same age categories were 4.54, 4.52, 3.51, and 2.75. Another study found that older men's level of sexual activity in later life is likely to be related to their level of activity before middle age (Martin, 1981).

Some research has considered the extent to which older men continue to fantasize about sex. Giambra and Martin (1977, p. 497) concluded, based on their study of 277 predominately white, middle-class adult men ranging from 24 to 91 years of age in the mid-1970s, that the "frequency and intensity of sexual daydreams declined with increasing age, and after age 65 virtually disappeared." These results are tempered by Brecher's (1984) finding that among men 50 and older, 80% report no decline in their use of fantasies compared to when they were 40.

Other research has considered the extent to which factors other than those directly or indirectly associated with aging are related to older men's sexuality, but multivariate research in this area is scarce. Research does indicate that sexual relations are highly correlated with the male's desire and ability to engage in sexual activity. Among older couples, research has indicated that males, not their female partners, typically determine the frequency and nature of sexual activity (Bretchneider & McCoy, 1988; Pfeiffer, Verwoerdt, & Wang, 1969; Verwoerdt, Pfeiffer, & Wang, 1969). Men tend to list reasons such as boredom, systemic physical illness, medication, and fatigue for their sexual abstinence (Diokno, Bromberg, Herzog, & Brock, 1988). Not surprising, older men have not ranked the lack of an available female partner as a reason for sexual cessation, perhaps because there are 1.47 women aged 65 and older and 2.12 women aged 80 and older for every man of those ages in the United States (Weeks, 1992).

In addition, Marsiglio and Donnelly (1991) found in their multivariate analysis of noninstitutionalized married persons 60 and older (men and women) that a partner's poor health was significantly related to decreased odds of having had sexual relations within the past month. However, the respondent's gender, personal health status, and a gender-by-partner's-health-status interaction term were not significant predictors of sexual relations within the past month or the frequency of sexual relations for those who were sexually active. Other research has suggested that women will readily give up their sexual roles in a relationship where the male is uninterested, unwilling, or unable to pursue particular sexual activities (Sviland, 1978).

Research has also indicated that female partners' debilitated health status, especially that of dementia, appears to be a significant hindrance to males' sexual interest and activity. Although masturbation levels remain high in older men whose spouses suffer from Alzheimer's disease, the frequency of sexual intercourse declines dramatically (Greer & Herkov, 1992). This may result from a man's guilt for having sex with someone who does not possess full faculties, even though they may have been married for more than 30 years.

Older Men's Sexuality and Interventions

There are several specific strategies for improving older men's ability to maintain an active and enjoyable sex life if they are interested. The three major approaches include penile prosthetic devices, androgen therapy, and sexual counseling and education. As noted earlier, many men will have some type of experience with impotence. It has only been within the past 15 years or so that professional and public attention has focused on the physical causes and treatments of impotence (Tiefer, 1986) and that attempts have been made to differentiate between organic and nonorganic causes (Bancroft, 1982; Krane, Siroky, & Goldstein, 1983; LoPiccolo, 1985). Before this recent shift in focus, it was generally believed that at least 90% of erectile dysfunction was psychological in origin, although clear documentation for this figure did not exist (Bancroft, 1982). More recent studies suggest that between 40% and 50% of impotence has an organic etiology (Tiefer, 1986).

Vascular disease is the most common organic cause of impotence (Morley & Kaiser, 1989), and thus penile prosthetic devices provide men experiencing erectile dysfunction with the opportunity to achieve an erection and have intercourse (Witherington, 1991). The first such device was marketed in the 1960s. Various types of devices have been developed and refined subsequently. For instance, Scott, Bradley, and Timm (1973) reported their work on a hydraulically driven inflatable penile prosthesis. This device mimicked more closely the process of erection and has undergone several modifications. The device currently consists of two expandable cylinders that are implanted within the corpora cavernosa (the spongy, vascular penis tissue). They are connected by tubing to a small activating and deactivating pump and a fluid-filled reservoir. The pump is situated subcutaneously in the scrotum; when given several squeezes, the pump transfers fluid from the reservoir to the expandable cylinders. A tumescent-type reaction occurs. Pressing a valve in the lower part of the pump causes the fluid to drain from the cylinders and return to the reservoir, allowing the penis to become flaccid.

Prosthetic devices are now available in several forms including semirigid, hinged, malleable, and inflatable (Roy, 1991). Each has its advantages and disadvantages. The noninflatable devices are easier to implant, cost less, and have no fluid to leak or valve to malfunction. The inflatable prostheses are more elaborate but are more expensive and may fail mechanically. Finally, a new prosthetic device, the Omni Phase[®], consists of a stack of round plastic segments through which a spring loaded cable runs. Manually bending the penis triggers the switch to shorten the cable, bringing the stack of round segments tautly together to produce an erection. On a second bending, the cable loosens and the prosthesis becomes flaccid. Postoperative infection remains a serious consequence of this kind of foreign body insertion. Research has indicated that a satisfaction rate of between 80% and 90% can be achieved with penile implants (McLaren & Barrett, 1992; Witherington, 1991; see also Jaworski, Richards, & Lloyd, 1992).

A second strategy, androgen therapy, has been used as a major modality for the treatment of impotence. Testosterone levels can be altered through oral preparations or intramuscular injections, the latter being the most commonly recommended approach. In addition, transdermal testosterone patches, placed on the scrotum, may produce physiological levels of the hormone but cost substantially more. The initial response to testosterone therapy is often salutary. However, the beneficial results may decline over time, perhaps because of the presence of coexisting causes of impotence such as vascular disease. This type of therapy is appropriate only for those patients with clear-cut hypogonadalism. Finally, testosterone therapy may be associated with several side effects, including breast enlargement, liver dysfunction, prostate congestion, and water retention. It is not recommended for patients with prostate cancer.

A third approach is relevant in cases where the underlying cause of sexual dysfunction is diagnosed to be psychological. To the extent that clinicians have assumed that psychological conflicts have been at the root of male erectile problems, diagnoses and treatments have focused on numerous psychotherapies with an emphasis on aging men's sexual self-concept. This bias is illustrated by the clinician's definitive use of the nocturnal penile tumescence device that records erections during REM sleep. Any erectile ability has historically been considered to indicate a psychological cause for male impotence. However, some erectile ability during sleep does not necessarily indicate a psychological cause of impotence (McKendry et al., 1983).

In those instances where psychological factors clearly do contribute in some way to men's sexual dysfunction, and assuming that these men are willing to discuss sexuality issues with others, specialists can impart basic knowledge about aging, sexual functioning, and specific sexual response techniques to them. Naivete in sexual matters and embarrassment are still quite common among older persons who grew up in the early 1900s. Specialists who allow a patient to express uncertainties and anxiety may promote a remedy to sexual problems by sorting fiction from fact. Fear of failure (performance anxiety), which often leads to actual failure, can be alleviated by empathic listening and advice. Although sex therapists and marriage counselors are likely to have the most expertise in providing psychosexual counseling, family physicians who have developed a long-standing rapport with their male patients (and their patients' partners) also can provide effective counseling.

The value of these counseling sessions could be supplemented by sex-education programs or workshops for older adults (Starr & Weiner, 1981). Lectures and workshops, perhaps in conjunction with groups such as the American Association of Retired Persons, could be designed to inform elderly persons about the various issues related to sexuality and aging. Research has shown that older persons increase their frequency and enjoyment of sexual activity when professionals inform them about sexual functioning and the aging process (Rowland & Hayes, 1978; White, 1982). Counseling sessions and group workshops could provide a useful service to older men (and their partners) who either were experiencing chronic erectile difficulties or were simply concerned about the aging process and its effect on their sexuality.

Summary

The conceptual model we presented in Figure 7.1 highlights the complex nature of older men's sexuality. This model, informed by social constructionist, symbolic interactionist, and life span perspectives, shows how older men's sexuality is affected by cultural, social, psychological, physiological, and medical factors. We discussed this model by clarifying how these interrelated factors are associated with emotional, cognitive, and behavioral aspects of older men's sexuality. Our approach, although taking into account physiological factors, emphasized the social and dynamic aspects of human sexuality.

In drawing on aspects of the scripting perspective, we underscored how older men develop their sexual self-concept and engage in sexual behavior within a gendered, sociocultural context. Understanding how older men's sexuality is affected by gender and culture is essential, given men's strong inclination to associate sexual prowess with masculinity and the fact that the physiological aging process is closely related to sexual response patterns for older men. We briefly described some of the key aspects of the physiological aging process and how they are related to older men's sexual response patterns. Although these changes do indeed sometimes have a profound impact on older men's sexual experiences, we indicated that there is considerable variation in the way men age and the way they respond to whatever changes do occur. We reiterated the value of focusing on the social and psychological dimensions to sexuality by noting that the nature of older men's relationships with their sexual partners is likely to influence how they cope with these changes.

Our discussion also revealed the need to develop more complex theoretical models of older men's sexuality. It would be useful, for example, to consider the interrelationship between factors associated with cultural and sexual scenarios, intrapsychic scripting, and interpersonal scripting for older heterosexual and homosexual men. In pursuing this line of inquiry, it would be important to determine what types of cultural or subcultural scenarios affect older men's sexual self-concepts. Do older men look toward middle-aged men or their own peers as a reference group? Or do older men internalize the general public's and health care professionals' images about older persons' limited sexuality (Cameron, 1970; La Torre & Kear, 1977)? How do the partners of older men influence how they feel about and express their sexuality? What types of emotional and sexual needs do unmarried older men experience, and what factors influence their sexuality decisions? Under what conditions are specific intervention efforts effective in improving older men's feelings about their sexuality? For example, what conditions or personal characteristics are associated with men's successful psychological adjustment to using a penile prosthesis?

In attempting to answer these and related questions, researchers would be well served to consider Libman's (1989, p. 565) question: "Has negative cultural conditioning imposed a norm to which the aging individual has become resigned or does the identified form of sexual expression in the aging reflect a characteristic pattern which is different from the one displayed by younger individuals but is no less satisfactory?" Researchers studying older men's sexuality should avoid making assumptions about the positive or negatives aspects related to a particular sexual lifestyle. Instead, they should examine older men's subjective views about the quality and quantity of their sexual activity in addition to documenting their sexual activity patterns.

Notes

1. We use the term *older men* to refer to those who are at least in their 60s. It is well understood that there is considerable variation in how individual men experience the physiological and social psychological aspects of the aging process. Thus some of the issues we address may be more or less relevant to particular "older men," and some issues may even be salient to younger men whose experiences are typical of much older men.

2. Although a comprehensive analysis of older men's sexual experiences would address gay men's sexuality as well as the sexuality of institutionalized men, such an analysis is beyond the scope of this chapter. In some respects the issues we discuss may be equally applicable to gay or heterosexual men, but there also may be unique differences among men with different sexual orientations. If these differences exist, they may not result directly from sexual orientation per se but from the specific experiences or philosophies of life shared by people who define their sexuality in a particular manner

(see Adelman, 1980; Herek, Kimmel, Amaro, & Melton, 1991; Kayal, 1984; Laner, 1978). Although some researchers (Gagnon & Simon, 1973; Kelly, 1977; Weinberg & Williams, 1974) have suggested that older gay men's experiences may be decidedly less appealing than those of heterosexual men because the trappings of youth are valued so heavily in the gay subculture, others have argued that hypothesized differences between straight and gay men have been exaggerated (Gray & Dressel, 1985; Kayal, 1984; see also Friend, 1990).

References

Adelman, M. R. (1980). *Adjustment to aging and styles of being gay: A study of elderly gay men and lesbians.* Unpublished doctoral dissertation, Wright Institute, Berkeley, CA.

Bancroft, J. (1980). Endocrinology of sexual function. *Clinical Obstetrics and Gynecology, 4,* 253-281.

Bancroft, J. (1982). Erectile impotence: Psyche or soma? *International Journal of Andrology, 5,* 353-355.

Blumstein, P., & Schwartz, P. (1983). *American couples: Money, work, and sex.* New York: William Morrow.

Brecher, E. M. (1984). *Love, sex, and aging.* Mount Vernon, NY: Consumers Union.

Bretchneider, J., & McCoy, N. L. (1988). Sexual interest and behavior in healthy 80- to 102-year olds. *Archives of Sexual Behavior, 17,* 109-129.

Cameron, P. (1970). The generation gap: Beliefs about sexuality and self-reported sexuality. *Developmental Psychology, 3,* 272.

Cooper, A. J. (1972). Diagnosis and management of endocrine impotence. *British Medical Journal, 2,* 34-36.

Dagon, E. M. (1983). Aging and sexuality. In N. Marcotte (Ed.), *Treatment interventions in human sexuality* (pp. 357-373). New York: Plenum.

Davidson, J. M., Chin, J. J., Crapo, L., Gray, G. D., Greenleaf, W. J., & Catania, J. A. (1983). Hormonal changes in sexual function and aging men. *Journal of Clinical Endocrinology and Metabolism, 57,* 71-77.

Diokno, A. C., Bromberg, J., Herzog, R., & Brock, M. (1988). Correlates of sexual dysfunction in the elderly. *Journal of Urology, 139,* 496A.

Ellis, B. J., & Symons, D. (1990). Sex differences in sexual fantasy: An evolutionary psychological approach. *Journal of Sex Research, 27,* 527-555.

Fleming, J. L. (1985). Occupational impotence. *Medical Aspects of Human Sexuality, 19,* 52-69.

Follingstad, D. R., & Kimbrell, C. D. (1986). Sex fantasies revisited: An expansion and further clarification of variables affecting sex fantasy production. *Archives of Sexual Behavior, 15,* 475-486.

Friend, R. A. (1990). Older lesbian and gay people: A theory of successful aging. *Journal of Homosexuality, 20,* 99-118.

Gagnon, J., & Simon, W. (1973). *Sexual conduct: The social sources of sexuality.* Hawthorne, NY: Aldine.

George, L. K., & Weiler, S. J. (1981). Sexuality in middle and late life. *Archives of General Psychiatry, 38,* 919-923.

Giambra, L. M., & Martin, C. E. (1977). Sexual daydreams and quantitative aspects of sexual activity: Some relations for males across adulthood. *Archives of Sexual Behavior, 6*, 497-505.

Gray, H., & Dressel, P. (1985). Alternative interpretations of aging among gay males. *The Gerontologist, 25*, 83-87.

Greer, R. A., & Herkov, M. J. (1992, December). *Sexuality in Alzheimer's disease patients.* Paper presented at Behavioral Neurology and Neuropsychology Conference, Orlando, FL.

Gross, A. E. (1978). The male role and heterosexual behavior. *Journal of Social Issues, 34*(1), 87-107.

Hegeler, S., & Mortensen, M. (1978). Sexuality and aging. *British Journal of Sexual Medicine, 5*, 16-19.

Herek, G. M. (1986). On heterosexual masculinity: Some psychical consequences of the social construction of gender and sexuality. *American Behavioral Scientist, 29*, 563-577.

Herek, G. M., Kimmel, D. C., Amaro, H., & Melton, G. B. (1991). Avoiding heterosexist bias in psychological research. *American Psychologist, 46*, 957-963.

Jaworski, T. M., Richards, J. S., & Lloyd, L. K. (1992). Retrospective review of sexual and marital satisfaction of spinal cord injury and diabetic males post penile injection or implant. *Urology, 40*, 127-131.

Kaplan, H. S., & Sager, C. J. (1971). Sexual patterns at different ages. *Medical Aspects of Human Sexuality, 5*, 10-23.

Kayal, P. M. (1984). Understanding gay and lesbian aging. *Journal of Society and Social Welfare, 11*, 409-431.

Kelly, J. (1977). The aging male homosexual: Myth and reality. *The Gerontologist, 17*, 328-332.

Kemper, T. D. 1990. *Social structure and testosterone.* New Brunswick, NJ: Rutgers University Press.

Kimmel, M. S. & Plante, R. F. (1992, August). *Sexual fantasies and gender scripts: Heterosexual men and women construct their ideal sexual encounters.* Paper presented at American Sociological Association meeting, Pittsburgh, PA.

Knussman, R., Christiansen, K., & Couwenbergs, C. (1986). Relations between sex hormone levels and sexual behavior in men. *Archives of Sexual Behavior, 15*, 429-445.

Krane, R. J., Siroky, M. B., & Goldstein, I. (1983). *Male sexual dysfunctions.* Boston: Little, Brown.

Laner, M. R. (1978). Growing older male: Heterosexual and homosexual. *The Gerontologist, 18*, 496-501.

La Torre, R. P., & Kear, K. A. (1977). Attitudes toward sex in the aged. *Archives of Sexual Behavior, 6*, 203-213.

Libman, E. (1989). Sociocultural and cognitive factors in aging and sexual expression: Conceptual and research issues. *Canadian Psychology, 30*, 560-567.

LoPiccolo, J. (1985). Diagnosis and treatment of male sexual dysfunction. *Journal of Sex and Marital Therapy, 11*, 215-232.

Marsiglio, W. (1988). Adolescent male sexuality and heterosexual masculinity: A conceptual model and review. *Journal of Adolescent Research, 3*(4), 285-303.

Marsiglio, W., & Donnelly, D. (1991). Sexual relations in later life: A national study of married persons. *Journal of Gerontology, 46*, S338-S344.

Martin, C. E. (1981). Factors affecting sexual functioning in 60-79 year old married males. *Archives of Sexual Behavior, 10,* 399-420.

Masters, W. H., & Johnson, B. E. (1966). *Human sexual response.* Boston: Little, Brown.

McKendry, J. B. R., Collins, W. E., Silverman, M., Krull, L. E., Collins, J. P., & Irvine, A. H. (1983). Erectile impotence: A clinical challenge. *Canadian Medical Association Journal, 128,* 653-663.

McLaren, R. H., & Barrett, D. M. (1992). Patient and partner satisfaction with the AMS 700 penile prosthesis. *Journal of Urology,* 147, 62-65.

Morley, J. E., & Kaiser, F. E. (1989). Sexual function with advancing age. *Medical Clinics of North America, 73*(6), 1483-1495.

Pfeiffer, E., Verwoerdt, A, & Wang, H.-S. (1969). The natural history of sexual behavior in a biologically advanced group of aged individuals. *Journal of Gerontology, 24,* 193-198.

Pleck, J. (1981). *The myth of masculinity.* Cambridge: MIT Press.

Plummer, K. (1982). Symbolic interactionism and sexual conduct. In M. Brake (Ed.), *Human sexual relations* (pp. 233-241). New York: Pantheon.

Rathus, S. A., Nevid, J. S., & Fichner-Rathus, L. (1993). *Human sexuality in a world of diversity.* Boston: Allyn & Bacon.

Rowland, K. F., & Hayes, S. N. (1978). A sexual enhancement program for couples. *Journal of Sex and Marital Therapy, 4,* 91-111.

Roy, J. B. (1983). Impotence: A surgically manageable disease. *Journal of the Oklahoma State Medical Association, 76,* 41-49.

Roy, J. B. (1991). Impotence. *Geriatric Medicine Today, 10,* 35-42.

Scott, F. B., Bradley, W. E., & Timm, G. W. (1973). Management of erectile impotence: Use of implantable inflatable prothesis. *Urology, 2,* 80-82.

Simon, W., & Gagnon, J. H. (1986). Sexual scripts: Permanence and change. *Archives of Sexual Behavior, 15,* 97-120.

Starr, B. D., & Weiner, M. B. (1981). *The Starr-Weiner report on sex & sexuality in the mature years.* New York: McGraw-Hill.

Sviland, M. A. (1978). A program of sexual liberation and growth in the elderly. In L. Solnick (Ed.), *Sexuality and aging* (pp. 96-114). Los Angeles: University of Southern California Press.

Thienhaus, Ole. J., Conter, E. A., & Bosmann, H. B. (1986). Sexuality and aging. *Aging and Society, 6,* 39-54.

Tiefer, L. (1986). In pursuit of the perfect penis: The medicalization of male sexuality. *American Behavioral Scientist, 29,* 579-599.

Tiefer, L. (1987). Social constructionism and the study of human sexuality. In P. Shaver & C. Hendrick (Eds.), *Sex and gender: Review of personality and social psychology* (pp. 70-94). Newbury Park, CA: Sage.

Turner, R. (1962). Role taking vs. conformity. In A. Rose (Ed.), *Human behavior and social process* (pp. 20-40). Boston: Houghton-Mifflin.

Verwoerdt, A., Pfeiffer, E., & Wang, H.-S. (1969). Sexual behavior in senescence I: Changes in sexual activity and interest in aging men and women. *Geriatrics, 24,* 137-154.

Weeks, J. (1986). *Sexuality.* Chichester, UK: Ellis Horwood.

Weeks, J. R. (1992). *Population: An introduction to concepts and issues* (5th ed.). Belmont, CA: Wadsworth.

Weinberg, M. S., & Williams, C. J. (1974). *Male homosexuals: Their problems and adaptations.* New York: Oxford University Press.

White, C. B. (1982). A scale for the assessment of attitudes and knowledge regarding sexuality in the aged. *Archives of Sexual Behavior, 11,* 491-502.

Williams, G. (1987). Erectile dysfunction: Diagnosis and treatment. *British Journal of Urology, 60,* 1-5.

Witherington, R. (1991). Mechanical devices for the treatment of erectile dysfunction. *American Family Physician, 43,* 1611-1620.

8

A Typology of Orientations Toward Household and Marital Roles of Older Men and Women

PAT M. KEITH

Patterns of gender role congruence over the life course have been investigated for the past several decades. Some of this work has addressed the continuity and discontinuity of individuals' work-family responsibilities and marital activities over the life course (e.g., Keith, Dobson, Goudy, & Powers, 1981; Sinnott, 1986). Other work has examined the congruence or incongruence of husbands' and wives' views of marital life across the family life cycle (e.g., Bowen & Orthner, 1983; Keith & Schafer, 1986, 1991). This chapter extends the latter research track by presenting a typology of older men's and women's frames of mind toward their household activities and marital roles.

Demographic characteristics, level of involvement in housework, fairness and disagreement as outcomes of marital interaction, and psychological well-being (self-esteem, depressive symptoms) were investigated to derive profiles of older husbands and wives. Use of the typology permitted consideration of responses to involvement in both household work and activities as a marital partner rather than involvement itself. An objective of this chapter is to develop profiles of older husbands and wives with varying orientations to their household and marital activities. Four types were premised on the assumption that individuals simultaneously may vary in assessments of their work in the household and of their competencies and rewards derived from being a spouse. That is, a person may be contented and feel capable in his or her life as a marital partner but be disgruntled or unrewarded by the tasks done around the home. Or individuals may find contentment in both spheres of life or discontentment in each.

This research is based on the premise that marriage is central to the structure and the emotional tone of the daily lives of many older persons (Atchley, 1992). For some persons, household and marital activities remain stable over the course of the marriage, whereas others may negotiate these tasks more frequently. Transitions taking place in the older family, including retirement, have been reflected in research on the division of household labor and marital relationships (Atchley, 1992; Dorfman, 1992; Keith & Schafer, 1991; Keith, Wacker, & Schafer, 1992).

Housework Once Again

It has been observed that most husbands do so little housework that research on it is "much ado about nothing" (Miller & Garrison, 1984, p. 328). Yet the disproportionate allocation of time to household work by men and women in relation to labor-force participation (paid work, volunteer work, homemaking, retirement) has prompted many research questions about men's and women's expectations for sharing in the family, conceptions of equity and fairness, consensus or disagreement about the extent of involvement, and the consequences for both spouses (Dorfman, 1992; Keith & Schafer, 1991).

Gender, Age, Housework, and Well-Being

Research on younger employed spouses generally has indicated that high levels of family work are associated with diminished well-being among women, whereas increased participation by men does not prompt psychological distress or depressive symptoms for them (Kessler & McCrae, 1982; Ross, Mirowsky, & Huber, 1983). Rather, male participation actually may aid their adjustment in the family and promote their overall well-being (Pleck, 1983). Younger husbands, for example, in marriages in which housework was divided equally enjoyed greater satisfaction with the division of labor (Benin & Agostinelli, 1988). Wives of husbands who did not share in household tasks reported more depressive symptoms than other wives (Ross, Mirowsky, & Huber, 1983), and those whose husbands did not do their fair share of work in the family enjoyed less marital satisfaction (Staines & Libby, 1986).

The type of tasks (i.e., "feminine" or "masculine") performed by an older man may well be associated with his own and his spouse's well-being. Involvement by men in so-called masculine tasks around the home contributed to the satisfaction of their wives (Dorfman, 1992) as well as to their own life satisfaction and self-esteem; shared feminine tasks were associated with life satisfaction of men (Keith, Dobson, Goudy, & Powers, 1981; Keith, Powers, & Goudy, 1981). Keith and Schafer (1991) observed that older men were distinguished from males of other ages by their significantly greater involvement in feminine tasks in the household (e.g., laundry, dishwashing). Earlier, Brubaker (1985) reported that task sharing (i.e., a less traditional division of labor) contributed to marital satisfaction of both older husbands and their wives.

But all research has not corroborated benign or positive outcomes of housework in the older family. One study of older spouses indicated that participation in cross-gender activities did not increase individual psychological well-being and that it diminished that of their partners (Keith & Schafer, 1991). Older husbands had more depressive symptoms if their wives were highly involved in masculine tasks, whereas their wives were distressed when the men participated more in feminine activities. Thus older spouses benefited from their high involvement in gender-typed activities and were disadvantaged by their spouses' cross-gender participation.

A less-traditional division of household labor has been linked with disagreement over work-family roles that was in turn associated with depressive symptoms among older women (Keith & Schafer, 1986). Even so, research on younger and older families suggests that some women may benefit from their husbands' involvement, especially in traditional feminine tasks (Benin & Agostinelli, 1988), and that husbands do not seem affected adversely by helping and may enjoy advantages (Brubaker, 1985; Pleck, 1983). It was expected that involvement in housework would differentiate the orientations of men toward household and marital roles less than those of women.

Marital Interaction and Psychological Well-Being

Disagreement and Fairness

Both disagreement and perceptions of fairness emanate from the interaction between husbands and wives, and they influence functioning in the household and in the marriage relationship (Bahr, Chappell, & Leigh, 1983). Perceptions of fairness (or equity) are derived from expectations and subsequent assessments about what individuals believe is the appropriate outcome from their efforts compared to those of a partner. Fairness and disagreement seem to be related to one another. Older men, for example, who felt inequitably treated with respect to their participation in tasks in the home also reported greater disagreement with their spouses (Keith & Schafer, 1985). In addition, husbands' satisfaction with retirement may be diminished by perceived inequity in household work (Vinick & Ekerdt, 1987). Older wives also may be depressed and dissatisfied in situations of inequity in feminine housework (Keith & Schafer, 1985).

Atchley (1992) observed that whether decision making and work are divided along traditional or nontraditional lines is likely less important than agreement between spouses about the values underlying the alternatives they select. This suggests that the actual division of labor, the qualitatively different work of husbands and wives, or the vastly disparate amount of time that spouses spend in running the home may be less important than how the distribution is regarded and whether it conforms to their values.

It is not surprising that disagreement is linked with diminished marital satisfaction (Bahr, Chappell, & Leigh, 1983). There is evidence that a supportive marriage, presumably one characterized by fairness and less dissonance, increases one's ability to manage stressful events and diminishes psychosomatic symptoms (Traupmann & Hatfield, 1983). Implications for the current research are that a more harmonious relationship with less disagreement should foster a situation in which spouses may feel more competent in and derive satisfaction from both household and marital roles. This research expected that marital relationships with more fairness and less disagreement would characterize types of men and women described as contented, whereas the discontented would more often have marital relationships fraught with disagreement and unfairness. Disagreement and inequity may undermine feelings of efficacy and satisfaction that might accrue from involvement as a partner or in household work.

Depressive Symptoms and Self-Esteem

Problems of interaction between spouses reflected in disagreement and unfairness may have consequences for evaluations of self and depressive symptoms. Unfair and argumentative relationships are erosive to the self and serve as a negative communication about one's worth. Psychological stress (e.g., diminished self-esteem or depressed mood) ensuing from impaired marital interaction, such as that which is unfair or marked by dissonance, can undermine feelings of competence and divert personal resources that in other circumstances would be devoted to attaining satisfaction and deriving benefits from marital and household relationships. Consequently, those with low self-esteem and depressive symptoms are left with diminished resources to devote to altering their orientations toward their marital and household roles.

Beck (1967) has observed that depressives hold a negative view of themselves and the future. Persons with depressed mood may display a conception of self premised on negative information including irrational pessimism. Such negativism may shape the way information about the self is processed. A hallmark of depressed mood is the salience of negative experiences over positive ones and the anticipation of negative prospects in the future. Consequently, individuals with diminished evaluations of themselves and negative views of the future were expected to devalue their marital and household experiences. It was anticipated that depressive symptoms and self-esteem especially would differentiate the polar types of contented and discontented individuals.

The focus of this chapter is thus on the intersection of older husbands' and wives' outlooks on household and marital roles (Figure 8.1). Rather than accounting for involvement in the household in later life or speculating about individual outcomes of such participation, I investigate profiles of four orientations toward household and marital roles. The chapter is based on the assumption that perspectives on household work and marital roles of older men and women are not always linear. That is, outlooks on household and marital roles may reflect contentment or discontentment, or they may be heterogeneous with one viewed as a source of pleasure and the other as a cause for disappointment or strain. This investigation should contribute to our understanding of the personal and psychological resources that men and women bring to old age and the characteristics of their marital interaction that may distinguish their views of an intimate relationship.

Procedures

Sample

Data were analyzed from 448 married men and 352 women 65 and older who were primary respondents for their households in the 1988 National Survey of Families and Households (Sweet, Bumpass, & Call, 1988). The main sample for the survey is a national, multistage area probability sample composed of approximately 17,000 housing units drawn from 100 sampling areas in the United States. The men and women studied were

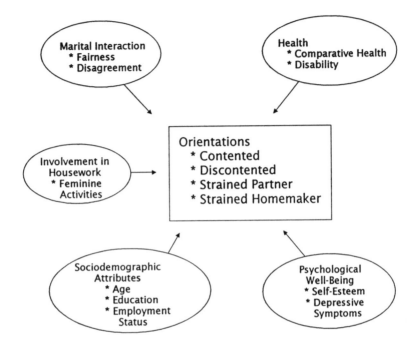

Figure 8.1. Correlates of Older Men's and Women's Orientations Toward Household Activities and Marital Roles

not married to one another. Although spouses were given an opportunity to complete a secondary questionnaire, the nonresponse rate for the selected questions would have limited the sample.

Women ranged in age from 65 to 97, with an average age of 71 years. Men ranged from 65 to 90 years of age ($X = 72$); 17% of the men and 10.5% of the women were employed (coded 0; not employed was coded 1). Men had completed an average of 10.7 years of education, compared with 11.14 years for women.

Measures

Housework

Respondents estimated the number of hours per week they spent doing each of five activities: preparing meals, washing dishes, cleaning house, shopping, and washing and ironing. These five activities, which represent types of household involvement primarily engaged in by women, were summed to form a housework scale. More feminine tasks were selected because they underscore differences between the work of men and women in the household—that is, male tasks around the house permit greater discretion about the time the activity is undertaken, and the activities often have a clearly defined beginning and end (Meissner, 1977). This measure focuses on some of the most routine, repetitive, and time-consuming tasks performed to maintain the household.

These five tasks formed a single factor in a factor analysis using a principal verimax rotation. Factor loadings for the five items ranged from .51 to .82 (alpha .72 for men, .62 for women).

Orientation Toward Household Work and Marital Roles

Rating six polar adjectives on a 7-point scale, respondents were asked to describe (a) the work they did around the house and (b) the things they did as a husband or wife as interesting-boring, appreciated-unappreciated, overwhelming-manageable, complicated-simple, lonely-sociable, and poorly done-well done. Scores of 1-7 were coded and summed across the six items so that a high-scale score represented a more positive assessment of their activities around the house and their marital roles. Scores for orientation toward housework for women ranged from 2.33 to 7.00 ($X = 5.33$, $SD = 1.01$, alpha = .62). Scores for men ranged from 2.17 to 7.00 ($X = 5.36$, $SD = 1.07$, alpha = .65). Scores for orientation toward marital roles of women ranged from 2.33 to 7.00 ($X = 5.69$, $SD = 1.02$, alpha = .74). Scores for men ranged from 1.50 to 7.00 ($X = 5.61$, $SD = 1.09$, alpha = .74).

Typology of Orientations Toward Household and Marital Roles

Based on orientations toward their involvement in work in the household and their activities as a marital partner, four types of older spouses were delineated. In one pattern called the *contented,* individuals felt competent and rewarded in both their household efforts and as a marriage partner (Table 8.1). The contented had scores on assessments of both household and marital involvement that were above the mean. Those who derived few benefits from either their household work or their activities as a spouse were described as *discontented.* Scores of the discontented were below the mean for both involvement in housework and in marital roles. The two interactive patterns were referred to as the *strained.* In these, one type of activity—marital role or household work—was assessed positively and the other negatively. Those called *strained partners* found little

Table 8.1 Typology of Orientations Toward Household Activities and
Marital Roles (in percentages)

	Men (N = 448)	Women (N = 352)
Contented	42	29
Discontented	25	40
Strained partner	8	21
Strained homemaker	25	10

rewarding about their marital roles but derived pleasure from their efforts
in household work, whereas *strained homemakers* felt disadvantaged by
the work they did around the house but were competent and benefited as
a marriage partner.

Fairness and Disagreement

Fairness was assessed by asking respondents how they felt about the
fairness in their relationship in terms of household chores and spending
money. Response categories were "very unfair to me" (1), "fair to both"
(3), "very unfair to her/him" (5). Responses to the two items were summed
with a higher score indicating greater advantages. Mean scores of women
ranged from 1 to 4 ($X = 2.93$, $SD = .33$); those of men ranged from 1 to 6
($X = 3.17$, $SD = .73$).

Disagreement was measured by summing responses to four questions:
"The following is a list of subjects on which couples often have disagreements. How often, if at all, in the last year have you had open disagreements about household tasks? money? spending time together? sex?"
Scores of women ranged from 1 to 4.75 ($X = 1.38$, $SD = .61$, alpha = .56);
those of men ranged from 1 to 4 ($X = 1.34$, $SD = .70$, alpha = .60).

Self-Esteem

Attitudes toward the self were assessed by responses of "strongly
disagree" (1) to "strongly agree" (5) to four statements: "On the whole, I
am satisfied with myself; I am able to do things as well as other people;
I feel that I'm a person of worth, at least on an equal plane with others; I
have always felt pretty sure my life would work out the way I wanted it
to." Responses were summed across the four items with a higher score

indicating more positive views of self. Scores for women ranged from 2 to 5 ($X = 4.03$, $SD = .55$, alpha = .57). Scores for men ranged from 2.25 to 5 ($X = 4.08$, $SD = .57$, alpha = .65).

Depressive Symptoms

Respondents were given a list of 12 ways they might have felt or behaved during the past week. Representative items were "On how many days during the past week did you: feel bothered by things that usually don't bother you? feel sad? not feel like eating? feel depressed? feel lonely? feel fearful?" Scores were summed across the 12 items with a higher score indicating more depressed mood. Scores for the number of times per week women experienced depressed moods ranged from 0 to 7 ($X = 1.25$, $SD = 1.56$, alpha = .92). Scores of men ranged from 0 to 6.92 ($X = 0.92$, $SD = 1.22$, alpha = .90).

Health

Two indicators of health were used. One indicator was whether health conditions limited activities (for example, caring for personal needs, moving about inside the house, doing household tasks, climbing stairs, walking six blocks) (1—not limited; 2—limited). More than one quarter (26%) of women and 30% of men had some health limitations. Comparative health was assessed by asking "Compared with other people your age, how would you describe your health?" (1—very poor; 5—excellent). Scores ranged from 1 to 5 for both men ($X = 3.75$, $SD = .89$) and women ($X = 3.69$, $SD = .89$).

Statistical Analyses

Bivariate analyses of the relationship between the typology and the characteristics of respondents were conducted using chi-square and analysis of variance. Discriminant analysis was then used to identify profiles of the types of orientations to housework and marital roles. Discriminant analysis is a multivariate statistical technique that may be used to identify characteristics that differentiate among groups. Standardized discriminant function coefficients indicate the relative contribution of a particular variable to the discriminating function; that is, coefficients represent the relative power of a variable when others are examined simultaneously.

Results

Housework in Older Families

Men and women estimated the number of hours per week they spent cooking, washing dishes, shopping, cleaning, and doing laundry. The scale of involvement in housework may be viewed as an indicator of gender equity in some of the most repetitious, time-consuming, and routine household tasks.

Reflecting little gender equity, these older men spent an average of 7.6 hours per week on housework compared to 34.77 hours spent by women. What is perhaps most telling is the disparity in the percentages of men and women who never engaged in the following particular tasks: doing laundry (77% men, 6% women), food preparation (51%, 2%), cleaning (49%, 5%), washing dishes (38%, 3%), and shopping (28%, 8%). Although these men and women were not married to one another, involvement in their respective households suggests that pursuits of older spouses continue to diverge. Older women, like their younger counterparts, performed substantially more and qualitatively different work in the home than men (Blair & Johnson, 1992).

Orientations Toward Household and Marital Roles

A typology was developed to reflect orientations to housework and one's activities as a husband or wife. A goal of the investigation was to distinguish among four types of spouses: the contented, the discontented, and two combined types—the strained partner and the strained homemaker. Men and women viewed their lives in the older family quite differently. Men were more often described as *contented* (42%) in their roles as spouses and around the home than were women (29%). Older men tended to find activities both as a spouse and in their work around the home more manageable, more appreciated, more simple, and more interesting. In contrast, women (40%) more often than men (25%) were identified as *discontented;* that is, they assessed their performance less positively in both spousal and homemaking activities. Thus women in the discontented pattern were more often burdened by both marital and housekeeping responsibilities. For example, women in this pattern felt less appreciated, found the activities more boring than interesting, and felt the tasks were less manageable.

Gender differences weres also observed in the combined type. Women (21%) more often than men (8%) were found in the *strained partner* type, in which individuals assessed their homemaking skills and the benefits derived from them more positively than their experiences as marital partner. In contrast, one quarter of the men compared with 10% of the women were in the *strained homemaker* type, in which they described their housework more positively. Men and women, of course, assessed markedly different levels of involvement in housework.

Multivariate Analysis

Discriminant analysis was used to develop profiles of the types of orientations toward housework and marital roles. Initial analyses for men and women included demographic characteristics (age, education, employment status, comparative health, disability), amount of involvement in housework, marital interaction variables (disagreement, fairness), and psychological well-being (self-esteem, depressive symptoms). Based on these analyses, reduced models were then tested and are described here (Table 8.2).

Men

In general, demographic characteristics failed to differentiate among patterns of orientation of men. Further, although it was not associated with the typology in the preliminary bivariate analysis, in the multivariate analysis, employment status, as a demographic variable, was linked with men's orientations (Table 8.2). In relation to marital and household orientations, depressive symptoms varied by employment status. Depressed retired men were more advantaged in their marital and household involvement than depressed employed men.

Preliminary analyses revealed that comparative health of contented men was better than that found in men who had negative experiences in both areas of family life (Table 8.2). Comparative health was also the only variable significantly related to the amount of involvement in housework by men, but it was a weak relationship ($r = .12, p < .05$). In the multivariate analysis, however, comparative health was not associated with family orientations. And in turn the amount of work around the house did not differentiate among orientations of men.

It had been anticipated that men in marital relationships characterized by disagreement and inequity would assess their household and marital experiences more negatively, but they did not. In the bivariate analysis, disagreement was associated with household and marital orientations ($F = 4.08, p < .01$). The contented experienced significantly less disagreement than the discontented. But the multivariate analysis indicated that disagreement was not a significant factor in differentiating types of household and marital orientations. Rather, self-esteem distinguished among types. Men, for example, who were contented with both their household work and role as a spouse were differentiated from the other three types by their high self-esteem and positive conceptions of themselves (Table 8.2). Self-esteem in particular was a resource for men in defining marital and household roles positively.

Depressive, pessimistic views of their lives were associated with negative outlooks on household and marital roles. A least-significant difference test indicated that men with the most positive responses to their role as a spouse and in homemaking reported significantly fewer depressive symptoms than discontented men or those who were strained homemakers. It was not inequity or disagreement as products of marital interaction that directly differentiated older men's orientations toward their marital and household roles. Rather, the confidence with which they viewed themselves and their skills and their optimism about the future made it possible for them to view their lives as spouses and housekeepers more positively. Furthermore, the correlations between marital interaction and psychological well-being were weak or not significant. Disagreement and fairness, for example, were correlated with self-esteem ($r = -.09, -.08$, n.s.) and with depressive symptoms ($r = .12, .11, p < .05$). In summary, in the multivariate analysis, fairness, disagreement, and amount of housework were unimportant in differentiating profiles of men's views of their marital and household roles.

Examination of the canonical discriminant functions at the group means (group centroids) for the one significant function indicated the contented were located farthest (.43) from the discontented (−.49) and closest to the strained partners (−.08) and strained homemakers (−.27). Thus the polar types—that is, the contented and discontented—were the least similar and were differentiated from one another by employment status and indicators of psychological well-being. And they were primarily distinguished from one another by self-esteem and depressive symptoms.

Women

The same demographic characteristics—qualities of marital interaction (disagreement and fairness), self-esteem, depressive symptoms, and amount of housework—were used in a discriminant analysis of housework marital role orientations for women as for men. A reduced model with just one

Table 8.2 Discriminant Analyses of a Typology of Orientations Toward Household Activities and Marital Roles (means, percentages, standardized discriminant functions)

	Contented Mean	SD	Discontented Mean	SD	Strained Partner Mean	SD	Strained Homemaker Mean	SD	Standardized Discriminant Function	F
Men										
Education	11.00	3.59	10.61	3.95	10.94	4.50	10.10	3.84	—	1.38
Health comparison	3.88	.86	3.59	.97	3.65	.87	3.72	.84	—	2.80*
Self-esteem	4.26	.48	3.90	.61	3.99	.58	3.97	.56	.75	11.08**
Depressive symptoms	.61	.88	1.33	1.55	.99	1.13	1.06	1.31	-.58	8.26**
Employment status (percentage employed)	13.4		19.3		14.3		18.8		.32	2.53
$\chi^2 = 57.02$, $df = 9$, $p < .001$, canonical correlation = .38										
Women										
Education	10.66	3.26	11.45	2.95	10.82	2.60	11.19	2.91	-.45	1.60
Health comparison	3.92	.84	3.43	.85	3.89	.78	3.52	1.50	.46	8.43*
Self-esteem	4.18	.54	3.80	.50	4.21	.47	3.97	.56	.50	12.76**
Depressive symptoms	.65	.97	1.79	1.78	.96	1.16	1.42	1.70	-.50	12.02**
Employment status (percentage employed)	12.6		9.2		11.1		11.1		—	.73
$\chi^2 = 71.72$, $df = 12$, $p < .001$, canonical correlation = .48										

*$p < .05$; **$p < .01$.

153

significant function is shown in Table 8.2. In contrast to orientations of men, those of women were differentiated by two demographic characteristics—education and comparisons of health. In a bivariate analysis, education was not significantly associated with the four types of orientations (Table 8.2). Rather, education was associated with the typology of housework and marital evaluations through its interaction with depressive symptoms. Except among the contented, low levels of education were accompanied with depressive symptoms. If women experienced success in both homemaking and marital roles (i.e., the contented), low levels of education were not accompanied by more depressive symptoms. For women in the other three types, however, greater levels of education seemed to be a buffer for depressed mood.

Comparison of health with that of peers differentiated among the patterns. Women who were contented and those who were strained partners enjoyed comparatively better health than their counterparts in the other patterns. Persons in these two types shared a positive orientation toward housework. Diminished health, however, was not associated with a reduction in the amount of time women spent in housework ($r = .04$, n.s.).

As among men, disagreement was related to the typology at the bivariate level ($F = 6.13$, $p < .001$). The contented had significantly less disagreement with their spouses than the discontented. Contrary to the exploratory hypothesis, in the multivariate analysis disagreement and the lack of fairness as outcomes of marital interaction did not directly differentiate among orientations to household and marital roles. Rather, any effect of fairness likely was mediated through its association with disagreement ($r = -.18$, $p < .01$), which was related to depressive symptoms ($r = .23$, $p < .01$). Inequity and disagreement combined to increase depressive symptoms of women in the discontented type. A breakdown analysis indicated that among discontented women those who felt unfairly treated and who experienced the greatest disagreement with their spouses also were substantially more depressed ($X = 2.40$) than women whose marriages were inequitable but accompanied by less disagreement ($X = 1.00$). A similar effect was not observed among men. In turn, depressive symptoms were a primary marker differentiating among the types of household and marital orientations.

As in the instance of their male counterparts, self-esteem and depressive symptoms differentiated among the four patterns for women. A bivariate analysis indicated that two types—the contented and strained partners—had substantially greater self-esteem than the discontented (Table 8.2). These two groups had in common their proficiency and benefits derived from housework. The contented had significantly fewer depressive symptoms than the discontented and strained partners who shared their dissatisfaction with their marital roles.

Examination of the canonical discriminant functions at the group means (group centroids) indicated that the contented and strained partners as a whole were differentiated from the discontented and strained homemakers. The contented and strained partners who shared positive assessments of their homemaking skills and benefits were more similar to one another. The contented (.57) were located farthest from the discontented (−.65) and closest to the strained partners (.36), with the strained homemakers in between (−.27).

Summary and Conclusions

Feeling competent, skilled, appreciated, and interested in household and marital roles simultaneously was the purview of older men more often than older women. In contrast, women more often were in circumstances resulting in less contentment in both household and spousal roles. In the mixed patterns (i.e., strained partners and strained homemakers), men more often were strained in the tasks of housework but experienced successes in their activities as a spouse, whereas women more often described positive activities as a homemaker and negative ones as a spouse. There was no evidence that these circumstances of older men and women were attributable to the amount of household involvement.

That men more frequently were contented in both household and marital roles may corroborate research indicating that they find marriage more satisfying and experience less negative affect than do women (Depner & Ingersoll-Dayton, 1985; Weishaus & Field, 1988; Quirouette & Gold, 1992). Furthermore, older males and females may have different expectations and preferences for their marital relationships. Men, for example, valued the instrumental care and activities of their wives more than affective aspects of their relationship (Wills, Weiss, & Patterson, 1974). In contrast, women may prefer more communication and affection than instrumental aid in the household. Unmet needs for interpersonal support in the marriage may in part explain why women more often select persons other than their marital partner as a confidant (Keith, Hill, Goudy, & Powers, 1984).

Differences in the way men and women regard marriage have significance for other aspects of their lives. Although women derive less satisfaction from marriage than men, it is a stronger predictor of their mental health (Gove, Hughes, & Style, 1983). Furthermore, the well-being of women is influenced more by their husband's perception of the marriage, whereas a man's well-being is less contingent on his wife's view (Quirouette & Gold, 1992). The tendency for women to be in the types in which their marital roles were evaluated more negatively (i.e., discontented or strained partner, 61% compared to 33% of men) may reflect the nature of interaction in the husband-wife dyad. Some of the assessments that were indicators of contentment in both household and marital roles were products of interaction with a partner—for example, feeling appreciated as a spouse or as a homemaker. Older men may receive significantly more supportive responses from their wives than women do from their husbands. The more limited support received by women may have been reflected in evaluations of their efforts as spouses and in household activities.

The research failed to support the following conclusion of Thompson and Walker (1989): "Among wives, unlike among husbands, there is a clear and positive connection between fair division of family work and marital and personal well-being" (p. 89). For these older men and women, the distribution of housework did not figure in their orientations to household and marital roles. The amount of household involvement also had no effect on outcomes of marital interaction (disagreement or fairness) or psychological well-being. Despite expectations to the contrary, fairness and disagreement did not directly affect men's or women's orientations toward household and marital roles. Perceptions of unfairness were associated with contentiousness between spouses, especially in women with depressive symptoms. It was depression that was important in distinguishing among types of orientations. This suggests once again that women's lives more than men's may be influenced more directly by the nature of interaction in the marriage. For men, depressive symptoms may have arisen from both marital interaction and the absence of employment.

The psychological resources (i.e., self-esteem and positive outlooks on life) that in part shaped older men's and women's views of their partnerships were remarkably similar. Conceiving of themselves, their present, and their future in a negative way, as reflected in low self-esteem and depressive symptoms, precluded positive assessments of their marital lives by some. Shoring up a diminished self and operating from a pessimistic vision for what is yet to be may exact enormous energy, perhaps leaving little reserve for attaining joy and appreciation from relationships in the household and marriage. Despite gender-related outcomes from marriage, the significance of attitudes toward the self and outlooks on life for framing conceptions of household and marital roles was quite comparable for these older men and women.

References

Atchley, R. (1992). Retirement and marital satisfaction. In M. Szinovacz, D. J. Ekerdt, & B. H. Vinick (Eds.), *Families in retirement* (pp. 145-158). Newbury Park, CA: Sage.

Bahr, S. J., Chappell, C. B., & Leigh, G. K. (1983). A great marriage, role enactment, role consensus, and marital satisfaction. *Journal of Marriage and the Family, 45,* 795-803.

Beck, A. T. (1967). *Depression: Clinical, experimental and theoretical aspects.* New York: Hoeber.

Benin, M. H., & Agostinelli, J. (1988). Husbands' and wives' satisfaction with the division of labor. *Journal of Marriage and the Family, 50,* 349-361.

Blair, S. L., & Johnson, M. P. (1992). Wives' perceptions of the fairness of the division of household labor: The intersection of housework and ideology. *Journal of Marriage and the Family, 54,* 570-581.

Bowen, G., & Orthner, D. (1983). Sex-role congruency and marital quality. *Journal of Marriage and the Family, 45,* 223-230.

Brubaker, T. H. (1985). Responsibility for household tasks: A look at golden anniversary couples aged 75 years and older. In W. A. Peterson & J. Quadagno (Eds.), *Social bonds in later life* (pp. 27-36). Beverly Hills, CA: Sage.

Depner, C. E., & Ingersoll-Dayton, B. (1985). Conjugal social support: Patterns in later life. *Journal of Gerontology, 40,* 761-766.

Dorfman, L. (1992). Couples in retirement: Division of household work. In M. Szinovacz, D. J. Ekerdt, & B. H. Vinick (Eds.), *Families in retirement* (pp. 159-173). Newbury Park, CA: Sage.

Gove, W. R., Hughes, M., & Style, C. B. (1983). Does marriage have positive effects on the psychological well-being of the individual? *Journal of Health and Social Behavior, 24,* 122-131.

Keith, P. M., Dobson, C. D., Goudy, W. J., & Powers, E. A. (1981). Older men: Occupation, employment status, household involvement, and well-being. *Journal of Family Issues, 2,* 336-349.

Keith, P. M., Hill, K., Goudy, W. J., & Powers, E. A. (1984). Confidants and well-being: A note on male friendship in old age. *The Gerontologist, 24,* 318-320.

Keith, P. M., Powers, E. A., & Goudy, W. J. (1981). Older men in employed and retired families. *Alternative Lifestyles, 4,* 228-241.

Keith, P. M., & Schafer, R. B. (1985). Equity role strains, and depression among middle aged and older men and women. In W. A. Peterson & J. Quadagno (Eds.), *Social bonds in later life* (pp. 37-49). Beverly Hills, CA: Sage.

Keith, P. M., & Schafer, R. B. (1986). Housework, disagreement, and depression among younger and older couples. *American Behavioral Scientist, 29,* 405-422.

Keith, P., & Schafer, R. (1991). *Relationships and well-being over the life stages.* New York: Praeger.

Keith, P., Wacker, R. R., & Schafer, R. B. (1992). Equity in older families. In M. Szinovacz, D. J. Ekerdt, & B. H. Vinick (Eds.), *Families in retirement* (pp. 189-201). Newbury Park, CA: Sage.

Kessler, R. C., & McCrae, J. A., Jr. (1982). The effect of wives' employment on the mental health of married men and women. *American Sociological Review, 47,* 216-227.

Meissner, M. (1977). Sexual division of labor and inequality: Labor and leisure. In M. Stephenson (Ed.), *Women in Canada* (pp. 160-180). Toronto: Women's Educational Press.

Miller, J., & Garrison, H. H. (1984). Sex roles: The division of labor at home and in the workplace. In D. H. Olson & B. C. Miller (Eds.), *Family studies yearbook* (Vol. 2, pp. 323-348). Beverly Hills, CA: Sage.

Pleck, J. H. (1983). Husbands' paid work and family roles: Current research issues. In H. Lopata & J. Pleck (Eds.), *Research in the interweave of social roles: Families and jobs* (Vol. 3, pp. 251-333). Greenwich, CT: JAI Press.

Quirouette, C., & Gold, D. P. (1992). Spousal characteristics as predictors of well-being in older couples. *International Journal of Aging and Human Development, 34,* 257-269.

Ross, C. E., Mirowsky, J., & Huber, J. (1983). Dividing work, sharing work, and in-between: Marriage patterns and depression. *American Sociological Review, 48,* 809-823.

Sinnott, J. D. (1986). *Sex roles and aging: Theory and research from a systems perspective.* Basel, Switzerland: Karger.

Staines, G. L., & Libby, P. L. (1986). Men and women in role relationships. In R. D. Ashmore & F. K. DelBoca (Eds.), *The social psychology of female-male relations: A critical analysis of central concepts* (pp. 211-258). San Diego, CA: Academic Press.

Sweet, J. A., Bumpass, L. L., & Call, V. R. A. (1988). *The design and content of the national survey of families and households* (Working Paper No. NSFH-1). Madison: University of Wisconsin, Center for Demography and Ecology.

Thompson, L., & Walker, A. J. (1989). Gender in families: Women and men in marriage, work, and parenthood. In A. Booth (Ed.), *Contemporary families: Looking forward, looking back* (pp. 76-96). Minneapolis, MN: NCFR.

Traupmann, J., & Hatfield, E. (1983). How important is marital fairness over the lifespan? *International Journal of Aging and Human Development, 17,* 89-101.

Vinick, B. H., & Ekerdt, D. J. (1987). *Activities and satisfaction among recently retired men and their wives.* Paper presented at 40th annual scientific meeting of the Gerontological Society of America, Washington, DC.

Weishaus, S., & Field, D. (1988). A half century of marriage: Continuity or change? *Journal of Marriage and the Family, 50,* 763-774.

Wills, T. A., Weiss, R. L., & Patterson, G. R. (1974). A behavioral analysis of the determinants of marital satisfaction. *Journal of Consulting and Clinical Psychology, 42,* 802-811.

9

Older Men's Friendship Patterns

REBECCA G. ADAMS

The field of adult friendship research is reaching maturity (Perlman, 1993). Most of the research on this topic has been conducted in the last 20 to 25 years, with a notable increase in quantity and quality of studies in the past decade. This mature stage of development is marked by the appearance of several monographs synthesizing and reviewing extant research (e.g., Allan, 1989; Blieszner & Adams, 1992; O'Connor, 1992; Rawlins, 1992) and by the availability of edited volumes focused on the friendships of the members of specific adult populations (see Adams & Blieszner, 1989, for a collection of chapters reviewing literature on older adult friendship; see Nardi, 1992a, for chapters examining men's friendships).

Gerontologists have focused more attention on friendship than other researchers have. This is probably the result of the centrality of the study of friendship to activity and disengagement theories, which preoccupied social gerontologists for decades, and because of the more recent interest in friends as a source of informal support for older adults (Adams, 1989). Despite this tendency of gerontologists to be interested in friendship, however, they have not often examined older men's friendships. The focus on women to the almost complete exclusion of men is characteristic of the research in many subfields of gerontology, largely because women comprise more of the older population than do men. The discrepancy between the number of studies focused on older men and those focused on older women is larger in the subfield of friendship than in many other gerontology subfields, perhaps because of the perception that friendship is less central to the lives of older men than to those of older women.

Although few researchers have focused exclusively on older men's friendships, more have studied friendship in populations including both genders. The contribution of these studies including both genders to our understanding of older men's friendships, however, is limited for three reasons. First, a surprising number of these studies do not include examinations of the effects of gender, but only analyses in which older men and older women are combined (Blieszner & Adams, 1992).

Second, when researchers do examine the effects of gender on friendship, they often use a gender-biased perspective, usually a female rather than a male perspective (Adams, 1988). A woman's perspective emphasizes what Wright (1982) called the face-to-face aspects of friendship (personalism and interpersonal sensitivity), whereas a man's perspective emphasizes the side-by-side aspects (instrumentality and activity centeredness). The gender biases of friendship researchers are reflected in the questions they ask about friendship and in the way they operationalize concepts. Female researchers have been more likely than male researchers to examine qualitative content or process (e.g., closeness, confiding, supportiveness), to ask nonglobal questions (as opposed to questions asking the respondent to summarize across friends), and to include the dyad as the unit of analysis (rather than focusing on friendships in general) (Adams, 1988).

Finally, when researchers do study gender differences and operationalize friendship in a way that approaches gender neutrality, they usually do not develop a theoretical explanation for why gender might have an effect (Adams & Blieszner, in press; Blieszner & Adams, 1992). They typically add the variable "sex" to a set of independent variables predicting friendship patterns, without discussing it conceptually and without including independent measures of gender as psychological disposition and as social structural position. This is unfortunate, because it is quite different, for example, to attribute the lesser intimacy of men's friendships to inadequate male psychological capacity rather than to their fewer opportunities to pursue such relationships.

To understand older men's friendships, it is necessary to study the effects of gender among older adults, as well as study the interactive effects of age and gender across the life course. Unfortunately, the limitations of the literature examining the effects of age on friendship mirror those of the literature examining the effects of gender on it. Researchers have conducted few studies of friendships across the life course; what we know about older adult friendship comes almost entirely from studies exclusively focused on that age group. When researchers do study friendships among adults of various ages, they either fail to examine age differences or they use the variable "age" as a proxy measure for both stage of life course and stage of development without distinguishing between these two aspects of aging. For example, Weiss and Lowenthal (1975) found that older adults tended to have more complex and multidimensional friendships than middle-aged or younger ones. They interpreted these results in light of differing age-related psychological needs and social norms, although they did not measure these needs or normative effects separately.

Studying the effects of age on friendship is further complicated by a need to separate out the effects of aging (growing older), period (time of measurement), and cohort (the interaction of age and period). To accomplish this, a theoretical rationale for setting one of these three effects to zero is needed, or at least a cross-sequential study design in which longitudinal studies of several cohorts are conducted should be done (see Maddox & Campbell, 1985, for a general discussion of this methodological dilemma). There have been virtually no longitudinal studies of older adult friend relationships (Adams, 1989) and no longitudinal studies including more than one cohort. Furthermore, none of the longitudinal studies of older adult friend relationships has focused on older men or has included reports of gender differences.

In addition to the problems already outlined, our knowledge of older men's friendships is further limited by problems characteristic of friendship research in general. On one hand, there is a lack of studies using representative samples and samples of general populations (Adams, 1989). This has limited our ability to make generalizations and to identify sources of variation. On the other hand, although friendship researchers have tended to study special populations or friendships in specific contexts, they have not identified how the characteristics of the special populations or contexts affect friendship (see Nardi, 1992b, for a discussion of how this affects what we know about men's friendships). Replications of both types of studies—the general and the specific—appear to be nonexistent.

Given these serious conceptual and methodological limitations of the literature bearing on older men's friendships, it is difficult to summarize the relevant findings. In a sense, we do not "know" anything about the friendships of older men; we only have clues. The rest of this chapter summarizes what can be gleaned from friendship research focused exclusively on older men and from research including gender comparisons, using a framework that Adams and Blieszner (1994) developed for this type of analysis.

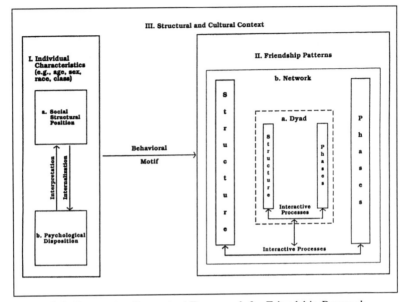

Figure 9.1. Integrative Conceptual Framework for Friendship Research

An Integrative Conceptual Framework

The framework posits that the social structural and psychological aspects of individual characteristics (such as age, sex, race, and class) operate together to shape behavioral motifs (the constellation of both the routine and unpredictable aspects of an individual's daily activities) that in turn influence friendship patterns (see Figure 9.1). Friendship patterns comprise dyadic and network structure and phases and the interactive processes connecting them. Internal structure consists of the degree of homogeneity, solidarity, and hierarchy between the members of friendship pairs and among friendship network members and the size, density, and configuration of the network. Phases reflect the developmental status of the friendship or network, whether in the formative, maintenance, or dissolution stage. Interactive processes denote the overt behavioral events and the covert cognitive and affective responses that occur when people interact (Kelley et al., 1983).

The elements of this integrative framework and the relationships among them vary by structural and cultural context. Structural and cultural contexts vary by their remoteness from the individual and thus from the immediate social environment in which friendships are formed and maintained (e.g., church, apartment building, senior center), to the community (e.g., ethnic and race subcultures), and finally to the larger social system (e.g., nations, historical time periods).

It is perhaps easier to see how the framework would work differently in different immediate social environments than in different communities or societies. For example, compare the effects of social status on friendship among older people who have relocated to a nursing home and among those who are still living independently. Nursing homes are equalizers. On entering a nursing home, residents often shed their social identities; the material reminders of their past statuses are often left in storage. Status differences are thus much more salient in shaping the friendships of those fortunate enough to age in place.

Friendship Patterns of Older Men

Using this integrative framework to organize what we know about older men's friendships immediately makes several substantive gaps in the literature apparent. First, there have been no studies of the phases of older men's friendships and no studies of older adult friendship phases that include gender comparisons. Second, although there have been some studies on the internal structure and some on the internal processes of older men's friendships, there have been few studies including measures of both. Finally, as mentioned in the introduction, although studies have been conducted in a variety of contexts and of different populations, systematic analyses of the effects of the characteristics of contexts or populations are not possible, because the researchers usually did not identify these characteristics.

In the following two sections, the findings bearing on the internal structure and processes of older men's friendships are summarized in sequence without discussion of their relationship to one another, without discussion of phases, and without systematic discussion of contextual and population effects. Also discussed are a few studies of the consequences of friendship for older men. The results of studies involving four types of samples are included in this synthesis: (a) those comparing men and women across stages of the life course, (b) those comparing older men and women, (c) those including men at various stages of the life course, and (d) those including only older men. See Table 9.1 for a list and description of the studies that are referenced in this chapter.

Table 9.1 Studies Including Information on Older Men's Friendships

Study	Population	Sample Type	N
Gender and life course comparisons			
Fischer and Oliker (1983)	Urban Northern California adults	Purposive	1,050
Fox, Gibbs, and Auerbach (1985)	Students in liberal arts classes	Availability	31
Weiss and Lowenthal (1975)	Families of high school students (including preretired)	Purposive	216
Gender comparisons of older adults			
Albert and Moss (1990)	Older adults	Unknown	225
Antonucci and Akiyama (1987)	National, 50+, married with at least one child	Probability	214
Blau (1961)	2 New York state health districts	Unknown	500
Bryant and Rakowski (1992)	National, 70+	Probability	473
Connidis and Davies (1990)	London, Ontario, Canada, 65+	Probability	400
Dykstra (1990)	Dutch elderly; 65+	Probability	322
Eckert (1980)	Single-room-occupancy hotel occupants in California	Availability	43
Ferraro, Mutran, and Barresi (1984)	Census survey of low-income aged and disabled	Probability	3,683
Fisher, Reid, and Melendez (1989)	Members of senior center in urban area	Unknown	55
Husaini, Moore, Castor, Neser, Whitten-Stovall, Linn, and Griffin (1991)	Black elderly in Nashville, Tennessee	Probability	600
Johnson (1983)	Acute care hospital admissions in San Francisco Bay Area	Saturation	167
Jones and Vaughan (1990)	Participants in community activities	Availability	76
Litwak (1989)	65+ in New York metropolitan area and 2 Florida counties	Availability/ Probability	1,818

Pihlblad and Adams (1972)	65+ in 64 small towns in Missouri	Probability	1,551
Powers and Bultena (1976)	60+ noninstitutionalized, in 5 Iowa counties	Unknown	269
Retsinas and Garrity (1985)	Nursing home residents, Pawtucket, Rhode Island	Unknown	145
Roberto and Scott (1986)	64+ in Southwestern city	Probability	116
Usui (1984)	60+ in Jefferson County, Kentucky	Probability	704

Stage of life course comparisons of men

Steuve and Gerson (1977)	Caucasian men, 21-64, living in primary families in Detroit metropolitan area	Probability	985

Older men only

Bossé, Aldwin, Levenson, Workman-Daniels, and Ekerdt (1990)	Community dwelling men, Boston area	Unknown	1,513
Cohen (1989)	Old homeless men on the Bowery	Availability	86
Elder and Clipp (1988)	World War II and Korean War veterans	Selected	149
Keith, Hill, Goudy, and Powers (1984)	Married Caucasian men in Midwestern state, 60+	Probability	1,200
Rubinstein (1986)	Older men living alone in Philadelphia	Availability	47
Tesch, Whitbourne, and Nehrke (1981)	Male residents of VA center in Bath, New York	Saturation	54

Internal Structure of Friendship Patterns

Size

The findings on the size of older men's friendship networks are inconsistent across studies, because the samples of the older population and the measures used to assess size differed. Several studies of more or less general populations examined the size of older men's friendship networks. Weiss and Lowenthal (1975) found that at all stages of life, men reported approximately one fewer friend than women did. In contrast, Fischer and Oliker (1983) found that, although there were no gender differences in number of friends among young adults and middle-aged parents, among middle-aged childless people and among the elderly, men reported fewer friendships than women did. In contrast, in their study of older adults in 64 small towns in Missouri, Pihlblad and Adams (1972) found that older men had more friends than older women.

Other studies of more specific populations also included measures of size of network. In the context of a nursing home, Retsinas and Garrity (1985) found no gender differences among the older residents in number of friendships. Approximately one third of the residents were loners; the median number of friendships was six; and the maximum number was also six. Blindness, being mute, tenure in the nursing home, and lack of lucidity were negatively related to number of friendships. Bossé, Aldwin, Levenson, Workman-Daniels, and Ekerdt (1990) reported that half of their sample of older men had at least some friends from work. Slightly fewer workers than retired men reported co-worker friends. In his study of old homeless men, Cohen (1989) found that the Bowery men had fewer informal (kin and nonkin) contacts than the 12 community men he studied for comparative purposes.

Homogeneity

The two most frequently studied types of network homogeneity are gender and age homogeneity. It is quite clear that older men have less gender-homogeneous friendship networks than do older women (Dykstra, 1990; Litwak, 1989; Powers & Bultena, 1976; Usui, 1984). Two studies suggested that older men and older women are equally likely to have age-homogeneous networks (Usui, 1984; Weiss & Lowenthal, 1975). In their study of men at six stages of life (including old fathers and postparents aged 50-64), Steuve and Gerson (1977) found that beyond age 29, there was a steady decline in age-similar friendships.

Both Dykstra (1990), who studied Dutch elderly, and Usui (1984), who studied the elderly in Jefferson County, Kentucky, reported on types of homogeneity that other friendship researchers have not studied among the elderly. Dykstra (1990) reported that never married and formerly married men had friendship networks characterized by lower marital status homogeneity than their female counterparts. Cohabiting men reported a higher degree of marital status homogeneity than their female counterparts. In contrast, Usui (1984) reported that older men had greater marital status homogeneity than older women did. This is not necessarily inconsistent with Dykstra's findings, because Usui did not include cohabitation as a marital status, and he controlled for the effects of race and marital status. He also reported no gender differences in education and race homogeneity.

Density

Network density is a measure of "the extent to which links which could exist among persons do in fact exist" (Mitchell, 1969, p. 18) and is expressed in terms of a percentage of all possible friendship links actually named. To measure density, the researcher must ask respondents about the interconnections among all of their friends. Because this is a time-consuming and thus expensive task, few studies of friendship network density have been conducted.

Two studies examined the density of the friendship networks of older men, but only in passing. Fox, Gibbs, and Auerbach (1985) reported that older and middle-aged men and young and middle-aged women had less-dense friendship networks than young men and older women did. Young men and older women tended to have friends who all knew one another and were friends with one another, and the others, including older men, knew their friends better than they knew one another. Although Steuve and Gerson (1977) did not discuss density in great detail, a measure of it was included in the Detroit Area Study data they analyzed. They did note that among older men there was no relationship between age homogeneity and density, but among younger men the denser the network was, the more age homogeneous the network was. They suggested that this was because age barriers to friendship are lowered with age.

Solidarity

Solidarity is the horizontal dimension of internal structure, or the degree of intimacy or closeness between dyad members (Brown, 1965).

Some researchers treat intimacy as a process variable rather than as a structural one, and the process character of friendship intimacy will be discussed shortly. But solidarity is a structural marker and a fairly widely used measure of the strength of social ties and of social distance (Marsden & Campbell, 1984). To measure network solidarity, it is necessary to determine the degree of emotional closeness between the members of each pair in the respondent's network. Few friendship researchers have done this (see Cohen & Rajkowski, 1982, for an exception, although they did not examine gender differences), and no friendship researchers studying older men or reporting gender comparisons have.

A few studies, however, suggested how network solidarity might vary by gender and across the life course. First, the authors of two articles suggested that older men interact less frequently than older women with intimate friends and that they reserve emotional closeness for family members (Fox, Gibbs, & Auerbach, 1985; Powers & Bultena, 1976). Because friendship networks tend to be homogeneous in terms of age and sex, this suggests that older men's friendship networks are probably lower in solidarity than older women's.

Although Steuve and Gerson (1977) did not study solidarity in its true sense, their work suggested that it does not vary across the life course. They included a measure of the percentage of friends with whom the respondent was intimate (not the percentage of all pairs in the friendship network that were intimate, which would be a true measure of solidarity). They reported the average percentage of intimate friends by life course category. Although they did not test for the differences among the means, it appears that the percentage of men's friendships that were intimate did not vary across the life course.

Friendships' Internal Processes

Cognitive

Cognitive processes reflect the internal thoughts that each partner has about her- or himself, the friend, and the friendship (Blieszner & Adams, 1992). Two of the cognitive processes involved in older men's friendships have been addressed: satisfaction with friendship and its definition or meaning.

The findings on friendship satisfaction are various. Antonucci and Akiyama (1987) reported that among the married people with at least one child whom they studied, older men were less satisfied with their friendships than were older women. In contrast, Jones and Vaughan (1990) reported no group differences in satisfaction with friends among the older married men, married women, and single women they studied. Roberto and Scott (1986) reported no overall gender differences in satisfaction with friends, but found that older men reported a greater level of satisfaction than did older women when overbenefited by their friends.

Other studies bearing on the cognitive processes of older men's friendships have addressed questions about the definition or meaning of friendship to those being studied. Fox, Gibbs, and Auerbach (1985) found that across all of the age groups they studied, men's and women's conceptions of friendship fell into instrumental and expressive categories, respectively. They also reported that the meaning of friendship deepened with age, particularly for men.

Weiss and Lowenthal (1975) listed six domains into which the descriptions of friendship their respondents gave fit: similarity, reciprocity, compatibility, structured dimensions, role model, and other. Men emphasized similarity more frequently than women, across all four stages of life. Women, on the other hand, were more likely to mention reciprocity.

Albert and Moss (1990) measured consensus on the attributes of closest friends and friends as a whole. Older men and women were equally likely to agree with others of their own sex and age. For older men, consensus about what is characteristic of a close friendship was higher than consensus about what is characteristic of a friend in general. For older women, the opposite was true. Across all marital status categories, older men ranked "someone to pass the time with" as a more important quality of all friends than women did. They also ranked "someone to feel comfortable with" for closest friends and "someone to count on" for all friends lower than older women did. Furthermore, Albert and Moss (1990) suggested that there are gender-linked differences in interpersonal culture. Consensus about close friendships appeared to matter less for older men than for older women. Consensus about all friendships was important for both older men and women, but for men deviation led to lower personal mastery and for women it led to depression.

Affective

Only one article listed in Table 9.1 addressed the topic of affective processes in older men's friendships. Affective processes encompass emotional reactions to friends and friendship. Empathy, affection, trust, loyalty, satisfaction, commitment, joy, and contentment are all positive or pleasurable emotions. Indifference, anger, hostility, and jealousy are examples of negative or unpleasant ones (Blieszner & Adams, 1992).

Fisher, Reid, and Melendez (1989) studied anger in friendships among older adults. They found that anger between age peers is related to envy and failure of friends to adapt successfully to the aging process. Although there were no gender differences in the tendency of older men and women to experience anger over unmet aging role expectations, this type of anger was more common among people in their 60s than among people in their 70s. Men were less likely than women to report envy in their friendships.

Behavioral

Behavioral processes are the action components of friendship. They include, for example, disclosure of thoughts and feelings, display of affection, social support, resource exchange, cooperation, accommodation to a friend's desires, coordination, sharing activities and interests, concealment, manipulation, conflict, and competition (Blieszner & Adams, 1992). Research on the behavioral aspects of older men's friendships includes discussions of social support, confiding, and companionship.

Several studies bear on the social supportiveness of older men's friendships. Because each study approached the topic somewhat differently and focused on different populations, it is difficult to make summary statements about the results. In their study of married older adults with at least one child, Antonucci and Akiyama (1987) reported no gender differences in the number of friends in the helping network. In their study of older married and widowed adults, Ferraro, Mutran, and Barresi (1984) found that married men were more likely than their female counterparts to have friendship support but that there was not a gender difference among the widowed. In his study of older single-room-occupant hotel dwellers, Eckert (1980) reported that men were less likely to be involved in supportive relationships than women. Similarly, Roberto and Scott (1986) reported that compared to older women, older men had less involvement in instrumental and expressive exchanges with friends. For men, both instrumental and emotional exchanges revolved around a shared activity.

Two studies examined equity in friendships. Roberto and Scott (1986) reported that older men were more likely than older women to be involved in equitable friendships. In contrast, in their study of senior adults (married men, married women, and single women), Jones and Vaughan (1990) reported no group differences in equity or reciprocity. They did observe that most of the people in their sample were slightly overbenefiting from their friendships.

Litwak (1989) examined the effect of the gender composition of the friendship support network rather than the effects of the gender of the respondent. He reported that the amount of help that older single men, older single women, and older married women received was not affected by the gender composition of their friendship network. Older married men, however, did better if they had both male and female friends.

In addition to these studies reporting gender differences, two studies focused exclusively on men reported on the social support they received from friends. Bossé, Aldwin, Levenson, Workman-Daniels, and Ekerdt (1990) reported that workers and retirees reported nearly identical levels of social support from friends. In his study of old homeless men, Cohen (1989) emphasized the importance of reciprocity in Bowery relationships. Small groups of three or four men slept together and took care of one another when they were drunk.

It is no surprise that the literature shows that older men are less likely to confide in friends than older women are (Connidis & Davies, 1990; Fox, Gibbs, & Auerbach, 1985). Several studies focused exclusively on men reveal more about their confiding relationships. Bossé, Aldwin, Levenson, Workman-Daniels, and Ekerdt (1990) found that, compared to retirees, workers reported more co-worker confidant friends and were more likely to talk to co-workers about problems. Keith, Hill, Goudy, and Powers (1984) reported that in their sample of older, Caucasian, married workers, 39% had a confidant outside of their family. In their study of veterans living in a residential facility, Tesch, Whitbourne, and Nehrke (1981) found that 68% had at least one friend in the facility, and half of these 68% had a confidant. Morale was not correlated with these measures.

Although researchers have not systematically examined what older men do when they are together, the authors of two studies discussed the importance of companionship to older men. Connidis and Davies (1990) reported that older men first turned to their spouses for companionship and then to friends, while for older women, the reverse was true. Rubinstein (1986) observed that men who successfully reorganized their lives after widowhood often mentioned having a friend who was important to them.

Proxy Measures of Interactive Processes

My discussion of processes focused on specific thoughts, feelings, and actions that take place between and among friends. Other process variables have received research attention as well. These include measures of how often and how long interactive processes occur and the variety of interactive processes that take place. These variables are proxy measures of process in the sense that they reveal only that interaction takes place but not the nature of the processes involved (Adams & Blieszner, in press; Blieszner & Adams, 1992). The underlying assumption of researchers who use these measures exclusively seems to be that a larger quantity and variety of process is better than less. The literature on older men's friendships includes many studies on frequency of interaction and duration, but none on the variety of interactive processes that take place among older men in general or among specific groups of them.

Several studies examined gender effects on older people's frequency of interaction with friends. The researchers involved in three studies found that gender did not affect frequency of interaction (Husaini et al., 1991; Johnson, 1983; Retsinas & Garrity, 1985); those involved in two reported that men talked to friends (Albert & Moss, 1990) and saw friends (Pihlblad & Adams, 1972) less frequently than women did; and those involved in one reported that men had more frequent contact with friends than women, but that fewer of their contacts were with intimate friends (Powers & Bultena, 1976). These findings probably reflect differences in the populations studied and measures of frequency of interaction more than they enlighten us about gender differences.

A few studies provided information on the connection between contact with friends and aging. Steuve and Gerson (1977) reported that, at all stages of life, the men they studied met with friends outside of their homes. Their frequency of interaction with friends declined through middle age and then stabilized. Pihlblad and Adams (1972) found that frequency of visiting friends declined with length of widowhood for men, but not for women. In a cross-sectional study, Blau (1961) reported that widowhood affected the social participation of both men and women more in their 60s (when widows and widowers are less common) than in their 70s. The impact of a loss of a spouse during the 60s was greater for men than for women. The difference in the friendship participation of married and widowed men disappeared in their 70s.

Although no studies included gender comparisons of duration of friendships, a couple of them did examine the connection between age and duration. Weiss and Lowenthal (1975) reported that for both men and women, the older the person was, the longer was the duration of his or her friendships. Steuve and Gerson (1977) reported the same finding and further analyses that showed that young men made new best friends much more frequently than older men and that older men held onto prior best friends longer. Elder and Clipp (1988) reported that heavy-combat veterans were more likely than other veterans to have enduring ties from the service.

Effects of Friendship

The perception, mentioned earlier, that friendship is less central to the lives of older men than to the lives of older women has not been systematically demonstrated by research. Few studies of the effects of friendship on older men's lives have been conducted, and the findings of existing studies are mixed. A couple of studies suggested that the common perception is correct. Husaini et al. (1991) found that talking with friends had positive effects on older black women's mental health and not on older black men's mental health. Similarly, Tesch, Whitbourne, and Nehrke (1981) reported that among older men in a domiciliary unit of a Veteran's Administration center, the extent of friendship with peers was not correlated with morale. But, in contrast, they reported that friendship was positively related to adjustment. Also contradicting the common perception are Bryant and Rakowski's (1992) finding that contact with friends lowered the risk of mortality for older African-American men and Elder and Clipp's (1988) discussion of the importance of maintaining ties with service mates for weakening memories of war and related stress.

Investigators need to examine the processes that connect friendship patterns and well-being rather than merely rubbing together scales measuring each of the two concepts as most have done. Duck (1990) has described this problem as similar to talking about the connection between ingredients and dinner without discussing cooking. For example, what are the differential effects of face-to-face versus side-by-side processes? Does one contribute more or differently to well-being than the other?

Conclusions

Applying the integrative conceptual framework (Adams & Blieszner, in press) to the research on older men's friendship reveals that not much is "known" about them. In part this is because of the conceptual and methodological limitations of previous studies. But researchers have neglected some aspects of older men's friendships entirely (e.g., friendships phases; most affective processes and many cognitive and behavioral processes; some aspects of internal structure, particularly hierarchy; the connections among structure, phases, and processes; contextual and population effects). Investigators have studied other aspects using inadequate measures. For example, because of the dearth of full-blown studies of the internal structure of older men's friendship networks, we only have hints about their solidarity. Still other aspects have been adequately studied, but only once or twice, using different measures on different populations.

Consistent findings across studies are rare enough that only a few scattered hypotheses can be generated. Compared to older women, older men: (a) have friendship networks lower in gender homogeneity, (b) have friendship networks equal to theirs in age homogeneity, and (c) are less likely to confide in friends. In addition, the evidence suggests that as men age, they (d) tend to maintain friendships longer than they did in their youth. This is not much, but it is a start.

So researchers interested in contributing to our knowledge of older men's friendship patterns need to replicate previously conducted studies and to design new ones including questions on neglected topics. Unexplored questions include but are not limited to the following:

1. How do men's friendships change as they age?
2. What affects the trajectories that older men's friendships follow?
3. How are the elements of older men's friendships interconnected? For example, are displays of intimacy more common when older men's friendship networks are dense? Are small networks higher in solidarity than large ones?
4. In what types of contexts are older men predisposed to friendship? What characteristics of contexts facilitate and inhibit the formation and maintenance of men's friendships?
5. What do older men do when they are together?
6. What are the effects of older men's friendships and by what process are these effects generated? Do older men's friendships contribute to their morale? Do they affect the way they cope with the aging process? Do they substantially affect their standard of living or lifestyle?

But merely asking unasked questions is not enough. These new studies should be designed to do one or more of the following: compare men and women across stages of the life course; separate out age, period, and cohort effects; distinguish between the sociological and psychological effects of age and gender; and identify other sources of variation in friendship patterns (especially class and ethnicity). Above all, researchers must continue to work toward the development of a gender-informed approach to the study of friendship so that older men's friendships can be examined on their own terms. This is an ambitious agenda, but at least the necessary methodological and conceptual tools are now available to friendship researchers.

References

Adams, R. G. (1988, November). *A gender-informed approach to friendship in late life.* Paper presented at 41st annual scientific meeting of the Gerontological Society of America, San Francisco.

Adams, R. G. (1989). Conceptual and methodological issues in studying friendships of older adults. In R. G. Adams & R. Blieszner (Eds.), *Older adult friendship: Structure and process* (pp. 17-41). Newbury Park, CA: Sage.

Adams, R. G., & Blieszner, R. (1989). *Older adult friendship: Structure and process.* Newbury Park, CA: Sage.

Adams, R. G., & Blieszner, R. (1994). An integrative conceptual framework for friendship research. *Journal of Social and Personal Relationships.*

Albert, S. M., & Moss, M. (1990). Consensus and the domain of personal relations among older adults. *Journal of Social and Personal Relationships, 7,* 353-369.

Allan, G. (1989). *Friendship: Developing a sociological perspective.* Hertfordshire, UK: Harvester Wheatsheaf.

Antonucci, T. C., & Akiyama, H. (1987). An examination of sex differences in social support among older men and women. *Sex Roles, 17,* 737-749.

Blau, Z. S. (1961). Structural constraints on friendships in old age. *American Sociological Review, 26,* 429-439.

Blieszner, R., & Adams, R. G. (1992). *Adult friendship.* Newbury Park, CA: Sage.

Bossé, R., Aldwin, C. M., Levenson, M. R., Workman-Daniels, K., & Ekerdt, D. J. (1990). Differences in social support among retirees and workers. *Psychology and Aging, 5,* 41-47.

Brown, R. (1965). *Social psychology.* New York: Free Press.

Bryant, S., & Rakowski, W. (1992). Predictors of mortality among elder African-Americans. *Research on Aging, 14,* 50-67.

Cohen, C. I. (1989). Social ties and friendship patterns of old homeless men. In R. G. Adams & R. Blieszner (Eds.), *Older adult friendship: Structure and process* (pp. 222-242). Newbury Park, CA: Sage.

Cohen, C. I., & Rajkowski, H. (1982). What's in a friend? Substantive and theoretical issues. *The Gerontologist, 22,* 261-266.

Connidis, I. A., & Davies, L. (1990). Confidants and companions in later life. *Journals of Gerontology, 45,* S141-S149.

Duck, S. (1990). Relationships as unfinished business: Out of the frying pan and into the 1990s. *Journal of Social and Personal Relationships, 7,* 5-28.

Dykstra, P. A. (1990). *Next of (non)kin.* Amsterdam: Swets & Zeitlinger.

Eckert, J. K. (1980). *The unseen elderly: A study of marginally subsistent hotel dwellers.* San Diego, CA: Campanile.

Elder, G. H., Jr., & Clipp, E. C. (1988). Wartime losses and social bonding. *Psychiatry, 51,* 177-198.

Ferraro, K. F., Mutran, E., & Barresi, C. M. (1984). Widowhood, health and friendship support in later life. *Journal of Health and Social Behavior, 25,* 245-259.

Fischer, C. S., & Oliker, S. J. (1983). A research note on friendship, gender, and the life cycle. *Social Forces, 62,* 124-133.

Fisher, C. B., Reid, J. D., & Melendez, M. (1989). Conflict in families and friendships of later life. *Family Relations, 38,* 83-89.

Fox, M., Gibbs, M., & Auerbach, D. (1985). Age and gender dimensions of friendship. *Psychology of Women Quarterly, 9,* 489-501.

Husaini, B. A., Moore, S. T., Castor, R. S., Neser, W., Whitten-Stovall, R., Linn, J. G., & Griffin, D. (1991). Social density, stressors, and depression: Gender differences among the black elderly. *Journals of Gerontology, 46,* P236-P242.

Johnson, C. L. (1983). Fairweather friends and rainy day kin. *Urban Anthropology, 12,* 103-123.

Jones, D. C., & Vaughan, K. (1990). Close friendships among senior adults. *Psychology and Aging, 5,* 451-457.

Keith, P. M., Hill, K., Goudy, W. J., & Powers, E. A. (1984). Confidants and well-being: A note on male friendship in old age. *The Gerontologist, 24,* 318-320.

Kelley, H. H., Berscheid, E., Christensen, A., Harvey, J. H., Huston, T. L., Levinger, G., McClintock, E., Peplau, L. A., & Peterson, D. R. (1983). Analyzing close relationships. In H. H. Kelley et al., *Close relationships* (pp. 20-67). New York: Freeman.

Litwak, E. (1989). Forms of friendships among older people in an industrial society. In R. G. Adams & R. Blieszner (Eds.), *Older adult friendship* (pp. 65-88). Newbury Park, CA: Sage.

Maddox, G. L., & Campbell, R. T. (1985). Scope, concepts, and methods in the study of aging. In R. H. Binstock & E. Shanas (1985), *Handbook of aging and the social sciences* (pp. 3-31). New York: Van Nostrand Reinhold.

Marsden, P., & Campbell, K. (1984). Measuring tie strength. *Social Forces, 63,* 482-501.

Mitchell, J. C. (1969). The concept and use of social networks. In J. C. Mitchell (Ed.), *Social networks in urban situations* (pp. 1-50). Manchester, UK: Manchester University Press.

Nardi, P. M. (Ed.). (1992a). *Men's friendships.* Newbury Park, CA: Sage.

Nardi, P. M. (1992b). "Seamless Souls": An Introduction to Men's Friendships. In P. M. Nardi (Ed.), *Men's friendships* (pp. 1-14). Newbury Park, CA: Sage.

O'Connor, P. (1992). *Friendships between women: A critical review.* New York: Guilford.

Perlman, D. (1993). Review of Adult Friendship and Friendship Matters. *Journal of Marriage and the Family, 55,* 246-248.

Pihlblad, C. T., & Adams, D. L. (1972). Widowhood, social participation and life satisfaction. *Aging and Human Development, 3,* 323-330.

Powers, E. A., & Bultena, G. L. (1976). Sex differences in intimate friendships of old age. *Journal of Marriage and the Family, 38,* 739-747.

Rawlins, W. K. (1992). *Friendship matters: Communication, dialectics, and the life course.* Hawthorne, NY: Aldine.

Retsinas, J., & Garrity, P. (1985). Nursing home friendships. *The Gerontologist, 25,* 376-381.

Roberto, K. A., & Scott, J. P. (1986). Friendships of older men and women: Exchange patterns and satisfaction. *Psychology and Aging, 1,* 103-109.

Rubinstein, R. L. (1986). *Singular paths: Old men living alone.* New York: Columbia.

Steuve, C. A., & Gerson, K. (1977). Personal relations across the life-cycle. In C. S. Fischer, R. M. Jackson, C. A. Steuve, K. Gerson, L. M. Jones, & M. Baldassare (Eds.), *Networks and places* (pp. 79-98). New York: Free Press.

Tesch, S., Whitbourne, S. K., & Nehrke, M. F. (1981). Friendship, social interaction, and subjective well-being of older men in an institutional setting. *International Journal of Aging and Human Development, 13,* 317-327.

Usui, W. M. (1984). Homogeneity of friendship networks of elderly blacks and whites. *Journal of Gerontology, 39,* 350-356.

Weiss, L., & Lowenthal, M. F. (1975). Life-course perspectives on friendship. In M. E. Lowenthal, M. Thurnher, D. Chiriboga, & Associates (Eds.), *Four stages of life* (pp. 48-61). San Francisco: Jossey-Bass.

Wright, P. H. (1982). Men's friendships, women's friendships, and the alleged inferiority of the latter. *Sex Roles, 8,* 1-20.

10

Men's Ties to Siblings in Old Age

Contributing Factors to Availability and Quality

SARAH H. MATTHEWS

Only recently have men come to be seen as appropriate targets for family research, and their ties to wives, children, and parents, have taken precedence over those to brothers and sisters. Even for women, sibling ties have received scant attention (Bedford, 1989). Finding data about men's sibling relationships in general and old men's in particular is much like searching for the proverbial needle in the haystack. This chapter, then, is as much a discussion of important factors to consider in adult sibling ties as it is of brothers in old age.

Men's ties to their siblings are likely to be of longer duration than any other relationship in their lives, especially in families in which children are closely spaced. Furthermore, the increase in divorce often results in tenuous ties between fathers and their children, making many men outsiders in their families of procreation. As a result, the family of orientation may play an increasingly important role in men's lives if they are to have any semblance of family life as middle-aged and old adults. Delineating factors that make visible and intelligible men's sibling relationships in old age is warranted.

Although it draws on the available literature, this chapter presents a framework within which to understand contingencies that are likely to affect men's ties to their siblings in old age. Most of the research literature

AUTHOR'S NOTE: Research was supported by Grant No. AG03484 from the National Institute on Aging.

focuses on frequency of contact, motivation for contact, or resources provided. Within these three areas, gender differences, of particular importance here, have been described (Noller & Fitzpatrick, 1993). What accounts for differences, however, has not been addressed systematically. Consequently, commonsensical notions of male and female identities are carried over into the routine analysis of sociological data (Morgan, 1990), and, in this case, into research about sisters and brothers. This chapter focuses on factors that are likely to affect men's sibling ties differently than women's in old age. Data collected from members of middle-aged and old sibling dyads that include at least one brother respondent are used for illustration. These respondents participated in the Older Families Study.1

The chapter begins with a discussion of the difficulty of gathering and interpreting family data from men. Demographic and life course variables that affect availability of siblings and the content and quality of sibling relationships through early adulthood into old age are then discussed. The importance of taking into account that sibling ties are embedded in family networks is stressed. This, in turn, leads to a discussion of the importance of size and gender composition of sibling groups as well as the significance of the way spouses and siblings-in-law fit into family networks.

Including Men in Research on Families

In American society many men are not accustomed to talking about their feelings. Answering a researcher's question about frequency of contact with his geographically closest sibling only requires a man to remember how often she or he has been seen. Responding to questions about his feelings toward that sibling is another matter. Evidence that men and women interpret differently questions about affect has been accumulating in the recent literature as more attention has been paid to men's relationships.

Francesca Cancian (1987) argues that there is a basic difference between men's and women's definitions of romantic love. She asserts that love became "feminized" in the last century so that when love is expressed in a "masculine" way, it is not recognized as such:

> Part of the reason that men seem so much less loving than women is that men's behavior is measured with a feminine ruler. Most research considers only the kinds of loving behavior that are associated with the feminine role, such as

talking about personal troubles, and rarely compares women and men on masculine qualities such as giving practical help or being interested in sexual intercourse. (p. 74)

As an example, Cancian cites a study in which a husband, "when told by the researchers to increase his affectionate behavior towards his wife, decided to wash her car, and was surprised when neither his wife nor the researchers accepted that as an affectionate act" (p. 76).

Although Cancian's focus is on heterosexual love, her ideas of gendered emotionality may apply to the way brothers and sisters describe their relationships. One respondent in the Older Families Study said of his brother, "When we were younger we were very competitive as twins. . . . We've gotten over that, become friends. When I was in the Peace Corps my brother handled all my finances." Few women would choose this to illustrate the depth of their feelings about a brother or sister. Another respondent from the study explained his relationship with his brother: "I may look to him for technical problems and he may look to me for financial problems he's having. He's always been good with mechanical things. We each have an area of expertise." Again, "expertise" would be an odd way for a woman to describe her ties to her siblings. Furthermore, if a social scientist were operationalizing "close," it is unlikely that he or she would choose "expertise" as an important element.

In her research on the significance of sibling ties to elderly men and women, Gold (1987, p. 205) writes:

Only men chose the word, "responsibility," to describe their reason for deeper concern [for a sibling, usually a sister]. Women, on the other hand, expressed more affective concern. . . . The men seemed to view the role of brother as an obligation that is instrumental in nature (e.g., I have a responsibility for her) while the women emphasized the expressive nature of their concern for the individual in that role.

Following Cancian, it could be argued that the underlying feelings of affection may very well be the same but that the way brothers and sisters express them are different. Both men and women emphasized the importance of sibling bonds but simply chose quite different terms to express their feelings about the relationship.

In their qualitative study of fathers' relationships with their adult sons and daughters, Nydegger and Mitteness (1991, pp. 252-253) also were struck by the difference between what the men said and the way that they said it:

When we asked the men in our study to discuss family relations in their own terms, we posed a difficult problem for them. Most men found it awkward; some were literally inarticulate. This was especially true in regard to terms of affection. . . . Paternal devotion was often expressed in the form of a supervisor's evaluation. However, there was no misinterpreting the glow of pleasure or expansiveness of pride which so often accompanied superficially prosaic, even meager, descriptions. . . . Thus accounts of fathers' emotional investment in children often have been distorted by persistent neglect of their distinctive mode of talking about relations.

Asking men to describe how they feel about their siblings in all likelihood presents a similar problem. Men appear to describe their positive feelings toward kin not in words of affection but in terms of accepted responsibilities, respect for one another, and gratifications with the attachments.

As a final caution it is important to keep in mind that men as a category are not homogeneous. To illustrate, one brother explained, "My brother is very, very logical and I'm much more intuitive and emotional." These two men describe their relationship very differently, even though they both are men.

The tendency for men and women to speak differently of close relationships is just that—a tendency. Nevertheless, these examples indicate that extreme caution must be used in interpreting gender differences. When they are found, and they frequently are, it is not clear whether it is because a "feminine yardstick" has been used inappropriately to gauge the degree of men's attachment to someone or whether the apparent differences are real.

Availability of Sibling Ties for Older Men

There are two prerequisites for a man to be a brother in old age. The first is determined very early in his life: His parents must have had more than one child. The second is that at least one of his siblings must still be alive.

The likelihood of these two things occurring varies by cohort. The current elderly, those born before 1930, had relatively large families compared to those who soon will join the ranks of the old. The latter were born during a time when fertility rates were relatively low—the Great Depression and World War II. Members of the former cohort, then, are more likely to have siblings than those of the latter.

Following a review of various Canadian surveys, Connidis (1989a, p. 12) concluded that the "vast majority of older Canadians (80-85%) have a living brother or sister." Lee, Mancini, and Maxwell (1990, p. 431) cite similar statistics for the United States: "Eighty percent of American children have siblings and 79 percent of Americans have living siblings in late adulthood" (see also McGhee, 1985; Suggs, 1989). The older a man is, of course, the more likely he is to be the sole survivor of his generation: "As many as 58% of those aged 85 and over may have no surviving siblings" (Hays cited in Connidis, 1989a, p. 12). Viewing this from a somewhat different angle, Cicirelli (1991, p. 294) writes, "On average about forty percent of the siblings of the elderly are dead." By the time people reach old age, they are likely to have experienced the death of a sibling (Moss & Moss, 1989), but a significant proportion still will have at least one.

Family size is only one important factor. The likelihood of having siblings in old age is not the same for men and women. Difference in life expectancy means that elderly men are more likely to have sisters than brothers and that a brother is unlikely to be the last living member of his generation. For example, in a sample of recent widows aged 60 and older, 71% reported having a living sister while only 58% reported having a living brother (O'Bryant, 1988). For a sample drawn in rural North Carolina and stratified to include equal numbers of Black and White respondents aged 65 and older, Suggs (1989) reports that almost one fourth of the 365 respondents said that they had no living siblings, with Black respondents twice as likely to have none. Of the 158 White respondents who reported having at least one living sibling, 73% had at least one living brother and 90% had at least one living sister. Of the 125 Black respondents with a sibling, 78% reported having at least one living brother and 94% at least one living sister. Sex differences in mortality also mean that both women and men are more likely to have widowed sisters-in-law than widowed brothers-in-law, a point whose significance is discussed below.

The content and quality of brothers' relationships with their siblings in old age also are the result of life course variation. As children move into adulthood and begin what Goetting (1986, p. 707) describes as the "second-life-cycle stage," behavior toward members of their families of orientation are no longer taken for granted. Siblings are very unlikely to continue to share a household. Brothers and sisters complete their education and join the labor force, some close to their parents' homes, others in different places near and far away. Some siblings marry; some marry and divorce; some marry, divorce, and remarry; and some remain single. Some have children, while others remain child free. These individual decisions affect the quality of relationships between siblings. Will they have equally prestigious occupations? Will they live in close proximity to one another? Will they like one another's spouses and will spouses-in-law like them? Will their children be close in age or enjoy playing together? Will they respect one another's lifestyles? Answers to these questions, often determined by decisions made in early adulthood, affect the nature of sibling ties throughout middle years and into old age. The number of combinations of these variables is so large that Victor Cicirelli (1991, p. 294) concludes, "The question is not whether variations in sibling connections exist, but what is the most fruitful way to describe them."

Embeddedness of Sibling Relationships

Even though they are ascribed, the content of sibling ties is often viewed as voluntary, open to negotiation between members of sibling dyads. Ann Goetting (1986, p. 707), for example, writes that in adulthood, "Sibling contact becomes voluntary and ties become loosened and diffused." Regardless of the quality of the connection, however, most Americans apparently are in agreement with the participants in Ross and Milgram's research (1982):

> [When] asked why they did not discontinue those relationships with siblings that had never been close, our participants were stunned. Most seemed to assume that sibling relationships are permanent. Some tried to explain, but did not get far beyond blood ties and family bonds. Very few, almost wistfully, realized that the question implied a choice—but the reality did not. (p. 231)

Graham Allan (1979, p. 102) also argues that the ties themselves are not voluntary in the way that friendships are: "One can have an ex-friend and an ex-roommate but not an ex-sibling."

Furthermore, ties are part of a network of relationships. For adult siblings this means that whenever two people in the family speak with one another, they are likely to relay information about other members. Parents often perform a "brokerage service" (Allan, 1979), passing on information about one sibling to the others. A sister in the Older Families Study, for example, described her current relationship with her brother: "Since he moved away, it hasn't been as close. My mother is the conduit. She keeps the communication flowing between us." When parents die, this service is likely to be performed by someone else in the family, typically a woman (Rosenthal, 1985).

Family embeddedness makes it possible for "sibling relationships to endure despite the comparatively limited exchange content involved in most of them" (Allan, 1979, p. 105). Sibling ties, unlike friendships, do not require the same type of active cultivation to endure. It is given that they will continue because they are expected to last a lifetime and are part of a network in which information is exchanged.

Ann Goetting (1986, p. 712) concludes that not only information but also services are likely to be exchanged: "It appears that many siblings provide aid to one another throughout their lives, yet no firm predictors of such behavior have been established." Much is made of siblings' being status equals whose relationships are reciprocal (Avioli, 1989). Janet Finch (1989, p. 45), for example, writes:

> Support between siblings contrasts with support between parents and children in two important ways. First, it seems less reliable, in the sense that whether it is offered depends very much upon personal circumstances and personal liking, at least in the majority White community. Except perhaps in rather trivial matters, there is no real sense that one can expect assistance from someone just because they are your brother or your sister. Second, it much more obviously is two-way support, built upon reciprocal exchanges between people who are in equivalent positions in genealogical terms. One would predict that where a particular sibling is not willing or able to give support they are unlikely to receive it, except perhaps if they have given assistance in the past.

The assertion, then, is that siblings cannot count on one another unless they are also friends.

This seems shortsighted. Aid to a sibling is likely to be in response to relatively transient needs. Even three years is a relatively short period of time when a 70-year relationship is the referent. Cross-sectional research designs are unlikely to show a high incidence of these transient circumstances. John Mogey (1991) argues that:

> "amity" operates in families: Goods and services, money and loving, flow from those who control these resources to those who have need of them. Those responding to the implicit demands of significant others, [do so] not to commands from superiors, nor as a result of bargains that are negotiated between status equals. . . . This self-regulating behavior is continuous between members of different generations and remains an important and essential form of social behavior in all modern societies. (p. 52)

John Mogey is describing parent-child relationships, but the principle of amity operates within generations as well. Several respondents in the Older Families Study indicated that siblings had provided help. One brother reported, "When I got divorced in 1977 John was there for me, so we got closer at that time." Another brother said of his sister, "Today my sister and I talk all the time and if she needs anything, I'm there." One sister said of her brother, "He had an unfortunate first marriage and he and his children lived with us [sister and mother] for six years." One brother who lived 2,000 miles away from his sister described his relationship with her:

> I'm closer to my sister in our adult years than when we were younger. I was the older brother and she always looked up to me and what I said usually went. If there was a crisis in my life she came and vice versa. When I was sick she came here and when she had trouble with her kids, I went there. . . . Our contact has always been very extensive. We see each other three to four times a year. It's the same relationship it has always been—close.

Siblings may come to one another's assistance as needed.

The fact that sibling ties exist within a family network may account for their purported unreliability. When parental support to adult children is not forthcoming, because parents either refuse or are dead, siblings may provide goods and services as well as emotional support. Sibling support, then, is not so much unreliable as rarely called upon because siblings are embedded not only in their families of orientation but also often in their families of procreation and friendship networks. Siblings, for many, are the "last resort":

> Siblings appear to function as an insurance policy for older persons. Although rarely called upon for instrumental aid, there is comfort and satisfaction in knowing that a sibling is there. Indeed, studies repeatedly suggest that it is the perceived availability of siblings and not the actual interaction with siblings that predicts psychological well-being in late life. (Avioli, 1989, p. 52)

Siblings who are single or child-free and who, therefore, are embedded in much smaller family networks, do receive more goods, services, and emotional support than those who are married with children. Jean Scott (1983, p. 51) reports that "childless persons and lifelong singles have more frequent contact and report greater closeness with siblings than do older married persons who have children." These research findings indicate that respondents do expect their siblings to come to their aid, if necessary. Amity, rather than reciprocity, may very well be operating in sibling as well as in intergenerational relationships, and there is no reason to believe that amity is gender-specific.

Size and Gender Composition of the Sibling Group

Once the embeddedness of sibling ties in family networks is acknowledged as central to understanding them, size and gender composition become important factors. Research that asks respondents to focus on the sibling to whom they feel emotionally closest lumps together answers from those who have no option but to choose their only sibling with answers from those who are allowed to choose one among many.

Clearly, having several siblings is different from having only one. First, the opportunity for sibling alliances occurs in larger groups. One brother in the Older Families Study described his two brothers:

I have different values than Peter and Carl. They are attorneys and feel different about money and success and lifestyle. That interferes with our working together and liking one another. We had a family reunion last June—sometimes unfinished business from growing up emerges and then there's some tension around that doesn't get resolved.

Brothers who are members of a dyad report similar feelings:

We were really much at odds when we were growing up and it is pretty much the same today. He is jealous of the fact that I am where I am financially and status-wise, and he is still struggling. He was always against whatever I was for and that is still in existence today. . . . He left when he was 18 for college vowing never to live here permanently. When he graduated, he left for good.

His brother's view was similar: "We don't entirely agree about a lot of things. We're in basic concert, but there's a lot of unfinished business from childhood. We have fundamental disagreements about whether it matters what happened in the past." Although the two sets of siblings have much in common, in the latter each brother stands alone, while in the former, one has an ally. These are very different experiences for all concerned.

Second, and in line with the previous point, larger sibling groups mean that comparisons can be made among siblings. Connidis (1993) reports from a random sample of elders in London, Ontario, that persons distinguish among their siblings. With the exception of sibling groups with six members, the proportion of respondents who considered no sibling a close friend declined as the number of siblings increased, from 34% for respondents in two-sibling groups to 8% for respondents in five-sibling groups. "The larger the family of orientation, the greater the likelihood of differentiating among siblings by considering some close friends and others not" (Connidis, 1989a, pp. 87-88). Different size sibling groups, then, do not only affect the likely availability of siblings in old age, but also embed sibling relationships in a more or less complex set of ties.

The gender composition of the sibling group also affects sibling ties. Most research on gender differences simply compares brothers to sisters, leaving out of the explanation the fact that the behavior associated with and the meaning of being a brother is embedded in a family network.

More sophisticated research focuses on the gender composition of sibling dyads—sister-sister, brother-sister, brother-brother—sometimes breaking down brother-sister into two groups depending on the gender of the respondent (Connidis, 1989b; Gold, 1989a; McGhee, 1985; Moss & Moss, 1989). For example, in Gold's analysis (1989b) of 60 sibling dyads—which she classified as intimate, congenial, loyal, apathetic, and hostile—she found that of the 13 brother-brother dyads, 79% ($n = 10$) were coded as either loyal or apathetic, while 53% of those that included at least one sister ($n = 47$) were coded as intimate or congenial.

Connidis (1993) has gone one step further to examine the gender composition of the sibling group—all sisters, all brothers, and mixed. By sorting sibling groups into these categories she was able to show that gender composition of the sibling group affects the likelihood of respondents' describing siblings as friends: "Men with sisters only are more likely than women with brothers only to consider no sibling a close friend. This suggests that being the only brother in a family of women creates a different dynamic than being the only sister in a family of men" (p. 18). Similarly, Barnett, Marshall, and Pleck (1992, p. 522) concluded from their study of adult son-parent relationships, "Sisters appear to keep married adult sons emotionally connected to their families of origin. Sons with sisters were more emotionally reactive to the quality of their relationships with their parents. In contrast, married sons without sisters appeared unresponsive to the affective tone of their relationships with their parents." These findings indicate that the way men experience family ties, including sibling ties, is influenced by the gender composition of the sibling group in their family of orientation.

Evidence that gender composition is an important consideration is also found in clinical work. Falconer and Ross (1988), for example, draw on their experience as family therapists to explore "the development of both children and parents" (p. 273) in "tilted" families, those in which all children are of the same gender. In their comparison of married couples who only had daughters with those who only had sons, they report that "a consistent pattern emerges that indicates higher conflict in the male-tilted families, with a lower level of expressed satisfaction" (p. 283).

Michael Farrell and Stanley Rosenberg (1981) argue that men are likely to rethink their sibling relationships when parents have problems in old age, but this clearly will not be the case for all brothers. Men differ. One brother from the Older Families Study described how his parents' old age affected his relationship with his brother:

> In the early 1970s, he moved to Florida and I was in Boston at the time. And I think after he moved to Florida, right around that time, my father died. . . . The distance made it difficult to communicate. Then the problems I mentioned before—well his . . . well I think he's selfish. That's my opinion. And then his general indifference regarding my mother, that hasn't helped. So I'd say we basically haven't gotten along except for a few years when we were going to school in the same place and there weren't any big problems.

Many other brothers, however, did report that increased contact because of aging parents had influenced positively their relationships with one another (Matthews, Delaney, & Adamek, 1989).

In summary, the evidence cited here indicates that brothers who have at least one sister are tied into their families of orientation differently from those in brothers-only families. Both number of siblings and gender composition of sibling groups influence the way brothers interact with their siblings in childhood, in middle age, and in old age.

Adding Siblings-in-Law

Graham Allan's placement of the sibling tie within the context of the kinship network draws spouses and siblings-in-law into the picture. In the United States, Canada, and Great Britain, there is a hierarchy of commitments such that when someone marries, spouse and children take precedence over the family of origin. Jane Aronson (1990, p. 242), for example, quotes an elderly mother whom she interviewed: "As my son said to me at one point: 'Mum, I'll come and help you as much as I can, but my first obligation's to my own family—you know, to my wife and children.' And I thought that was kind of callous . . . and then I thought afterwards, 'I did the same thing, you know, with my mother.' "

There is, however, a gender difference in the degree to which adult children are expected, even encouraged, to pull away from their families of origin when they marry. In her description of kinship as work, Micaela de Leonardo (1992) writes:

> We think of [American] kin-work tasks such as the preparation of ritual feasts, responsibility for holiday card lists, and gift buying as extensions of women's domestic responsibilities for cooking, consumption, and nurturance. American men in general do not take on these tasks any more than they do housework and child care—and probably less, as these tasks have not yet been the subject of intense public debate. (p. 252)

Because it is less common for American men than women to perform kin-work tasks, a wife's brothers and sisters are likely to receive more attention than her husband's and thus her family becomes part of his active kinship network. Similarly, Nyddeger and Mitteness (1991) write, "Strong mother-daughter bonds and wives' kin-keeping function result in a de facto asymmetry that tends to weaken the ties between sons and their parents. . . . In extreme cases, the son's family ties may be severed" (p. 260). A son's withdrawal from bond-maintaining interaction with his parents is also likely to include his siblings, at least to some degree.

Farrell and Rosenberg (1981), in their research on middle-aged men's relationships with parents, provide insight into the way men's attachment to their families of orientation and consequent ties to siblings may be attenuated. They argue that "in the process of shifting allegiance to the wife's family, the men seem to idealize their styles and values, coming to view their own families of origin in a very negative light" (p. 178).

> The shift away from the husband's parents and toward the wife's seems also, at least in part, to be the consequence of the wife's more reliable efforts to maintain familial ties and integrate her husband into the extended kin network. The result is a tendency toward a growing relationship or even intensive identification with the wife's father, with increasing coolness or openly negative feelings expressed toward one or both of the husband's parents . . . both husband and wife have reasons for defining her family as "their" family in this life phase. For the wife it permits the continuance of more comfortable closeness with her family of origin, for the husband a means of separating from his parents while still garnering support. The couple often justifies these

needs by blaming his family, defining them as impossible and idealizing hers. (pp. 179-180)

Research by Nydegger and Mitteness (1991) on fathers' relationships with their adult children adds support to Farrell and Rosenberg's argument. They found that "fathers are more negative about sons than daughters (more dissatisfied, worried, angered, etc.)" (p. 257). "Sons, interpreting their fathers' behavior as critical and intrusive, either learn techniques of information management (Nydegger & Mitteness, 1988) or curtail visiting. The tendency of sons to distance themselves from the family during the early years of career and marriage is widely reported. . . . Avoidance of oversight is one motive" (p. 259). Men who have sisters, however, may continue to be included in the family network as part of their sisters' kin-keeping activities. Connidis cites research by Irish (1964), who found that:

contact is greater with the wife's than the husband's family. Women are in greater contact with all relatives than men, while men are in greater contact with in-laws than women. The consequence for sibling interaction is that contact between two sisters or a brother and a sister is more common than that between two brothers. (Connidis, 1989b, p. 83)

Marriage, then, has different effects on men's ties to families of orientation not only because kin keeping is part of wives' responsibilities, but also because sons perceive and may be encouraged by their wives to perceive that they are more harshly judged by parents than by parents-in-law. Brothers without sisters have the least resistance to these spousal influences, while brothers with at least one sister have in her a sibling whose kin-keeping activities will include him in the family network (Connidis, 1989b).

Siblings-in-law are an important factor for another reason. In-law relations, although not as negative as stereotypes suggest, nevertheless are problematic. The degree to which persons who marry into a family are accepted by and embrace its members is likely to have repercussions for sibling ties still evident 40 or 50 years later. Allan (1979) found that one of the apparent explanations for very close or "special" relationships between siblings was how well siblings-in-laws got along. About his working-class respondents he writes, "An important aspect of nearly all the working-class respondents' 'special' relationships was the spouse's relationship to the sibling and to the sibling's spouse" (p. 110). About the same "special" relationships of two of his middle-class respondents, he concludes, "It is doubtful if either of these sibling relationships would have developed the way they had if the respondents had not found the sibling-in-law to be so compatible and come to regard him or her as a friend" (p. 110). At least some of the sibling ties that were not described as close presumably are the result of siblings-in-law having less than high regard for one another.

Similarly, Ross and Milgram (1982) report that their respondents felt that marriages had influenced their sibling relationships. Some participants:

> felt that their siblings' marriages enhanced sibling relationships. They attributed this to their respect and liking for the siblings' spouses, and in general to the spouses' ability to fit into the family in terms of values, goals, and interests. Conversely, participants who felt that marriage detracted from sibling relationships attributed this to the siblings' spouses' different religion, ethnic background, socioeconomic status, and/or educational level. (p. 231)

Two thirds of marriages were described as detracting from sibling relationships. Of these, more than half were reported about siblings who were the same sex as the respondent, more often brothers than sisters. In this exploratory study, then, brothers and their respective wives had the most difficulty establishing close relationships.

Two brothers from the Older Families Study suggested that their relationship had improved after one of the brothers divorced. One said, "As I said, the basis of our relationship through his first marriage was really bad." His brother also said that their relationship had improved and they had "much more contact now that I have a new wife." Acknowledging the importance of ties between in-laws, one man said of his brother, "We get along fine. Our children are close. We talk once a week or thereabouts. . . . Our wives, too, are close. It's a four-way deal."

A sister and a brother complained about one another's spouses, but both indicated that their relationship had changed recently:

> My brother and I were never that close. I was the kid sister then and now. There was no reason for us to have had a relationship. . . . We don't get together socially. It's my sister-in-law who has been closer to her family. Until recently my brother and I had no real relationship but now it's changed, not because of mother but due to his illness. It's made him need me a little more. His wife is running away from it and takes constant vacations and leaves him home alone.

Her brother also felt that he had recently become closer to his sister, but for a different reason: "My relationship with my sister is at its peak now. . . . I have been more willing to support her since her husband died six years ago. My brother-in-law was tough. I was not close to my sister for years because of it. We were close growing up." In-law ties affect the content and quality of sibling relationships. This last example also illustrates the point made above that even when neither is particularly good, amity still remains part of the tie and may be drawn upon when circumstances change to allow its expression.

Not all siblings marry, of course, and being unmarried is one factor that increases individuals' attachment to siblings, as evidenced by strength of feelings of closeness, more frequent interaction, and closer geographical proximity (Connidis, 1989a). The routes to being single are many, and each is likely to have a different consequence for brothers' ties to their siblings. Some men, by choice or by chance, are ever single. Other men divorce and remain unmarried or are single between marriages. Still others are widowed.

An unmarried brother may meet more often with his siblings or even live with them. For example, in the past when gay men were more likely to hide their same-sex relationships from family members, pressure to attend gatherings of their families of orientation continued, whereas married siblings might have been excused to celebrate with their in-laws or to spend less time "at home." By the same token, unmarried brothers may be included in their siblings' families. Men who are ever single, for whatever reason, like their female counterparts (who have received a great deal more attention; see Allen, 1990), may be more likely to be involved with their families of origin.

At the other extreme are single men who have been cut off from family life—men who are unlikely to be included in gerontological research on families. Residents of public housing in a converted hotel in downtown Los Angeles, for example, were disproportionately men. None appeared in old age to have ties to siblings or to children, although presumably many had both (Smithers, 1985).

When men divorce and remarry, they are likely to become involved with their current wives' families. A second wife may be viewed by a man's parents and siblings as an improvement. Alternatively, particularly if men have had children in a previous marriage, their parents and siblings may feel divided loyalties.

Men in old age are more likely than women to be married. Two brothers, then, typically are both married, while brother-sister dyads are likely to have different marital statuses, with the sister unmarried and the brother married. Brothers and their wives, then, can interact as couples, while a brother's sister may be a "third wheel" in social situations. This may account for Connidis's (1989b) finding in her London, Ontario, study: "Sisters see one another more often than brothers, but brothers see one another more often than brother-sister pairs" (p. 91). In a similar vein, O'Bryant (1988) found that widows' brothers-in-law provided more help than their brothers. Her explanation is that a wife mediates her husband's contributions to her sister but not to his sister. Wives view unmediated contributions as competitive and thus discourage them. Connidis (1989b) also found that "[s]ibling pairs in which at least one member is single are in more frequent contact than are married pairs" (p. 91). In old age, brothers are less likely than sisters to be single and are less likely to be in the position of casting about for a "replacement" (Jerrome, 1981).

Conclusion

It should be clear by now that Cicirelli's (1991) assertion has merit—that is, that the important question is not whether there is variation, but what is the best way to describe it in sibling relationships. For each sibling group, the factors discussed above and others such as family history, sibling rivalry, and geographic proximity come together in a unique way. Rather than present a model of relationships among variables, this chapter has attempted to highlight differences between men's and women's lives that influence ties to siblings in old age. It has not used gender as a convenient, dichotomous variable but as an important, theoretically relevant perspective. Furthermore, it has not focused on old age per se, but on influences throughout men's lives that set the stage for interaction with and quality of sibling ties in old age.

The chapter has taken a sociological rather than a developmental perspective. Men's feelings about their siblings in old age are in all likelihood influenced by nearness to death. Old age is a time for life review and, for elderly persons, their siblings may be among the few people who have been part of their entire lives. This indeed makes them "something special" (Gold, 1987)

There is variation, however, with respect to the degree to which siblings have been and have had the opportunity to be active and emotionally supportive throughout one another's lives. This variation is patterned, with gender being one of the most significant elements. It is not simply the difference between men and women, however, but the more invisible expectations about the way each is expected to participate in their families of orientation and in their marriages.

Women more than men are expected to care about relationships and be able to talk about them. This puts men at a disadvantage in a way often unrecognized by researchers. Men's descriptions of family ties in general and sibling ties in particular are likely to be less "rich" than their sisters'. Men's shorter life expectancy means that they and their brothers are more likely than women to be married when they die—to be embedded in their marriages and families of procreation in a way that their widowed sisters are less likely to be. Men's sibling ties are part of a family network in which information and services are exchanged so that the size and gender composition of their sibling groups affect involvement in their families of orientation. Men without sisters are likely to be more distant from both their parents and brothers. Furthermore, because maintenance of family ties is women's work, wives have the opportunity to focus more on their own rather than on their husbands' relatives. The choice of a marriage partner, then, is a critical but often unanticipated component that affects the quality of ties to siblings in old age.

None of these factors, however, is ironclad, as the words of those who participated in the Older Families Study indicate. Each family has its own culture that mediates or allows free reign to some or all of the factors identified here. Predicting the final outcome is impossible. The goals of this chapter, then, are to alert researchers to important variables outside of individuals that pattern sibling ties of older men and to provide social actors with information that will enable them to make informed decisions as lifelong members of their families of orientation.

Note

1. The Older Families Study was designed to explore whether and how siblings share responsibility for parents who were at least 75 years old. Age of the parents, not of the siblings, qualified respondents for the study. Most respondents were at least middle-aged and some were old, but they are by no means typical elderly siblings because at least one of their parents is still alive. The chapter's focus on life course variation of men and women rather than developmental stage is the justification for using these respondents to illustrate the points made here.

References

Allan, G. A. (1979). *A sociology of friendship and kinship.* Sydney, Australia: Allen & Unwin.

Allen, K. (1990). *Single women, family ties.* Newbury Park, CA: Sage.

Aronson, J. (1990). Old women's experiences of needing care: Choice or compulsion. *Canadian Journal on Aging, 9,* 234-247.

Avioli, P. S. (1989). The social support functions of siblings in later life: A theoretical model. *American Behavioral Scientist, 33,* 45-57.

Barnett, R. C., Marshall, N. M., & Pleck, J. H. (1992). Adult son-parent relationships and their association with son's psychological distress. *Journal of Family Issues, 13,* 505-525.

Bedford, V. (1989). Sibling research in historical perspective: The discovery of a forgotten relationship. *American Behavioral Scientist, 33,* 6-18.

Cancian, F. M. (1987). *Love in America: Gender and self development.* New York: Cambridge University Press.

Cicirelli, V. G. (1991). Sibling relationships in adulthood. In S. K. Pfeifer & M. B. Sussman (Eds.), *Families: Intergenerational and generational connections* (pp. 291-310). New York: Haworth.

Connidis, I. A. (1989a). *Family ties and aging.* Toronto: Butterworths.

Connidis, I. A. (1989b). Siblings as friends in later life. *American Behavioral Scientist, 33,* 81-93.

Connidis, I. A. (1993). *The effect of gender on older sibling ties: An expanded view.* Unpublished manuscript, University of Western Ontario, London, Ontario.

de Leonardo, M. (1992). The female world of cards and holidays: Women, families, and the work of kinship. In B. Thorne & M. Yolom (Eds.), *Rethinking the family: Some feminist questions* (pp. 246-261). Boston: Northeastern University Press.

Falconer, C. W., & Ross, C. A. (1988). The tilted family. In M. D. Kahn & K. G. Lewis (Eds.), *Siblings in therapy: Life span and clinical issues* (pp. 273-296). New York: Norton.

Farrell, M. P., & Rosenberg, S. D. (1981). *Men at midlife.* Boston: Auburn House.

Finch, J. (1989). *Family obligations and social change.* Cambridge, UK: Polity.

Goetting, A. (1986). The developmental tasks of siblingship over the life cycle. *Journal of Marriage and the Family, 48,* 703-714.

Gold, D. T. (1987). Siblings in old age: Something special. *Canadian Journal on Aging, 6,* 211-227.

Gold, D. T. (1989a). Sibling relationships in old age: A typology. *International Journal of Aging and Human Development, 28,* 37-51.

Gold, D. T. (1989b). Generational solidarity: Conceptual antecedents and consequences. *American Behavioral Scientist, 33,* 19-32.

Irish, D. P. (1964). Sibling interaction: A neglected aspect in family life research. *Social Forces, 42,* 279-288.

Jerrome, D. (1981). The significance of friendship for women in later life. *Aging and Society, 1,* 175-197.

Lee, T. R., Mancini, M., & Maxwell, J. W. (1990). Sibling relationships in adulthood: Contact patterns and motivations. *Journal of Marriage and the Family, 52,* 431-440.

McGhee, J. L. (1985). The effects of siblings on the life satisfaction of older siblings. *Journal of Marriage and the Family, 47,* 85-91.

Matthews, S. H., Delaney, P. J., & Adamek, M. E. (1989). Male kinship ties: Bonds between adult brothers. *American Behavioral Scientist, 33,* 58-69.

Mogey, J. (1991). Families: Intergenerational and generational connections—conceptual approaches to kinship and culture. In S. K. Pfeifer & M. B. Sussman (Eds.), *Families: Intergenerational and generational connections* (pp. 47-67). New York: Haworth.

Morgan, D. H. J. (1990). Issues of critical sociological theory. In J. Sprey (Ed.), *Fashioning family theory* (pp. 67-106). Newbury Park, CA: Sage.

Moss, S. Z., & Moss, M. S. (1989). The impact of the death of an elderly sibling: Some considerations of a normative loss. *American Behavioral Scientist, 33,* 94-106.

Noller, P., & Fitzpatrick, M. A. (1993). *Communication in family relationships.* Englewood Cliffs, NJ: Prentice Hall.

Nydegger, C. N., & Mitteness, L. S. (1988). Etiquette and ritual in family conversation. *American Behavioral Scientist, 31,* 702-716.

Nydegger, C. N., & Mitteness, L. S. (1991). Fathers and their adult sons and daughters. In S. K. Pfeifer & M. B. Sussman (Eds.), *Families: Intergenerational and generational connections* (pp. 249-266). New York: Haworth.

O'Bryant, S. L. (1988). Sibling support and older widows' well-being. *Journal of Marriage and the Family, 50,* 173-183.

Rosenthal, C. J. (1985). Kinkeeping in the familial division of labor. *Journal of Marriage and the Family, 47,* 965-974.

Ross H. G., & Milgram, J. I. (1982). Important variables in adult sibling relationships: A qualitative study. In M. E. Lamb & B. Sutton-Smith (Eds.), *Sibling relationships: Their nature and significance across the lifespan* (pp. 229-248). Hillsdale, NJ: Lawrence Erlbaum.

Scott, J. P. (1983). Siblings and other kin. In T. H. Brubaker (Ed.), *Family relationships in later life* (pp. 47-62). Beverly Hills, CA: Sage.

Smithers, J. A. (1985). *Determined survivors.* New Brunswick, NJ: Rutgers University Press.

Suggs, P. K. (1989). Predictors of association among older siblings: A black/white comparison. *American Behavioral Scientist, 33,* 70-80.

11

Older Men as
Fathers and Grandfathers

JEANNE L. THOMAS

The last two decades have witnessed more frequent and varied portrayals of father-child relationships and increased professional recognition of fathers' roles in young children's development (e.g., Bozett & Hanson, 1991; Lamb, 1981). Popular culture and professional literatures provide fewer images of older men's relationships with adult children and with grandchildren. Indeed, the reification of the nuclear family implies that men and women past voting age have little involvement with either their fathers or their mothers. Scholars of family gerontology inform us that most middle-aged and older parents have close and satisfying relationships with their adult children and their grandchildren. But much of that work, like much research on parenthood earlier in the life cycle, has concentrated on mothers' relationships with their adult children and—particularly in recent years—on women's involvement in family caregiving.

Clearly, an examination of older men's relationships with their children and grandchildren is long overdue. Recent reviews of the literature in family gerontology provide a historical perspective but generally do not stress gender as an organizing variable or examine the interplay among gender, class, and race as they affect family relationships in old age (e.g., Mancini, 1989; Mancini & Blieszner, 1989). A review and critique taking this approach can provide impetus and guidelines for increased research on fatherhood and grandfatherhood and their significance in the lives of middle-aged and older men. To the extent that contemporary American fathers are no longer primarily distant breadwinners, as were many fathers

197

in earlier cohorts (e.g., Lamb, 1981), relationships with children and grandchildren should correspondingly be correlates of adaptive functioning in the future. Thus the study of fatherhood and grandfatherhood in middle and later adulthood will become a research priority for the 21st century. This chapter begins with an overview of classic and contemporary theoretical perspectives relevant to fatherhood and grandfatherhood in middle and later adulthood.

Theoretical Perspectives

Carl Jung (1933) offered one of the earliest life span theories of personality development. Jung proposed that it is only in the latter half of life that full personality development is possible; at that time, all aspects of the personality are ripened and are integrated into a balanced whole. This process of individuation includes the synthesis of the anima, understanding and expression of nurturing impulses, into the middle-aged man's personality (as well as the integration of the complementary animus into the middle-aged woman's personality). More recently, Daniel Levinson (1977; Levinson, Darrow, Klein, Levinson, & McKee, 1978) has discussed much the same process as an essential component of men's personality development in middle adulthood.

Although Jung did not explicitly consider the implications of this process for older men's experience as fathers and grandfathers, his description implies that these arenas to care for others may be particularly rewarding for middle-aged and older men. David Gutmann's (1975, 1977; Neugarten & Gutmann, 1958) research suggests that integration of nurturing impulses into middle-aged and older men's personality does in fact occur, and further that fatherhood shapes the tempo of that process. Using projective materials obtained in Western and non-Western cultures, Gutmann (1975) shows that young men, confronting the early years of parenthood, channel energy into productivity:

> They tame the extremes of their nature, deploying aggression toward production, curbing passive tendencies, and generally accepting, even with good humor, the responsibilities and sacrifices that come with the productive stance. . . . They work very hard to increase flocks, fields, or business clienteles; and they do not indulge the "softer" yearnings toward comfort and pleasure that could interfere with their effectiveness in productive roles. . . . They divest themselves of the passive dependent traits *that might prove lethal to their children.* (pp. 179-180, emphasis in original)

Gutmann (1975) goes on to explain that middle-aged and older men, with the demands of providing for the material needs of young children behind them, "begin to live out directly, to own as part of themselves, the passivity, the sensuality, the tenderness—in effect, the 'femininity'—that was previously repressed in service of productive instrumentality" (p. 181). Thus psychodynamic work accords a key role to fatherhood in understanding individual development in middle and later life. Erikson's psychosocial theory of personality development (Erikson, 1950; Erikson, Erikson, & Kivnick, 1986) continues this theme and is a frequently invoked framework for research on intergenerational relations. Erikson proposes that personality growth occurs as the individual achieves a dynamic balance between opposing tendencies; at different points in the life cycle, different polarities are of predominant concern. In middle adulthood, the developmental issue is to balance tendencies toward generativity—the need to provide for the establishment and welfare of succeeding generations—with tendencies toward stagnation or self-indulgence. In later adulthood, this concern recedes, and the need to balance feelings of satisfaction with past commitments and feelings of regret becomes more important.

Both of these psychosocial transitions have clear relevance to fatherhood and grandfatherhood. Although he acknowledges that having children is neither necessary nor sufficient for attaining an adaptive balance between generativity and stagnation, Erikson (1950) does identify parenthood as a primary vehicle for that task. In his discussion of the need to balance senses of ego integrity and despair, Erikson notes the importance of reminiscence—a process that may be triggered by experiences with grandchildren and adult children.

Both frameworks, then, highlight fatherhood and grandfatherhood as vehicles for personal growth. On the basis of both classical psychodynamic theory and psychosocial theory, one would predict that middle-aged and older men's levels of adjustment and their experiences with children and grandchildren would be associated. As we see in the remaining sections of this chapter, this prediction has been tested repeatedly, with mixed outcomes. Meta-analysis and similar empirical techniques should be used at this point to evaluate the strength of the association between fatherhood and well-being and to identify variables that moderate the association.

More recent theoretical approaches to the study of family gerontology stem from a contextual perspective (e.g., Bengtson, Rosenthal, & Burton, 1990; Matthews & Sprey, 1989). Using this approach, individual relationships are examined as nodes in an elaborate network of family relationships and as reflections of the cultural setting in which they unfold. This viewpoint, applied to the study of fatherhood and grandfatherhood in later life, offers promise of increased attention to diversity in these experiences as a function of such variables as fathers' marital status, family size, race, sexual orientation, and so forth. These sources of variation have largely been ignored in research on fathers and grandfathers to date.

Furthermore, the contextual approach (unlike psychodynamic approaches such as Erikson's and Gutmann's) provides a basis for examining men's experience as fathers and grandfathers at varying points in the life cycle. As Hagestad and Neugarten (1985) note, age provides an increasingly inaccurate index of individuals' status in their family life cycles: Some men become fathers in adolescence, whereas others remain childless until their 40s. Although psychologists and sociologists have studied early and delayed transitions to motherhood, the impact of becoming a father in early adolescence—or a grandfather in early adulthood—is as yet unexplored. Similarly, there is virtually no published research describing the consequences of delaying fatherhood until the 30s or 40s. Understanding these experiences demands considering fatherhood within the context of men's other family roles and relationships, their responsibilities and ties outside the family, and the cultural setting in which they become fathers.

Older Men as Fathers

As noted earlier, the literature on relationships between adult children and older parents for the most part describes either young and middle-aged adults' relationships with their mothers or with their parents (gender unspecified). Few researchers have explicitly considered fatherhood in middle and later adulthood or even made extensive contrasts between men's and women's reactions to relationships with adult children. Given this caveat, what can we say about these relationships?

The Launching Stage

One logical starting point for examining relationships with adult sons and daughters is the "launching stage" of the family life cycle, when children move toward adult status through such steps as attending college, initiating careers, getting married, establishing households, and the like. Research on families generally, and research on fathers particularly, in the launching stage presents two contrasting perspectives. Some portray the

launching period as a conflict-filled period of crisis in family development; even in the absence of interpersonal strife, the middle-aged father
is believed to experience intrapsychic crisis. Other researchers, however,
paint a more sanguine portrait. This work suggests that most fathers
perceive the launching of their adult sons and daughters as a nonevent at
worst and a welcomed and expected transition at best.

In what ways, and on what bases, has the launching period been
characterized as a crisis period for middle-aged fathers? Some early work
identified tension in relationships between middle-aged men and their
sons and daughters (e.g., Borland, 1978; Brim, 1976; Levinson et al.,
1978). This conflict apparently stemmed in part from intergenerational
conflicts in values. In part, the conflict reflected fathers' awareness of
their own declining physical strength and attractiveness and their con-
stricting life options—at the very time that they saw these qualities
blossoming in their sons and daughters. By contrast, others proposed that
stereotypes of remote, uninvolved fathers belied the distress that fathers
experience on their sons' and daughters' departure from the parental home
(Back, 1971; Lewis, Freneau, & Roberts, 1979).

It is no surprise that recent scholars have found that middle-aged men
experience stress, sometimes extreme stress, in reaction to crises such as
divorce, drug and alcohol problems, and unemployment in their newly
launched children's lives (e.g., Huyck, 1989; Greenberg, 1991). Other
work shows that middle-aged fathers' psychological distress is associated
with their young adult children's perceptions that their relationships lack
intimacy and emotional intensity (Harvey, Curry, & Bray, 1991).

These findings notwithstanding, it seems that the launching period is
more often a neutral or positive experience than a negative one. Lowenthal
and Chiriboga's (1972) classic research on the "empty nest" transition
revealed that few mothers or fathers considered this transition a major one
and that most reacted to it positively. Other early research suggested that
parenthood had less impact on middle-aged men's general psychological
well-being after the launching period than before (e.g., Clausen, 1976;
Tamir, 1982). Fathers who have launched their children report greater
personal happiness than those with children still at home, and they worry less
about their children and about family finances (Roberts & Zuengler, 1985).

Scholars have also found that middle-aged fathers (and mothers) psychologically rehearse their adult children's departure from home and feel
well-prepared for the transition (Greene & Boxer, 1986). Fathers in the
launching period continue to feel involved in their children's lives and
ready to help their sons and daughters as necessary; fathers are more likely

than mothers in this stage to take pleasure in entering a new phase of parenthood and to take pride in their children's successful initiation of adult undertakings (Huyck, 1989).

Indeed, it appears that fathers, like mothers, are more likely to be distressed if their "nest" fails to empty on schedule—or is refilled because of crises in adult sons' and daughters' lives. Fathers in recent research, while ready to help their young adult children and often taking pleasure in so doing, also reported that providing this support was stressful (Greenberg, 1991; Huyck, 1989). In one study, the fathers most likely to report stress in these "prolonged parenting" situations were those who expressed less satisfaction with parenting in general (Huyck, 1989). For older fathers (ages 57-79) in this study, distress related to parenting was significantly associated with general psychological well-being; this association may reflect fear that children might not eventually overcome current problems, difficulty in reworking their relationship with children as they and the children matured, or generational differences in their own or their children's expectations for the relationship.

Some work, then, portrays the launching period as a stressful crisis, and other research yields a description of a far less tumultuous period; however, there is a common theme in discussions of fatherhood during this period of the family life cycle. Scholars agree that providing young adult children with ongoing support of various kinds—practical help, financial assistance, advice and moral support, and shelter—is as central to men's experience as fathers in the launching period as it is earlier in the life cycle.

Although research has described fathers' reactions to the supportive function of their role, scholars have not yet identified the circumstances that determine which fathers experience the greatest joy, and which experience the greatest stress, from providing support as they launch their children. Developmental status, for example, requires further consideration. Do younger fathers confronting relatively high levels of career pressures and financial demands encounter more stress than older, more established and affluent fathers? Or do emerging concerns with parent care make providing support for young adult children a more stressful experience for older fathers than for younger ones?

Researchers also have not examined which types of support contribute to fathers' satisfactions or distress. Do fathers who continue to financially support their adult children—and thereby maintain the "productive parental role" that Gutmann describes—report less distress than fathers who take on a more nurturing role by providing emotional support and advice?

Nor have researchers yet considered ways in which such variables as race and ethnicity, social class, biological versus stepfather status, and marital status mediate reactions to this function of fathering during the launching period. Using a contextual perspective (see above), all of these dimensions alone and in combination may affect the extent to which providing support is stressful or satisfying. And the strategies that fathers—and mothers—use as they cope with stresses of the launching period remain unexamined. Do men and women use similar strategies, or do they confront these problems differently? All of these issues should shape research on fathers of young adult sons and daughters in the future.

**Middle-Aged and Older Fathers'
Relationships With Sons and Daughters**

In discussing parents' relationships with young adult sons and daughters, Greene and Boxer (1986) proposed that renegotiation was the predominant theme. Maintaining satisfying relationships while young adults establish independent households, launch careers, and form their own families requires both parents and adult children to restructure their relationship by reframing expectations, channels of communication, and occasions for interaction. Renegotiation is equally important for sons, daughters, and fathers as their relationships endure through middle adulthood and old age. As fathers and adult children confront such age-related events as the birth of grandchildren, retirement, or chronic illness, it is continually necessary for both parties to restructure their relationship if the bond is to endure. In that sense, relationships between fathers and adult children must be characterized by change throughout adulthood.

A closer look, however, reveals that this process of change is best described as a process of maintaining a dynamic balance. Key features of relationships between parents and adult children remain stable for years or even for decades. For example, the expectations that fathers and their adult children have for the kinds of help that they will exchange, and for when and why they will get together, will undoubtedly change. Nonetheless, the general assumptions that help will be exchanged, that affection is fundamental to the relationships, and that father and adult children will see one another regularly remain constant.

In this section, I review research on fathers' relationships with adult sons and daughters who are young and middle-aged adults. The initial focus is on relatively objective aspects of these relationships: geographic proximity and frequency of contact between the generations. Considered next are the more "subjective" aspects of the relationships: feelings of affection and exchanges of assistance. The section closes with a brief discussion of family caregiving in the context of relationships between older fathers and adult children.

Proximity and Contact

One of the best-documented findings in family gerontology is that most middle-aged and older adults and their children prefer to live near but not with one another, and that most families are successful in implementing their preference (e.g., Bengtson, Rosenthal, & Burton, 1990). Multigenerational households, although never a common American living arrangement, have grown even less frequent since the 1960s (Crimmins & Ingegneri, 1990). Fathers are less likely than mothers to live with children and grandchildren, a difference that probably stems from gender differences in mean longevity (Coward, Cutler, & Schmidt, 1989). The gender difference in frequency of multigenerational living may also reflect deliberate choice, however. Mancini and Blieszner (1989) noted in their review that older fathers were less likely than older mothers to endorse the idea of living with their children if they were unable to care for themselves or did not want to live alone.

Most older parents live within a 30-minute drive of at least one adult son or daughter, although many also have other children living farther away (Moss, Moss, & Moles, 1985). Over the past 30 years the percentage of older parents who have an adult son or daughter living very close—within 10 minutes—has decreased slightly, although the percentage who have adult children living within 30 minutes of travel has not changed (Crimmins & Ingegneri, 1990). Older Hispanic-Americans, in general, live closer to kin than do older non-Hispanic people (Markides & Mindel, 1987).

As these data describing intergenerational proximity suggest, most older fathers (and mothers) generally see their adult sons and daughters often. Most older parents report that they have seen an adult son or daughter within the last week or so, and many report that have seen an adult child within the last day or so (e.g., Aldous, 1987; Bengtson, Rosenthal, & Burton, 1990; Crimmins & Ingegneri, 1990; Shanas, 1979; Treas & Bengtson, 1987). In a recent study of rural elderly Canadians, Carol Harvey and her colleagues (1991) found that fathers' frequency of contact with offspring was negatively related to the fathers' life satisfaction. Perhaps these fathers' dysphoria aroused children's concern and prompted frequent visiting; alternatively, fathers may have been distressed by visiting frequency that they considered excessive; and, of course, it is possible that this correlation does not reflect a causal relationship at all.

Feelings of Affection

In examining feelings of affection between middle-aged and older fathers and their adult children, most researchers have used quantitative scales with which fathers (and, in some cases, their adult children) rate the levels of such qualities as trust, understanding, fairness, and the like in their relationships. Using this approach, older fathers and mothers typically report strong feelings of affection for their sons and daughters—feelings that the adult children typically reciprocate (e.g., Aldous, 1987; Bengtson, Rosenthal, & Burton, 1990; Treas & Bengtson, 1987). In her study of older mothers and fathers, Aldous (1987) found that mothers and fathers when interviewed separately did not differ in their descriptions of the affective quality of their relationships with children. Other research shows that older African-Americans and Hispanic-Americans are particularly likely to describe their relationships with adult children as close, warm, and affectionate (e.g., Bengtson, Rosenthal, & Burton, 1990; Taylor, 1988).

Older parents generally portray these relationships as embodying greater levels of positive affect and attitudinal similarity than the children themselves do (Bengtson & Kuypers, 1971). Peterson and Peterson (1988) recently reported that older fathers described their relationships with adult children as embodying greater equity than the children themselves did. The adult children in this study were more likely to believe that they were overbenefited in the relationships than to describe the relationships as equitable.

But understanding the feelings of affection—and the negative feelings—that characterize relationships between fathers and adult children requires going beyond a quantitative research approach; qualitative methodology is crucial for examining feelings between fathers and adult children. Nydegger and Mitteness (1991) took such an approach in their Fatherhood Project, in which they conducted semistructured interviews with men aged 45 to 80 and one of their adult children; interviews with both the fathers and children dealt with the history and quality of family relationships. These interviews, like more structured quantitative approaches, highlight the strong feelings of affection that middle-aged and older men express for their adult children.

The Fatherhood Project further reveals an important influence of fathering: Men identified fundamental differences in their relationships with sons as compared to daughters (Nydegger & Mitteness, 1991). Fathers believed that rearing sons and daughters entailed different problems and sources of satisfaction; they found it easier to understand their sons than their daughters; and they were more demanding and critical of their sons than of their daughters. However, fathers whose daughters had adopted traditionally male occupational roles described their relationships with these daughters as embodying many of the same functions as relationships with sons. As in bonds with sons, fathers were concerned about socializing their daughters into the male work world, easing their career entry, and monitoring their progress. This project makes an important contribution in specifying ways in which child gender moderates the quality of adulthood relationships between fathers and children; similar approaches, in which possible moderating effects of family structure, race, and social class are considered, would be equally valuable.

Exchanging Support

Hill's (1968) classic study of three-generation families illustrates the long-term reciprocal patterns of intergenerational support that characterize most American families. Hill interviewed grandparents in their 60s and 70s, parents in their 40s and 50s, and young adults in their 20s and 30s; much of the interview focused on ways in which these relatives exchanged help over a year's time. Hill found that these exchanges were characterized by a high level of reciprocity, as members of each generation both gave and received help; further, he identified the "middle" parent generation as having a patron-type status with regard to the older and younger generations. In other words, the middle-aged parents in these families provided more help to their young adult children and to their own elderly parents than they received from members of either generation.

More recent research confirms that Hill's (1968) portrait of intergenerational support patterns is still accurate 25 years later. Contemporary scholars continue to report that young adults, their middle-aged parents, and their elderly grandparents exchange help in such forms as child care, care during illness, emotional support and advice, help with household tasks or home repairs, housing, transportation, and financial support and advice and that the middle-aged generations are typically pivotal in these exchanges (e.g., Aldous, 1987; Bengtson, Rosenthal, & Burton, 1990; Nakao, Okabe, & Bengtson, 1988). Because contemporary American families are increasingly likely to include four or more adult generations, however, the networks of help exchanges are correspondingly more complex than Hill's (1968) early report indicated. Men and women generally provide different kinds of help to family members. Whereas women most often help by providing care during illness, emotional support, and help with housekeeping, men are more likely to help by giving money, maintaining financial records and providing financial advice, or helping with home or automobile repairs, home maintenance, and yard work (Chappell, 1990; Coward & Dwyer, 1990). Both mothers and fathers help their adult children selectively: most resources are directed toward children that the father believes to be most in need of support (Aldous, 1987). Never-married and divorced adult children, particularly daughters, are especially likely to be singled out for paternal attention.

For fathers, acting as a resource for adult children in need may be stressful—as it may be for mothers. However, the source of stress is different for men and women (Greenberg & Becker, 1988). Interviews with parents who were helping adult children cope with serious problems such as divorce, difficulties in childrearing, unemployment and career crises, serious illness, and so forth showed that mothers typically noted the stress that their children's problems caused them personally. Fathers, however, were more likely to be distressed over the anxiety that their wives experienced and thus were indirectly affected by their children's life problems.

Of course, middle-aged and older fathers find pleasure, as well as pain, in helping their adult sons and daughters. Lewis (1990) identifies sources of gratification that fathers derive from helping adult children, including the ability to provide amenities to children that were impossible earlier in the life course and the foundation that helping provides for maintaining influence over adult children. Lewis (1990) also notes, as does Antonucci (1990), that middle-aged fathers and mothers may regard help that they provide to adult sons and daughters as "deposits" in a metaphorical "support bank." In other words, by helping their adult children when they are relatively rich in physical health and material resources middle-aged parents ensure that their children will help them as they encounter age-related constriction of health and wealth.

Emotional reactions to helping adult children, however, do not reflect simply the fact that help is provided, or the impact that helping has on the spouse. Perceptions of the extent of equity in exchanges of help with adult children are also important. Harvey, Curry, and Bray (1991) found that among elderly rural Canadian parents, fathers' happiness was positively related to the extent to which the fathers believed that their children could "count on" them but was negatively related to the extent to which the fathers believed that they could "count on" their children. Thomas (1988) found that fathers and mothers aged 60 to 74 who reported an even balance between the amounts of help that they gave to and received from children were more satisfied with children's help than were parents reporting less balanced exchanges.

Fathers and Family Caregiving

Even the most cursory survey of the literature on intergenerational relations highlights family caregiving as a principal topic throughout the 1980s and 1990s. Researchers have considered gender in caregivers' experiences, contrasting husbands and wives or sons and daughters. Considerations of the elderly care recipients' reactions to the help that they receive from their adult children are rare; in the studies that are available, gender alone has not been identified as a predictor of parents' evaluations of adult children's help (e.g., Thomas, 1988). But gender may interact with family orientation to produce distinct reactions to receiving help from children. Lee and Shehan (1989) found that men who had low filial responsibility expectations experienced decreased morale when receiving aid from children, although women who held such expectations experienced increased morale.

Men are more likely to provide care for their elderly parents or parents-in-law than they are to receive care from their adult children. Primary caregivers, who take major responsibility for the everyday, routine needs of a frail older individual, are usually the spouse if the spouse is living; an adult child is the most likely primary caregiver if there is no living spouse. Given sex differences in longevity, the wife is more likely to be an older man's primary caregiver than his sons or daughters are.

Nonetheless, the relationship between elderly father and adult child is a context for family caregiving, because approximately two thirds of the primary caregivers in the United States receive assistance from secondary caregivers who take on tasks (such as transportation and home repairs) that come up intermittently (Stone, Cafferata, & Sangl, 1987). Whereas primary caregivers are usually the spouse or daughter of the frail older person, secondary caregivers are typically sons-in-law, sons, grandchildren, siblings, or nonrelatives (Tennstedt, McKinlay, & Sullivan, 1989). Thus an aged father who receives long-term care from his wife as a primary caregiver probably also receives care from his adult children and their families. Unfortunately, research on family caregiving thus far has included little examination of secondary caregivers' reactions to providing care and no published accounts of care recipients' reactions to secondary caregivers' assistance.

Men as Grandfathers

The 1980s were, in a sense, a "renaissance" period for grandparenthood research. Scholars built on early descriptive studies by examining individual differences in reactions to grandparenting and linkages between grandparenthood and mental health. In the early 1990s, custodial grandparents became a focal point for research. Scholars described the circumstances under which grandparents took on parental relationships with grandchildren and the impacts that this choice had for the grandparents. What have these waves of research told us about men's reactions to grandfatherhood?

Reactions to Grandfatherhood

Neugarten and Weinstein (1964) conducted interviews with grandparent couples and identified the primary significance that each grandparent found in the role, as well as each individual's "style" of grandparenting. In their view, gender differences were less intriguing than age and cohort differences in these dimensions. However, they did note that grandfathers were less likely than grandmothers to find significance in grandchildren as a source of biological renewal, perhaps because most of the participating couples were maternal grandparents. Neugarten and Weinstein (1964) also found that grandfathers were more likely than grandmothers to serve as a "reservoir of family wisdom" by providing grandchildren with special skills and knowledge, and that grandfathers in their sample were not "surrogate parents" who regularly took care of grandchildren while the parents worked.

More recent work elaborates the picture of gender differences in grandparenting. Cherlin and Furstenberg (1985, 1986), using a nationally representative sample of grandparents, found that grandfathers were more likely to have "active" relationships with grandchildren—in which they regularly and frequently exchanged services or had a nearly parental influence—than passive relationships in which exchanging services or providing influence were not readily apparent. These active relationships were particularly striking for grandfathers with grandsons. Furthermore, some scholars report that grandfathers tend to provide instrumental types of help (e.g., financial assistance, career guidance) to grandchildren and their families, in contrast to the expressive support (e.g., advice, sympathy, guidance in interpersonal matters) that grandmothers more often give (Cherlin & Furstenberg, 1985; Hagestad & Speicher, 1981).

In one of the few observational studies of grandparenthood, Tinsley and Parke (1988) found that infants were rated as less cute, alert, and excitable when interacting with their grandfathers than with their grandmothers or with either parent. Although observer ratings did not differ for grandfathers as compared to grandmothers or either parent, the authors suggested that grandfathers may be—in a global sense—less competent interactive partners with young infants than grandmothers or parents are. Thomas (1986a, 1986b, 1989) found that grandmothers enjoy grandparenthood more than grandfathers do, and that grandfathers express higher levels of obligation to offer childrearing advice and take care of grandchildren than grandmothers do. In contrast to Neugarten and Weinstein's (1964) results, contemporary grandfathers in one sample found the extension of their family through a new generation and opportunities to indulge grandchildren more meaningful than grandmothers did (Thomas, 1989).

Grandfatherhood and Mental Health

On a practical and clinical level, the most important question may be whether grandparenthood offers any psychological benefit to grandfathers. Kivnick (1982a, 1982b, 1985) identified associations between the symbolic meaning attributed to grandparenthood and grandparents' mental health. For grandfathers, emphasis on grandparenthood was positively related to life satisfaction and morale: Men who found grandparenting pleasant and important enjoyed life in general.

Specific relationships with individual grandchildren, as well as warm feelings about being a grandfather in general, are important. Thomas (1990a) examined associations between the relationship with the oldest grandchild in the two-parent household geographically closest to a grandparent and the grandparent's mental health. The grandparent's feelings of satisfaction and nurturance in the relationship were positively associated with mental health, although the extent to which the grandparent wielded authority in the relationship (by disciplining the grandchild, for example) was not.

Emerging Roles for Grandfathers

Research on the impact of divorce on grandparents' family roles largely supports a "latent function" view of grandparenthood. According to this perspective, grandparents have the most active role in times of family crisis or disruption (e.g., Clingempeel, Colyar, Brand, & Hetherington, 1992; Thomas, 1990b). Grandparents are typically called on to take a more active role in grandchildren's upbringing when the children are in a single-parent household. In taking such an active role, however, grandparents must be masters of diplomacy. Thomas (1990b) found that single mothers cited grandparents' ability to provide help and support as the primary advantage of having grandparents in the family, but they identified grandparents' interference in childrearing as the primary disadvantage.

Recent research on custodial grandparenting suggests that this latent function of grandparenthood—at its most extreme level—can entail considerable stress for grandfathers (and grandmothers). Burton (1992) interviewed African-American grandparents and great-grandparents who were rearing grandchildren because of parental drug addiction. Grandfathers, as well as grandmothers and great-grandmothers, reported role-related stress that they attributed to neighborhood dangers, the demands of providing care not only for their grandchildren but also for other family members, and the physical, psychological, and economic demands of meeting young children's needs. Virtually all felt that they could benefit from both instrumental and emotional support as they managed these stresses. At the same time, these men and women willingly accepted their roles as custodial grandparents and derived satisfaction from the close involvement in their grandchildren's lives.

Shore and Hayslip's (in press) work with a predominantly Caucasian sample shows that Burton's (1992) findings extend beyond the African-American community. These researchers compared overall reactions to grandparenthood, relationships with grandchildren, and psychological well-being for custodial and noncustodial grandparents. Custodial grandparents expressed lower levels of satisfaction with grandparenting, more negative perceptions of the grandparent-grandchild relationship, and lower levels of overall well-being.

Racial Variation in Grandfatherhood

Researchers in the 1980s explicitly considered racial and ethnic differences in grandparent-grandchild relationships, although not always making race-by-gender comparisons. In contrast to Neugarten and Weinstein's (1964) portrayal of Caucasian grandparents, Markides and Mindel (1987) reported that grandparents in Hispanic families often play important roles in their grandchildren's upbringing by passing along family history and ethnic heritage, providing support in times of crisis, and having strong influence over family decisions. Mexican-American grandparents are more likely than grandparents in other Hispanic groups to be involved with grandchildren on an everyday basis (Bengtson, 1985). Unfortunately, there is little information about Native American grandparents' relationships with their grandchildren. The available data suggest, however, that Native American grandparents have important roles in their grandchildren's lives. Approximately 25% of Native American grandparents regularly care for at least one grandchild, and—like grandparents in other racial groups—most live near at least some of their grandchildren and regularly exchange support with family members (National Indian Council on Aging, 1981).

African-American grandparents have been studied more extensively than have grandparents in other groups. Kivett's (1991) work suggests that grandfatherhood has a distinct character for African-American men. She found that the role of grandfather was more central for African-American men than for Caucasian men and was an important source of affection. Researchers have noted that African-American men today experience grandfatherhood through a wider variety of family structures than in the past as a consequence of changing mortality and fertility patterns (Burton & Dilworth-Anderson, 1991). An African-American grandfather may be part of a verticalized intergenerational family, in which there are relatively many generations, but relatively few members per generation. In this case, an African-American man might be a great-great-grandfather, a great-grandfather, a grandfather, and a father—but have only a few offspring in each generation. Alternatively, he might be a member of an age-condensed family, which is characterized by shortened age distance between generations. An African-American grandfather in this type of family may be merely 25 years older than his grandchildren, rather than the more traditional age distance of 40 years or more. A third structure is the substitutional family structure, in which an older man has a small kin network and consequently is involved in the support networks of remote or fictive kin.

Future Directions

This review has suggested productive directions for subsequent research on intergenerational relations and their importance in the lives of older men. Throughout the chapter, I have noted such steps in the context of specific issues. These suggestions include the need for meta-analytic studies of associations between reactions to fatherhood and grandfatherhood and psychological well-being, identification of factors that distinguish men experiencing different amounts and types of stress as fathers and grandfathers, research on fathers and family caregiving, and—perhaps most important—far more extensive study of racial and ethnic diversity in fatherhood and grandfatherhood. These are promising avenues for future work.

But there are other inviting research directions as well. Descriptive research would be welcome on topics that have remained unexplored to date, including relationships between older homosexual fathers and their children and grandchildren. Scholars might consider, for example, the kinds of relationships that homosexual fathers have with their sons as compared to their daughters, or how fathers' custody or visitation arrangements affect their relationships with children and partners. And, as great-grandfatherhood becomes more frequent, research describing that experience and its variation according to the age, race, gender, and proximity of great-grandchildren will grow in importance.

Researchers should also move beyond descriptive work and initiate explanatory studies that account for the portraits of fatherhood and grandfatherhood that previous work has yielded. As noted earlier, explanations are needed for why some fathers encounter stress when providing help to children (or when launching their young adult children into independent lifestyles), whereas others find the experience satisfying. To the extent that earlier descriptive studies have identified racial and ethnic variation in fatherhood and grandfatherhood, explanatory research specifying the values or pressures within the culture and subculture that might account for these differences would be enlightening.

As noted at the outset of the chapter, a contextual perspective offers a useful framework for such explanatory work. Among the topics that could be addressed using this approach are ways in which older men's career involvements and career transitions are related to their relationships with adult children and with grandchildren, and ways in which fatherhood and grandfatherhood unfold in various nontraditional family forms. By placing older men's experiences as fathers and grandfathers in the broader context of other family relationships and involvements outside the family, the contextual viewpoint may provide a sound basis for understanding these bonds as they occur in the 1990s and beyond.

References

Aldous, J. (1987). New views on the family life of the elderly and the near-elderly. *Journal of Marriage and the Family, 49*, 227-234.

Antonucci, T. C. (1990). Social supports and social relationships. In R. H. Binstock & L. K. George (Eds.), *Handbook of aging and the social sciences* (3rd ed., pp. 205-226). San Diego, CA: Academic Press.

Back, K. W. (1971). Transition to aging and the self-image. *Aging and Human Development, 2,* 296-304.

Bengtson, V. L. (1985). Diversity and symbolism in grandparental roles. In V. L. Bengtson & J. F. Robertson (Eds.), *Grandparenthood* (pp. 11-25). Beverly Hills, CA: Sage.

Bengtson, V. L., & Kuypers, J. A. (1971). Generational differences and the developmental stake. *Aging and Human Development, 2,* 249-260.

Bengtson, V. L., Rosenthal, C., & Burton, L. (1990). Families and aging: Diversity and heterogeneity. In R. H. Binstock & L. K. George (Eds.), *Handbook of aging and the social sciences* (3rd ed., pp. 263-287). San Diego, CA: Academic Press.

Borland, D. C. (1978). Research on middle age: An assessment. *The Gerontologist, 18,* 379-386.

Brim, O. G. (1976). Theories of the male mid-life crisis. *Counseling Psychologist, 6,* 2-9.

Bozett, F. W., & Hanson, S. M. H. (1991). *Fatherhood and families in cultural context.* New York: Springer.

Burton, L. M. (1992). Black grandparents rearing children of drug-addicted parents: Stressors, outcomes, and social service needs. *The Gerontologist, 32,* 744-751.

Burton, L. M., & Dilworth-Anderson, P. (1991). The intergenerational family roles of aged black Americans. *Marriage and Family Review, 16,* 311-330.

Chappell, N. L. (1990). Aging and social care. In R. H. Binstock & L. H. George (Eds.), *Handbook of aging and the social sciences* (3rd ed., pp. 438-454). San Diego, CA: Academic Press.

Cherlin, A., & Furstenberg, F. F. (1985). Styles and strategies of grandparenting. In V. L. Bengtson & J. F. Robertson (Eds.), *Grandparenthood* (pp. 97-116). Beverly Hills, CA: Sage.

Cherlin, A., & Furstenberg, F. F. (1986). *The new American grandparent: A place in the family, a life apart.* New York: Basic Books.

Clausen, J. A. (1976). Glimpses into the social world of middle age. *International Journal of Aging and Human Development, 7,* 99-106.

Clingempeel, W. G., Colyar, J. J., Brand, E., & Hetherington, E. M. (1992). Children's relationships with maternal grandparents: A longitudinal study of family structure and pubertal status effects. *Child Development, 63,* 1404-1422.

Coward, R. T., Cutler, S. J., & Schmidt, F. E. (1989). Differences in the household composition of elders by age, gender, and area of residence. *The Gerontologist, 29,* 814-821.

Coward, R. T., & Dwyer, J. W. (1990). The association of gender, sibling network composition, and patterns of parent care by adult children. *Research on Aging, 12,* 158-181.

Crimmins, E. M., & Ingegneri, D. G. (1990). Interaction and living arrangements of older parents and their children: Past trends, present determinants, future implications. *Research on Aging, 12,* 3-35.

Erikson, E. H. (1950). *Childhood and society.* New York: Norton.

Erikson, E. H., Erikson, J. M., & Kivnick, H. Q. (1986). *Vital involvement in old age: The experience of old age in our time.* New York: Norton.

Greenberg, J. R. (1991). Problems in the lives of adult children: Their impact on aging parents. *Journal of Gerontological Social Work, 16,* 149-161.

Greenberg, J. S., & Becker, M. (1988). Aging parents as family resources. *The Gerontologist, 28,* 786-791.

Greene, A. L., & Boxer, A. M. (1986). Daughters and sons as young adults: Restructuring the ties that bind. In N. Datan, A. L. Greene, & H. W. Reese (Eds.), *Life-span developmental psychology: Intergenerational relations* (pp. 125-149). San Diego, CA: Academic Press.

Gutmann, D. (1975). Parenthood: A key to the comparative study of the life cycle. In N. Datan & L. H. Ginsberg (Eds.), *Life-span developmental psychology: Normative life crises* (pp. 167-184). San Diego, CA: Academic Press.

Gutmann, D. (1977). The cross-cultural perspective: Notes toward a comparative psychology of aging. In J. E. Birren & K. W. Schaie (Eds.), *Handbook of the psychology of aging* (pp. 302-326). New York: Van Nostrand Reinhold.

Hagestad, G. O., & Neugarten, B. L. (1985). Age and the life course. In R. H. Binstock & E. Shanas (Eds.), *Handbook of aging and the social sciences* (2nd ed., pp. 35-61). New York: Van Nostrand Reinhold.

Hagestad, G. O., & Speicher, J. L. (1981, April). *Grandparents and family influence: Views of three generations.* Paper presented at biennial meeting of the Society for Research in Child Development, Boston.

Harvey, C. D. H., Bond, J. B., & Greenwood, L. J. (1991). Satisfaction, happiness, and self-esteem of older rural parents. *Canadian Journal of Community Mental Health, 10,* 31-46.

Harvey, D. M., Curry, C. J., & Bray, J. H. (1991). Individuation and intimacy in intergenerational relationships and health: Patterns across two generations. *Journal of Family Psychology, 5,* 204-236.

Hill, R. (1968). Decision making and the family life cycle. In B. L. Neugarten (Ed.), *Middle age and aging* (pp. 286-295). Chicago: University of Chicago Press.

Huyck, M. H. (1989). Midlife parental imperatives. In R. A. Kalish (Ed.), *Midlife loss: Coping strategies* (pp. 115-148). Newbury Park, CA: Sage.

Jung, C. G. (1933). *Modern man in search of a soul.* New York: Harcourt Brace Jovanovich.

Kivett, V. R. (1991). Centrality of the grandfather role among older rural black and white men. *Journal of Gerontology: Social Sciences, 46,* S250-S258.

Kivnick, H. Q. (1982a). Grandparenthood: An overview of meaning and mental health. *The Gerontologist, 22,* 59-66.

Kivnick, H. Q. (1982b). *The meaning of grandparenthood.* Ann Arbor, MI: UMI Research Press.

Kivnick, H. Q. (1985). Grandparenthood and mental health: Meaning, behavior, and satisfaction. In V. L. Bengtson & J. F. Robertson (Eds.), *Grandparenthood* (pp. 151-158). Beverly Hills, CA: Sage.

Lamb, M. E. (1981). *The role of the father in child development* (2nd ed.). New York: John Wiley.

Lee, G. R., & Shehan, C. L. (1989). Elderly parents and their children: Normative influences. In J. A. Mancini (Ed.), *Aging parents and adult children* (pp. 117-133). Lexington, MA: Lexington Books.

Levinson, D. J. (1977). The mid-life transition: A period in adult psychosocial development. *Psychiatry, 40,* 99-111.

Levinson, D. J., Darrow, C. N., Klein, E. B., Levinson, M. H., & McKee, B. (1978). *The seasons of a man's life.* New York: Knopf.

Lewis, R. A. (1990). The adult child and older parents. In T. H. Brubaker (Ed.), *Family relationships in later life* (2nd ed., pp. 68-85). Newbury Park, CA: Sage.

Lewis, R. A., Freneau, P. J., & Roberts, C. L. (1979). Fathers and the postparental transition. *Family Coordinator, 28,* 514-520.

Lowenthal, M. F., & Chiriboga, D. (1972). Transition to the empty nest. *Archives of General Psychiatry, 26,* 8-14.

Mancini, J. A. (1989). *Aging parents and adult children.* Lexington, MA: Lexington Books.

Mancini, J. A., & Blieszner, R. (1989). Aging parents and adult children: Research themes in intergenerational relations. *Journal of Marriage and the Family, 51,* 275-290.

Markides, K. S., & Mindel, C. H. (1987). *Aging and ethnicity.* Newbury Park, CA: Sage.

Matthews, S. H., & Sprey, J. (1989). Older family systems: Intra- and intergenerational relations. In J. A. Mancini (Ed.), *Aging parents and adult children* (pp. 63-77). Lexington, MA: Lexington Books.

Moss, M. S., Moss, S. Z., & Moles, E. L. (1985). The quality of relationships between elderly parents and their out-of-town children. *The Gerontologist, 25,* 134-140.

Nakao, K., Okabe, T., & Bengtson, V. L. (1988, February). *Reciprocity across generations in social support.* Paper presented at annual meeting of the International Network for Social Network Analysis, Sunbelt Social Network Conference, San Diego, CA.

National Indian Council on Aging. (1981). The 1981 White House Conference on Aging: The Indian issues. *National Indian Council on Aging Quarterly, 4,* 1.

Neugarten, B., & Gutmann, D. (1958). Age-sex roles and personality in middle age: A thematic apperception study. *Psychology Monographs, 72,* 1-33.

Neugarten, B. L., & Weinstein, K. K. (1964). The changing American grandparent. *Journal of Marriage and the Family, 26,* 199-204.

Nydegger, C. N., & Mitteness, L. S. (1991). Fathers and their adult sons and daughters. *Marriage and Family Review, 16,* 249-256.

Peterson, C. C., & Peterson, J. L. (1988). Older men's and women's relationships with adult kin: How equitable are they? *International Journal of Aging and Human Development, 27,* 221-231.

Roberts, C. L., & Zuengler, K. L. (1985). The postparental transition and beyond. In S. M. H. Hanson & F. W. Bozett (Eds.), *Dimensions of fatherhood* (pp. 196-216). Beverly Hills, CA: Sage.

Shanas, E. (1979). Social myth as hypothesis: The case of the family relations of older people. *The Gerontologist, 19,* 3-9.

Shore, R. J., & Hayslip, B. (in press). Custodial grandparenting: Implications for children's development. In A. Gottfried & A. Gottfried (Eds.), *Redefining families: Implications for children's development.* New York: Plenum.

Stone, R., Cafferata, G. L., & Sangl, J. (1987). Caregivers of the frail elderly: A national profile. *The Gerontologist, 27,* 616-626.

Tamir, L. M. (1982). *Men in their forties: The transition to middle age.* New York: Springer.

Taylor, R. J. (1988). Aging and supportive relationships among black Americans. In J. S. Jackson (Ed.), *The black American elderly: Research of physical and psychosocial health* (pp. 259-281). New York: Springer.

Tennstedt, S. L., McKinlay, J. B., & Sullivan, L. M. (1989). Informal care for frail elders: The role of secondary caregivers. *The Gerontologist, 29,* 677-683.

Thomas, J. L. (1986a). Age and sex differences in perceptions of grandparenting. *Journal of Gerontology, 41,* 417-423.

Thomas, J. L. (1986b). Gender differences in satisfaction with grandparenting. *Psychology and Aging, 1,* 215-219.

Thomas, J. L. (1988). Predictors of satisfaction with children's help for younger and older elderly parents. *Journal of Gerontology: Social Sciences, 43,* S9-S14.

Thomas, J. L. (1989). Gender and perceptions of grandparenthood. *International Journal of Aging and Human Development, 29,* 269-282.

Thomas, J. L. (1990a). Grandparenthood and mental health: Implications for the practitioner. *Journal of Applied Gerontology, 9,* 464-479.

Thomas, J. L. (1990b). The grandparent role: A double bind. *International Journal of Aging and Human Development, 31,* 169-177.

Tinsley, B. R., & Parke, R. D. (1988). The role of grandfathers in the context of the family. In P. Bronstein & C. P. Cowan (Ed.), *Fatherhood today: Men's changing role in the family* (pp. 236-250). New York: John Wiley.

Treas, J., & Bengtson, V. L. (1987). The family in later years. In M. B. Sussman & S. K. Steinmetz (Eds.), *Handbook of marriage and the family* (pp. 625-648). New York: Plenum.

12

Older Men and the Family Caregiving Orientation

LENARD W. KAYE
JEFFREY S. APPLEGATE

Men are a distinct minority among the elderly. Older men who are involved to a significant degree in caring for an older incapacitated family member constitute yet another, even smaller minority among the elderly population. Perhaps for both these reasons, our understanding of the experience of older husbands, sons, and other men in the family constellation who are caring for a dependent relative is woefully inadequate. Our knowledge of older male caregiving is also sparse because conventional wisdom and stereotypical thinking have led us to assume that older men lack the inclination and capacity to meet the physical and emotional needs of another person.

If, as Rubinstein (1986) argues, the aged male is the "forgotten" man often known by others primarily through stereotypes, impressions, and anecdotes, then the aged male family caregiver has been virtually dismissed from societal consciousness. Consequently, the research that does exist on older men, rather than considering their "other-oriented" nurturant capabilities, has focused instead on the "self-oriented" individualistic stresses that males often confront during the latter stages of life, including the personal effects of retirement, widowerhood, disease and disability, rolelessness, and sexuality (Solomon, 1982). The demands

AUTHORS' NOTE: The research on which this chapter is based was supported by a grant from the Andrus Foundation of the American Association of Retired Persons.

associated with assuming the caregiver function have seemingly been lost in the shuffle.

Although our understanding of the challenges and rewards of family caregiving for men remains grossly underdeveloped, recent evidence suggests that there may be more males engaged in helping other relatives than previously assumed. In addition, older men's family caring activities consume a significant portion of their lives, both in terms of time and physical and emotional commitment.

This chapter reports on research that profiles the characteristics of these caring men and the presence of what we will characterize as a family caregiving orientation among older caring men in particular, largely husbands and older sons providing help for their incapacitated wives and mothers or fathers, respectively.

The degree to which a caregiving orientation pervades the older male population is, of course, debatable. Yet we maintain that evidence suggests that such a helping orientation is clearly discernible and growing in influence. More specifically, we will speak to the presence of an "other-oriented" nurturant orientation among a cohort of older men. Both the rewards and burdens of older adult caregiving will be identified, as well as the core characteristics of their experiences as family carers. A detailed profile of the older man observed most commonly to exhibit such a family caregiving orientation also will be constructed.

Demographics and the Sociology of Family Caregiving

The traditional assumption in our society has been that women will shoulder the majority of family caregiving responsibilities. Wives and daughters primarily, and daughters-in-law and other female members of the family unit secondarily, are perceived naturally to assume the central role of helping incapacitated relatives in their old age (Brody, 1990). Women's grounding in connectedness, it is argued, cultivates in them a powerful ethic of caring and responsibility for others that subsequently orients them toward empathic relationships with other persons. In contrast, men are believed to be socialized according to an ethic of justice that focuses on the rules, procedures, and rights of relationships (Gilligan, 1982). Accordingly, it can be reasoned that caregiving—whether of infant, child, or elder—has been assigned to women. At the same time, this work has been viewed as less prestigious than the work of providing financially for the family, which has been assumed by men and carried out outside the home (Kaye & Applegate, 1990a). As a result, women have occupied the domestic center of family life while men have kept their distance at its perimeter (Gutmann, 1987), the latter coming to know the world in terms of separation rather than through interpersonal connection (Belenky, Clinchy, Goldberger, & Tarule, 1986).

Although such sociological interpretations have dominated our way of explaining the presumed gender role bifurcation in family roles generally, and family caregiving in particular, recent data on the demographics of helping suggest their usefulness is waning. Referred to is research that confirms that while women may still be providing the majority of family caregiving assistance in the home, men, and older men in particular, are significantly more involved than previously assumed. For example, a national survey of 2,999 Americans (1,069 men and 1,930 women) conducted for the Commonwealth Fund (1992) by Louis Harris and Associates, Inc., highlights men's contributions at work, as volunteers, and as caregivers. Specifically, the survey discovered that men over age 55 play a larger role than usually credited as volunteers and caregivers. Of all older men, 25% are volunteering, 28% are caring for others, and 50% who have children or grandchildren are helping to care for them. Among married couples, 1.6 million men are caring for sick or disabled spouses, 1.2 million are caring for sick or disabled parents, and 2.1 million men are caring for sick or disabled friends or neighbors. Furthermore, 14% (3.1 million) of all men (as compared to 10% or 2.9 million women) age 55 and older are willing and able to volunteer. Most important, perhaps, is that this same study highlighted the underestimated vitality of the older-than-75 population. Of this age cohort, 22% are caring for others who are sick and disabled, whether they be spouses, other relatives, or friends and neighbors.

A study by the American Association of Retired Persons and Travelers Companies Foundation has estimated that one quarter of the 7 million elder caregivers in this country are men (Weinstein, 1989). Other researchers estimate that as many as one third of elder caregivers are men (Zarit, Todd, & Zarit, 1986). Conservatively speaking, therefore, there are at least 1.7 million, and possibly as many as 2.3 million, men caring for elderly relatives in the United States. Stone and Kemper (1989) have estimated that there are 13.3 million potential caregivers in the United States who have disabled parents or spouses 65 years of age and older. Substantial proportions of this potential provider group are men as well, and, in particular, older men. Recent research on adult children's perceptions of their responsibility to provide care for dependent elderly parents further reinforces men's apparent commitment, at least morally, to the caregiving function. Wolfson, Handfield-Jones, Glass, McClaran, and Keyserlingk (1993) found no difference between sons and daughters in their sense of moral obligation or their actual ability to provide various types of supportive care to a dependent elderly parent.

The current and potential future size of the group of males who assume family caregiving functions for older disabled relatives notwithstanding, men, as noted at the outset of this chapter, remain the "forgotten carers" (Arber & Gilbert, 1989). Researchers have focused their investigative efforts on women generally, and daughters in particular (Brubaker, 1990; Carlson & Robertson, 1990; Harper & Lund, 1990; Kaye & Applegate, 1990a; Mancini & Blieszner, 1989). Lack of knowledge of men's caregiving experience has in turn led to misunderstandings about their roles and motivations as family carers (Parker, 1989).

A review of the research that has been produced on the male caregiving experience confirms that men have usually been characterized as performing an extremely circumscribed range of concrete and instrumental-type caregiving tasks for disabled members of the family, including such activities as home repair and maintenance, transportation, financial management, yard work, and dealing with bureaucratic organizations (Horowitz, 1985; Montgomery & Kamo, 1989; Rathbone-McCuan & Coward, 1985). It has been further argued that men tend to avoid performing tasks that require personal, hands-on assistance such as grooming, bathing, and dressing the family care recipient as well as other functions that are likely to be replete with affective connotation such as the provision of emotional support, engagement in individual problem solving, and the offering of companionship (Kaye & Applegate, 1990a).

The Research Study

Data reported here are drawn from a combined national and local (Philadelphia metropolitan area) sample of 178 men involved in family caregiving with an older adult (Kaye & Applegate, 1989). A combination of highly structured survey questionnaires and intensive face-to-face interviews were used as strategies to collect information about these men's caregiving experiences. Although there was considerable range in the ages of the men in this research, the majority were older than 60, with the average age in the upper 60s. Slightly more than 50% were 70 and older. The sample, representing men who were or had recently been

participating in support group programs for elderly caregivers, was dominated by married white males living with and caring for their spouses and
financially managing reasonably well. A minority of the sample com-
prised nonspousal males, primarily older sons caring for a very old and
disabled mother or father. More than 90% of the care recipients were
female, and almost 70% were 70 and older.

Profiling the Characteristics of the Older Male Caregiver

It has been widely reasoned that men's traditional sex-role socialization
has confined them to providing family care from the emotional periphery,
where they focus primarily on instrumental task performance associated
with providing and protecting. Recent research, however, suggests that as
a consequence of the women's movement, contemporary men are being
granted cultural permission to be nurturant and to care for others. Gutmann
(1987) and Lowenthal, Thumber, and Chiriboga (1975) maintain that
mid-life and late-life men in particular may become naturally more
nurturant and concerned for those around them.

The men in our study were assessed as to how they viewed themselves
along an affective-instrumental continuum. We used a shortened version
of a gender-orientation index developed by Bem (1974) in which subjects
were asked to assess the extent to which they would describe themselves
according to traditional masculine and feminine terminology. Subjects'
scores suggest a considerable degree of androgyny in these older men's
perceptions of themselves. Subjects tended to describe themselves with a
combination of instrumental (e.g., "self-sufficient," "analytical," "competitive," "forceful," and "aggressive") and affective (e.g., "gentle,"
"compassionate," "loving," "yielding," and "warm") adjectives. Closer
review of the overall rating pattern, however, disclosed that these men
actually viewed themselves as displaying significantly more affective
than instrumental qualities. Although they did rate self-sufficiency as
being of greatest importance (reflecting the societal imperative for men
to be independent), the next four adjectives receiving the highest ratings
were all of the affective type. The three lowest ranking adjectives were
of the instrumental type (see Table 12.1). Overall, these men, all engaged
in elder family caregiving to a significant degree, saw themselves as
possessing substantial measures of affective, nurturant, and expressive
personality traits usually associated with femininity, but they tempered
this personality orientation with a high valuation for autonomy and
self-sufficiency. And, as we will see, these men were providing care that

Table 12.1 Male Caregivers' Self-Descriptions From Adjectives
Representing Masculine or Feminine Personality Traits

Adjectives	Mean[a]	SD	Rank
Self-sufficient	4.30	.81	(1)
Gentle	4.07	.86	(2)
Compassionate	3.99	.92	(3)
Warm	3.98	.89	(4)
Loving	3.89	.94	(5)
Analytical	3.52	1.17	(6)
Yielding	2.80	.97	(7)
Competitive	2.80	1.26	(8)
Aggressive	2.54	1.15	(9)
Forceful	2.53	1.04	(10)

a. Scoring 1-5: 1 = *rarely or never*, 2 = *sometimes*, 3 = *often*, 4 = *usually*, 5 = *almost always*.

reflected considerable integration of affective and instrumental dimensions (Kaye & Applegate, 1990b).

It is noteworthy that subjects' views of their gender orientation, as measured by the above index, did not vary significantly in relation to their marital status, employment status, age, physical health, or whether they were caring for a spouse or another relative. The common experience of heavy engagement in family caregiving appears, from our perspective, to be the consistent feature in the lives of these men that is associated with their distinctive orientation to role performance. Of course, in the absence of a comparison group of noncaregiving men, we can only put forward this presumed association as a postulate.

In addition to displaying strong androgynous traits, the male oriented to family caregiving appears to be driven to help others as much or more by love and affection as by duty and obligation. Ungerson (1987) concurs, maintaining that women are more likely to be motivated by the need to be dutiful when it comes to addressing the needs of others. Subject after subject in our research spoke of their unabiding commitment to and concern for the care recipient, whether it be a spouse, mother, or father. Even though caregiving was found to be extremely demanding for many, a long-standing sense of deep affection and intimacy surfaced regularly in our discussions with the men in the local sample. Theirs was an uncompromising love, and they were able to express it in no uncertain terms through their caregiving efforts.

Stoicism and the Performance of Tasks

Most of the literature on caregiving tends to document that even for those men who become engaged in helping another, the experience is not an intense one. Men tend, it is argued, to provide intermittent as opposed to continuous care and to assist infrequently with particular categories of help such as personal care and household chores (Finley, 1989; Horowitz, 1985: Olesen, 1989; Stoller, 1990). Furthermore, researchers have asserted that men are more likely to marshal external resources when caring for a relative, including additional help secured from other family members as well as community service programs (Snyder & Keefe, 1985). Specifically, husbands, more than wives, are said to secure supplemental aid from their adult children and other relatives when caring for a sick spouse (Antonucci & Akiyama, 1987; Johnson, 1983; Pruchno, 1990; Stoller & Cutler, 1992; Zarit et al., 1986).

Our data contradict much of the research cited above. We suggest that older men generally, and older husbands in particular, who have assumed primary caregiving responsibilities (i.e., they are the dominant providers of assistance for the dependent person) neither restrict themselves to a circumscribed range of helping tasks nor reach out to a significant degree to obtain the help of others in easing their caregiving burden. Rather, we propose that the differences between the male and female caregiving experience may not be near as great as we have been led to believe for those serving as primary caregivers and displaying a family caregiving orientation. Further, we postulate that gender-related differences in caregiving patterns will be reduced even further for those caregivers who carry out their caregiving inclinations in coresidence with an elderly person who is severely impaired, especially in the emotional domain. Recent research tends to give credence to the importance of the latter two variables— coresidence and severity of care recipient incapacity—in understanding the caregiving experience (Moss, Lawton, Kleban, & Duhamel, 1993; Tennstedt, Crawford, & McKinlay, 1993).

The male caregivers we surveyed, three fifths of whom resided with the person to whom they were providing care, were performing an exceedingly wide range of tasks associated with elder caregiving, from hand-holding to housecleaning and laundry, home repair, and hands-on personal care. In contrast to the stereotype of male caregiving as primarily instrumental, our subjects provided emotional support and companionship functions most frequently and felt most competent and satisfied in performing this category of assistance as opposed to more concrete tasks. Concrete, home-maintenance tasks were performed slightly less fre-

Table 12.2 Frequency of Male Caregivers' Performance of Caregiving Tasks

Tasks	Mean[a]	SD	Rank
Providing companionship/emotional support	2.76	.59	(1)
Help with paying bills/writing checks	2.70	.84	(2)
Marketing or shopping	2.54	.82	(3)
Help with writing letters/filling out forms	2.43	.92	(4)
Escorting to doctor's office	2.41	.97	(5)
Help with legal matters	2.31	.99	(6)
Laundry	2.29	1.14	(7)
Preparing meals	2.26	1.17	(8)
Household cleaning	2.23	1.10	(9)
Home repairs	2.22	1.21	(10)
Help with medications/injections	2.02	1.31	(11)
Arranging for outside services	1.97	1.16	(12)
Help with dressing	1.83	1.30	(13)
Help with eating meals	1.73	1.31	(14)
Help with grooming	1.72	1.23	(15)
Help with telephoning	1.63	1.25	(16)
Help with bathing	1.61	1.37	(17)
Speaking for elder at community agencies	1.54	1.14	(18)
Help with going to the bathroom	1.44	1.23	(19)
Help getting in and out of bed	1.41	1.33	(20)
Supervising help provided by paid workers	1.35	1.32	(21)
Supervising help provided by relatives/friends	1.23	1.23	(22)

a. Scoring 0-3: 0 = *never*, 1 = *rarely*, 2 = *sometimes*, 3 = *often*.

quently. Although the men in our sample did provide personal hands-on care and care supervision less often than other categories of care, they nevertheless did engage in such activities periodically (see Table 12.2).

The male who is oriented to caregiving is capable of committing himself to extended periods of care for long durations. Our subjects displayed an unusually responsible and persevering attitude toward care. These men had engaged in the caregiving enterprise for long periods of time (three or more years in most cases) and for extended hours each week (the majority were providing care for more than 60 hours per week). Furthermore, more than a quarter of these men were simultaneously bearing the burden of full- or part-time employment, including the responsibilities associated with careers in the professional, managerial or administrative, sales, clerical, and service domains. Caregiving men are not necessarily driven to seek out other resources to substitute for their own. In fact, their approach to caregiving, as reflected in our sample, might well be described as stoic. Although they acknowledged that the recipients of their caring ministrations could benefit from additional increments of help, these men and their care recipients tended to benefit minimally from other family and community resources. It was highly unusual for these men to be receiving supplementary assistance from more than one other relative. And aid from other family members declined noticeably over time (Applegate & Kaye, 1990). Furthermore, these men made minimal use of the services of community health care workers such as those affiliated with respite, adult day care, senior center, visiting nurse, homemaker or home health aide, and friendly visiting programs.

Bearing Up to the Burden of Care

The older caregiving man, like other family caregivers, is subject to significant degrees of stress and strain (Gatz, Bengtson, & Blum, 1990; Teresi, Toner, Bennett, & Wilder, 1988-89). Although men have the tendency to downplay or even deny the difficulties experienced during caregiving (Barusch & Spaid, 1989; Borden & Berlin, 1990; Fitting, Rabins, Lucas, & Eastham, 1986; Young & Kahana, 1989), the price to be paid for a caregiving orientation is both considerable and undeniable. Often the burden is exacerbated by the older man's own frailties and limitations. Indeed, more than 40% of the subjects we surveyed confirmed that their health limited to some degree the care they were able to provide. These men also reported their emotional or mental health to be only fair and recorded only moderate levels of personal satisfaction with life as measured by their feelings of loneliness, frequency of worrying, general perceptions of life, and overall satisfaction with life.

It is noteworthy that our subjects did not express significantly divergent points of view about their personal well-being. Levels of caregiver satisfaction did not significantly vary across a range of respondent subgroups, including those varying in terms of employment status, marital status, age, financial status, or education. Even for men in reportedly good health, the physical and emotional demands of caregiving proved to be great.

The burden of caregiving did appear to express itself in varying ways for different older men. One 63-year-old man caring for his 84-year-old blind and stroke-paralyzed mother put it this way: "Because of my angina, I can't lift my mother. She's dead weight, so it's hard to move her around." Another 79-year-old man caring for his 76-year-old wife with Alzheimer's put it in simple terms: "When you're old you get tired." And for a 65-year-old man caring for his 66-year-old wife with brain damage suffered in an accident, the lament went as follows: "It's made an older man out of me. I come home and work, get up and do work."

For other older men, the demand of caregiving expressed itself in the form of forfeited dreams of freedom in older age. One 67-year-old man caring for his 92-year-old mother with dementia said, "It's a hassle and a nuisance. I can't get away to travel or go away for even one day." "It's tied me down. I can't travel; I miss that the most," disclosed a 76-year-old man caring for his 82-year-old wife with Alzheimer's disease. A 71-year-old man caring for his 84-year-old hydrocephalic, seizure-disordered sister bemoaned, "I'd always planned to be free." A 63-year-old man caring for his 84-year-old blind mother summed it up well by admitting, "I had looked forward to retirement—but I can't leave now."

The demands associated with caring for Alzheimer's patients can be expected to be especially commonplace for men generally (given that more women are diagnosed with the disease) and particularly onerous for the older male caregivers in particular (Quayhagen & Quayhagen, 1988), especially spousal caregivers (George & Gwyther, 1986). We propose that the demand characteristics of Alzheimer's caregiving, which derive from the chronic, irreversible, and rapidly deteriorating nature of the disease, surpass those of other types of illnesses. At the emotional level, the state of dementia commonly associated with Alzheimer's disease and related disorders symbolizes in no uncertain terms the decline and impending demise of the individual (Parks & Pilisuk, 1991). In turn, it serves as a reminder (especially for caregivers, who are aging themselves—like the subjects in our research) of their own frailties and inevitable decline (Sommers, 1985). Indeed, working with Alzheimer's patients was, in our research, a predictor of increased stress and burden for caregivers.

Caregiving can also be extremely isolating and insular for the older man engaged heavily in the experience. The responsibilities of being a primary caregiver inevitably replace time that could have been spent with others (Parks & Pilisuk, 1991). Men who find themselves increasingly isolated because of heavy caregiving responsibilities may also experience a sense of role demand overload or role conflict (Mui & Morrow-Howell, 1993) as they inevitably become involved in carrying out a greater number of caregiving tasks that may have traditionally resided outside the domain of their expertise. In particular, older men may experience a sense of role strain as the caregiving situation requires more than their financial and physical resources will allow. Such feelings may escalate eventually to the point of reflecting feelings of role engulfment and loss of self (Skat & Pearlin, 1992).

Discussion

Further Thoughts on the Caregiver Orientation

This chapter argues that there may well be a nurturant orientation associated with family caregiving. As such, this perspective on helping significant others is evidenced, we propose, not only among women but also in specialized forms among men, and perhaps among older men in particular. Older male spousal caregivers appear to typify one such categorization of this helping orientation. Their relationship with their spouse appears to be unique because it is potentially the most supportive of all intimate family relationships (Anderson & McCulloch, 1993).

Our observations lead us to conclude that the husband's orientation to care is played out through the importation of workplace skills into the home. Such skills emphasize the attributes of structure, organization, independence, and a "tough-it-out" attitude. Such men resist the resources of others, including the offerings of assistance from other family members and the various supportive services available through community agencies. They tend to submerge themselves in the tasks of caring. In effect, the business site "workaholic" becomes a domestic, caregiving "workaholic." However, embedded in this commitment to care evolves a unique and quite intimate support relationship.

The caregiving orientation in older men tends to promote the likelihood of an insular experience for them. Such men appear to grapple regularly with an ongoing tension that displays itself as a dual set of motivating drives—those of obligation versus love for the care recipient.

The conceptualization of the caregiving orientation in older men presses us to redefine traditional views of family elder caregiving among male helpers. Revised definitions will need to incorporate the likelihood of men contributing extended hours and a longer-term time commitment to performance of the family helping function. Revised, too, would be the range of specific tasks and activities that men would be expected to perform given the extensive nature of the task repertoire evidenced in this analysis.

Older Men and Caregiving Careers

The concept of a caregiving "career" is a particularly useful one for characterizing the experiences of the older men described here, especially of husbands caring for their impaired spouses (Montgomery & Hatch, 1986). The "work" of caring for another family member apparently promotes in these men, as it traditionally has done for many women in terms of the performance of domestic labor, a powerful and unabiding sense of responsibility (Lewis, 1987).

To pursue the caregiving-work analogy, like positions in the workplace, these men's caregiving roles change over time, never becoming fully established or immutable (Montgomery & Datwyler, 1990). And, as is the case for a salaried position, relative levels of responsibility and accountability can be expected to escalate over time. This is probably especially the case for those men caring for those with Alzheimer's disease and related disorders (a common situation for older male spouses caring for their wives). In such cases, the disease propels the care provider and the care recipient through progressive stages of impairment requiring more and more skill and expertise on the part of the helper. Under these conditions, men will likely engage initially in the provision of "semicare" in which the help provided is almost imperceptible (Stoller, 1990). Caring then progresses to informal assistance and help with financial and medical affairs, to the performance of concrete household-maintenance tasks, and ultimately to the provision of extensive and personalized hands-on care. Caring thus proceeds through a sequence of stages characterized by increasingly intense and extended periods of assistance with a wide range of tasks associated with daily living (Lewis, 1987).

The older man oriented to caregiving appears to assume primarily "care-provision" responsibilities (i.e., direct service provision) and, less often, more supervisory "care-management" functions (i.e., the coordination of services provided by others). Although Archbold (1983) maintains that family "care managers" tend to have higher incomes and are thus more able to obtain community services to meet their relative's needs, our data suggest that financial capacity may be less a factor in predicting engagement in the care-management function than a caregiving orientation. Indeed, our subjects were reasonably secure financially and yet resisted bringing home-based community services into the home and thus had little reason to function as care managers. They remained frontline providers of support even though the receipt of community services such as respite care has been shown to contribute significantly to the reduction of caregiver burden (Knight, Lutzky, & Macofsky-Urban, 1993; Skelly, McAdoo, & Ostergard, 1993).

Although others have argued that men unlike women tend to withdraw prematurely from their caregiving "careers," we contend that men who display a nurturant orientation do not. In accord with other research that speaks to the influence of the generation variable on caregiving career patterns (Montgomery & Borgatta, 1987; Montgomery & Kamo, 1989), we also find that older as opposed to younger men may be more inclined to commit themselves to long-term caregiving responsibilities.

Rationality With Feeling

The caregiver orientation in older men is characterized by displays of "rationality with feeling"—that is, the approach for these men during caregiving appears to be quite task-oriented and systematic at the same time that considerable intimacy is expressed. The two usually opposing inclinations appear to meld together to create the older male's unique recipe for family caring. The rational side of caregiving is evidenced in the manner by which men acknowledge the stress and strain associated with helping others; that is, they tend to admit to only moderate levels of burden associated with the experience. On the other hand, these men apparently derive considerable satisfaction from the provision of social and emotional support. An "industrial" technique may be used by these men to maintain their caring, yet relatively stoic, stance. They seem to practice "masculine domesticity." Put differently, instrumental approaches are adopted in the performance of a variety of social support and related functions.

The scenario described above appears to be reflective especially of the experiences of those men caring for severely mentally impaired relatives (e.g., those suffering from Alzheimer's). The intensity of this mentally debilitating disease and the resultant demand for assistance it places on the caregiver appear to exacerbate these men's isolating and "stiff-upper-lip" inclinations. Caring for Alzheimer's victims may accelerate the development of the caregiver orientation by forcing the helper to call up that much sooner the special combination of workmanship and nurturant traits that are essential to caring adequately for such individuals. We believe a separate set of behavioral rules may operate for these men as compared to younger generations of male caregivers who are less likely to be spouses or older sons of an individual with irreversible mental impairment.

Fighting the Stigma of Caring

All things considered, we consider it to be quite impressive that the male caregiver orientation manages to surface at all in this society given the forces that continuously aim to dissuade men from "doing" caregiving. The barriers to men's caregiving evidenced in our research are multiple and include the following.

1. Female relatives often "assume" that the tasks of helping are theirs to perform and attempt to reclaim or usurp the role from men who have already assumed the helping function and are performing its concomitant tasks. This experience is particularly common when daughters visit their parents and presume it is their responsibility to step in and take over for their fathers even though they may not have been asked to do so.
2. Society itself presumes that it is out of character and inappropriate for men to do "women's work."
3. Employers tend to frown on men who satisfy family caregiving responsibilities at the expense of job performance.
4. Government refuses to supply monetary support for family caregiving tasks that would imbue men's performance with the customary and classic gauge for determining the value and worth of such tasks.
5. Elder care recipients have their own traditional, often distorted, expectations of the tasks that are appropriate and inappropriate for men to perform.

Taken together, men's orientation to care, or lack thereof, is shaped and patterned inevitably by the expectations and prescriptions of a multitude of individuals and societal institutions. To varying degrees, men are commonly viewed to be inadequate, inexperienced, incapable, and uncomfortable or embarrassed when helping others, especially when performing personal, hands-on tasks. Men with nurturant strivings must therefore resist these expectations, which can be transmitted both directly (through overt expression and direction as to what caregiving tasks men should and should not engage in) and in more subtle manner (through cloaked displays of hesitation and embarrassment by those who experience men performing the caregiving function).

Assessing the Risk of a Caring Orientation

In effect, we have argued that a caregiving orientation carries with it a strong element of risk. More precisely, a strong orientation to caregiving may serve to predict those individuals who are likely to experience increments in conflict and stress during the course of helping another. This risk, in our view, may well be greater, relatively speaking, for men as compared to women, given the former's stoic or unbending helping posture. The application of LaRossa and LaRossa's (1981) conflict sociological model of the transition to parenthood proves useful in assessing the relative level of conflict likely to be experienced by primary male caregivers. LaRossa and LaRossa (1981) developed their model based on the experiences of parents caring for children. We find that one can draw parallels between the transition to parenthood and the transition to caring for an incapacitated older family member, and thus the model is useful for our purposes.

Briefly explained, LaRossa and LaRossa (1981) identified four contingency variables that could be expected to affect the caregiver's sense of conflict (or *stress,* in our terms) at various points:

1. the degree of protectiveness felt by the caregiver,
2. the value placed on free time by the caregiver,
3. the interchangeability of available caregiving coverage, and
4. the legitimacy of the division of labor during caregiving.

Increases in contingency variables 1 and 2 (feelings of protectiveness and the value placed on free time) were hypothesized by the authors to increase the likelihood of conflict felt by the caregivers. Conversely, increases in contingency variables 3 and 4 (interchangeability of available caregiving coverage and legitimacy of the division of labor during caregiving) were predicted to decrease the likelihood of felt conflict.

Given the hypothesized relationships among the four contingency variables and the construct of conflict in the LaRossa and LaRossa (1981) model, we would predict that men who display a family caregiving persona and carry primary elder caregiving responsibilities will experience escalated feelings of conflict or stress. We find our subjects to be very protective of their elder care recipients (they feel a great sense of responsibility for care), to lack flexibility in terms of the interchangeability of coverage (they are firmly and almost exclusively enmeshed in the caregiving role), to have little free time set aside for themselves, and to receive little or no recognition for the caregiving tasks they perform. Thus men displaying a caregiving orientation evince, according to our analysis, a characteristic pattern of contingencies that would predict high levels of internal conflict while caring for a relative. Consequently, the extent to which these men withstand such disincentives to caregiving and remain committed to the responsibility over the long haul is all the more impressive and noteworthy.

Epilogue

Our sample appears quite skewed in the direction of reflecting a cohort of men who display a caregiver orientation. Our definitions, views of task performance, and division of labor are premised on data drawn from White middle-class men. The sample depicts what may therefore be a mainstream white experience. Largely absent from our discussion (and the work of other researchers) are descriptions of lower working-class and racial/ethnic minority families' caregiving experiences. Consequently, the demographic bias inherent in our sample could well have skewed our vision of the caregiving persona.

The fact that our subjects were mostly primary care providers and involved with caregiver support groups may also separate them from the larger aggregate of men involved in family caregiving to varying degrees. As such, it is probably best to consider this work to be generative in nature with subsequent analyses building on the propositions presented here. Nevertheless, our data do document the existence of a subgroup of older men who are significantly engaged in promoting the well-being of dependent family members through personalized and intense caregiving.

Future researchers would be advised to delve deeper into the male caregiver persona. The key research question would appear to be: To what extent and in what ways is a caregiving orientation manifested in men varying in terms of their relative position in the family, age, socioeconomic status, race and ethnicity, and relationship to the care recipient? We predict that the number of men displaying this orientation to family care is far greater than conventional wisdom suggests. Considerable flexibility in the expressions of care evidenced anecdotally among African-American and other minority male caregivers further encourages us to think in this manner.

We further predict that the number of older male caregivers will swell in the years ahead, coming to represent a critical source of help for families that include incapacitated elder members. Men's presence among the ranks of those who provide family care will grow increasingly strong in part because of the current generation of older men who are serving as exemplars of males who are able to allow themselves to be caring, emotionally connected, and persevering even while carrying the responsibility of family care. The male caregiving orientation is destined to flourish and in so doing will reduce considerably the extent to which gender bias is reflected in the provision of family caregiving.

References

Anderson, T. B., & McCulloch, B. J. (1993). Conjugal support: Factor structure for older husbands and wives. *Journal of Gerontology: Social Sciences, 48,* S133-S142.

Antonucci, T. C., & Akiyama, H. (1987). An examination of sex differences in social support among older men and women. *Sex Roles, 17,* 737-749.

Applegate, J. S., & Kaye, L. W. (1990). The integrity of family support networks used by male caregivers of the elderly. *Family Perspective, 24,* 275-287.

Arber, S., & Gilbert, N. (1989). Men: The forgotten carers. *Sociology, 23,* 111-118.

Archbold, P. G. (1983). Impact of parent-caring on women. *Family Relations, 32,* 39-45.

Barusch, A. S., & Spaid, W. M. (1989). Gender differences in caregiving: Why do wives report greater burden? *The Gerontologist, 29,* 667-676.

Belenky, M. F., Clinchy, B. M., Goldberger, N. R., & Tarule, J. M. (1986). *Women's ways of knowing.* New York: Basic Books.

Bem, S. L. (1974). The measurement of psychological androgyny. *Journal of Consulting and Clinical Psychology, 42,* 155-162.

Borden, W., & Berlin, S. (1990). Gender, coping, and psychological well-being in spouses of older adults with chronic dementia. *American Journal of Orthopsychiatry, 60,* 603-610.

Brody, E. M. (1990). *Women in the middle: Their parent-care years.* New York: Springer.

Brubaker, T. H. (1990). Families in later life: A burgeoning research area. *Journal of Marriage and the Family, 52,* 959-981.

Carlson, K. W., & Robertson, S. E. (1990). The influence of impairment on the burden experienced by spouses of partners with dementia. *Canadian Journal of Rehabilitation, 3,* 213-222.

Commonwealth Fund. (1992, June 25). *The nation's great overlooked resource: The contributions of Americans 55+* (Americans Over 55 at Work Program). New York: Author.

Finley, N. J. (1989). Theories of family labor as applied to gender differences in caregiving for elderly parents. *Journal of Marriage and the Family, 51,* 79-86.

Fitting, M., Rabins, P., Lucas, M. J., & Eastham, J. (1986). Caregivers for dementia patients: A comparison of husbands and wives. *The Gerontologist, 26,* 248-252.

Gatz, M., Bengtson, V. L., & Blum, M. J. (1990). Caregiving families. In J. E. Birrin & K. W. Schaie (Eds.), *Handbook of the psychology of aging* (3rd ed., pp. 404-426). San Diego, CA: Academic Press.

George, L. K., & Gwyther, L. P. (1986). Caregiver well-being: A multidimensional examination of family caregivers of demented adults. *The Gerontologist, 26,* 253-259.

Gilligan, C. (1982). *In a different voice.* Cambridge: MA: Harvard University Press.

Gutmann, D. (1987). *Reclaimed powers: Toward a new psychology of men and women in later life.* New York: Basic Books.

Harper, S., & Lund, D. A. (1990). Wives, husbands, and daughters, caring for institutionalized and noninstitutionalized dementia patients: Toward a model of caregiver burden.
International Journal of Aging and Human Development, 30, 241-262.

Horowitz, A. (1985). Sons and daughters as caregivers to older parents: Differences in
role performance and consequences. *The Gerontologist, 25,* 612-617.

Johnson, C. (1983). Dyadic family relations and social support. *The Gerontologist, 23,*
377-383.

Kaye, L. W., & Applegate, J. S. (1989). *Unsung heroes? A national analysis and intensive
local study of males and the elderly caregiving experience* (final report to the AARP
Andrus Foundation). Bryn Mawr, PA: Bryn Mawr Graduate School of Social Work &
Social Research.

Kaye, L. W., & Applegate, J. S. (1990a). *Men as caregivers to the elderly: Understanding
and aiding unrecognized family support.* Lexington, MA: Lexington Books.

Kaye, L. W., & Applegate, J. S. (1990b). Men as elder caregivers: A response to changing
families. *American Journal of Orthopsychiatry, 60*(1), 86-95.

Knight, B. G., Lutzky, S. M., & Macofsky-Urban, F. (1993). A metaanalytic review of
interventions for caregiver distress: Recommendations for future research. *The Gerontologist, 33,* 240-248.

LaRossa, R., & LaRossa, M. M. (1981). *Transition to parenthood: How infants change
families.* Beverly Hills, CA: Sage.

Lewis, J. (1987). *Daughters caring for mothers.* Technical report to the Rockefeller
Foundation. London: London School of Economics.

Lowenthal, M. F., Thumber, M., & Chiriboga, D. (1975). *Four stages of life: A comparative study of women and men facing transitions.* San Francisco: Jossey-Bass.

Mancini, J. A., & Blieszner, R. (1989). Aging parents and adult children: Research themes
in intergenerational relationships. *Journal of Marriage and the Family, 51,* 275-290.

Montgomery, R. J. V., & Borgatta, E. (1987). *Effects of alternative family support
strategies.* Final report to the Health Care Financing Administration. Baltimore, MD:
Department of Health and Human Services.

Montgomery, R. J. V., & Datwyler, M. M. (1990). Women & men in the caregiving role.
Generations, 14(Summer), 34-38.

Montgomery, R. J. V., & Hatch, L. R. (1986). *Caregiving career lines.* Paper presented at
39th annual scientific meeting of the Gerontological Society of America, Chicago.

Montgomery, R. J. V., & Kamo, Y. (1989). Parent care by sons and daughters. In J. A.
Mancini (Ed.), *Aging parents and adult children* (pp. 213-227). Lexington, MA: D. C.
Heath.

Moss, M. S., Lawton, M. P., Kleban, M. H., & Duhamel, L. (1993). Time use of caregivers
of impaired elders before and after institutionalization. *Journal of Gerontology: Social
Sciences, 48,* S102-S111.

Mui, A. C., & Morrow-Howell, N. (1993). Sources of emotional strain among the oldest
caregivers: Differential experiences of siblings and spouses. *Research on Aging, 15,*
50-69.

Olesen, V. L. (1989). Caregiving, ethical and informal: Emerging challenges in the
sociology of health and illness. *Journal of Health and Social Behavior, 30,* 1-10.

Parker, G. (1989). Unending work and care. *Work, Employment & Society, 3,* 541-553.

Parks, S. H., & Pilisuk, M. (1991). Caregiver burden: Gender and the psychological costs
of caregiving. *American Journal of Orthopsychiatry, 61,* 501-509.

Pruchno, R. A. (1990). The effects of help patterns on the mental health of spouse caregivers. *Research on Aging, 12,* 57-71.

Quayhagen, M. P., & Quayhagen, M. (1988). Alzheimer's stress: Coping with the caregiving role. *The Gerontologist, 28,* 391-396.

Rathbone-McCuan, E., & Coward, R. T. (1985, November). *Male helpers: Unrecognized informal supports.* Paper presented at 38th annual scientific meeting of the Gerontological Society of America, New Orleans, LA.

Rubinstein, R. L. (1986). *Singular paths: Old men living alone.* New York: Columbia University Press.

Skat, M. M., & Pearlin, L. I. (1992). Caregiving: Role engulfment and the loss of self. *The Gerontologist, 32,* 656-664.

Skelly, M. C., McAdoo, C. M., & Ostergard, S. M. (1993). Caregiver burden at McGuire Veterans Administration Medical Center. *Journal of Gerontological Social Work, 19,* 3-14.

Snyder, B., & Keefe, R. (1985). The unmet needs of family caregivers for frail and disabled adults. *Social Work in Health Care, 10,* 1-14.

Solomon, K. (1982). The older man. In K. Solomon & N. B. Levy (Eds.), *Men in transition: Theory and therapy* (pp. 205-240). New York: Plenum.

Sommers, T. (1985). A woman's issue. *Generations, 10*(Spring), 9-13.

Stoller, E. P. (1990). Males as helpers: The role of sons, relatives, and friends. *The Gerontologist, 30,* 228-235.

Stoller, E. P., & Cutler, S. J. (1992). The impact of gender on configurations of care among married elderly couples. *Research on Aging, 14,* 313-330.

Stone, R. I., & Kemper, P. (1989). Spouses and children of disabled elders: How large a constituency for long-term care reform? *Milbank Quarterly, 67,* 485-504.

Tennstedt, S., Crawford, S., & McKinlay, J. B. (1993). Determining the pattern of community care: Is coresidence more important than caregiver relationship? *Journal of Gerontology: Social Sciences, 48,* S74-S83.

Teresi, J., Toner, J., Bennett, R., & Wilder, D. (1988-89). Caregiver burden and long-term care planning. *Journal of Applied Social Sciences, 13,* 192-214.

Ungerson, C. (1987). *Policy is personal: Sex, gender and informal care.* London: Tavistock.

Weinstein, G. W. (1989, October). Help wanted—the crisis of elder care. *Ms.,* pp. 73-79.

Wolfson, C., Handfield-Jones, R., Glass, K. C., McClaran, J., & Keyserlingk, E. (1993). Adult children's perceptions of their responsibility to provide care for dependent elderly parents. *The Gerontologist, 33,* 315-323.

Young, R. F., & Kahana, E. (1989). Specifying caregiver outcomes: Gender and relationship aspects of caregiver strain. *The Gerontologist, 29,* 660-666.

Zarit, S. H., Todd, P., & Zarit, J. (1986). Subjective burden of husbands and wives as caregivers: A longitudinal study. *The Gerontologist, 26,* 260-266.

13

Making Gender
Visible in Public Policy

JUDITH G. GONYEA

It is increasingly evident that men and women do not experience the same quality of life in their later years. The central question to be explored in this chapter is whether these gender differences are derived only from the variations in personal, social, and economic resources men and women bring to the Third Age of their lives or whether they are also the result of political decisions regarding entitlements, rewards, and resources. The analysis will not only encompass the interaction of gender and age but also examine how ethnicity or race intertwines with age and gender to influence well-being. It is the thesis of this chapter that inequities experienced earlier in life are often exacerbated in old age and that governmental policies have been differentially effective in raising men and women and persons of color out of poverty.

This chapter reinforces a theme emphasized throughout the text that gender is more than a biological factor and aging is more than an organic process. Both also have important social meanings. Gender is a relational construct—that is, definitions of masculinity and femininity are interdependent. Further, these definitions have historically reinforced power relations of men over women because masculinity is associated with traits of "authority and mastery," while femininity is associated with traits of "passivity and subordination" (Kimmel, 1986, p. 521). As Hendricks (1990) states, "Discussing gender is not the same as merely discussing what it means to be a woman or a man. The focus must be on the relative impact, and to do that both genders must be considered" (p. 5). Aging is also a social process. Aging can be measured in terms of the passage of chronological time or years, but the meaning of age can also be assessed through membership in a particular age cohort (e.g., coming of age in the Depression or being a baby boomer) or in terms of the passage of normative life events (e.g., graduation, marriage, parenthood, retirement). Analysis of the combined effects of gender and age is important if we are to understand how being a male frames the aging experience. Indeed, all societies assign social status and distribute resources according to value systems that include beliefs about gender and age (Levy, 1988). Public policies are formal statements regarding a society's strategies or goals concerning the allocation of social positions, roles, and resources. In this concluding chapter, I explore one macro-micro interaction of gender and aging, namely, how policy events in the United States have differentially influenced the well-being of elders. Most important are public policies that focus on maintaining or improving the economic status of older Americans.

The Economic Status of the Aging Population

Before analyzing the gender-based assumptions that underlie our aging policies, we must first understand the economic status of older men and women and the factors that contribute to the different resources and needs they bring to their aging years. In the 1960s and 1970s, the popular image of the aging population was that it was poor, physically infirm or frail, ill-housed, socially isolated, and politically powerless. These deprivations were felt to be no fault of the elderly themselves and thus helped secure a "permissive consensus" for governmental action (Hudson, 1978, p. 430). In recent years, however, this compassionate stereotype has been replaced with a scapegoating view of the aged (Binstock, 1983). This new singular image portrays the older population as affluent, politically powerful, not bearing their fair share of taxes, and receiving a disproportionately high percentage of governmental benefits (Catchen, 1989). Both stereotypes homogenize and treat the elderly as a single class, ignoring the great diversity within the aging population, especially in terms of gender and ethnicity (Nelson, 1982). Future cohorts of the aging population will be increasingly diverse. By 2020, 21% of the population will be persons of color, and by 2050 that segment will increase to 33%, from today's 14% (U.S. Bureau of the Census, 1989). The economic condition of the United States' aging population has improved over the past 30 years both in absolute and relative terms. In 1959, approximately 35% of the elderly were officially poor as compared to approximately 20% of the general population, whereas by 1990, 12.2% of the elderly were poor as opposed to 13.5% of the general population. If we expand our analysis to include the "near poor" (incomes at 125% of the poverty line) then we find that 19% (more than 5.7 million) of the elderly as compared to 26.1% of children and 14.4% of other adults were among the ranks of the poor and near poor in 1990 (U.S. Bureau of the Census, 1991).

Many of the economic gains witnessed since the 1960s are a result of government income-maintenance programs. Yet these economic improvements are not evenly distributed throughout the aging population. Table 13.1 presents the percentage of poor and near poor by age, sex, and race or ethnicity for the older population in 1990. These data underscore that men, especially white men, are least likely to experience or be at risk of poverty. Moreover, this is a surprisingly recent development. In 1959, 35% of older men and 36% of older women had incomes below the poverty line—that is, they equally suffered economic deprivation; by 1990, however, older men had a 7.6% poverty risk as compared to a 15.4% risk for women (U.S. Government Accounting Office, 1992).

Analysis by race reveals that older African-American men are five times as likely (27.8%) and older Hispanic men are three times as likely (18.6%) than older white men (5.6%) to be among the ranks of the poor. Across all ethnic groups, the risk of poverty increases with aging. For white men age 65 to 74, not quite 5% are in poverty; and by age 75, that risk increases to 7.8%. However, for African-American men age 65 to 74, one in four is poor, and by age 75, the rate of poverty is 34.4%; similarly for Hispanics age 65 to 74, the poverty risk increases from 20.6% to 26.2% when men reach age 75 and older.

Table 13.1 also dramatically demonstrates the interactive effects of gender, race, and age on the experience of poverty. The poorest group of elderly are African-American women over the age of 75 (43.9%) followed by Hispanic women 75 years and older (30.1%). Gerontologists refer to this phenomenon as the double and triple jeopardies of aging that confront women and persons of color.

Table 13.1 Percentage of Poor and Near Poor Elderly Persons by Age, Sex, and Race or Ethnicity, 1990

Sex and Age	White		Black		Hispanics[a]		Total	
	Poor	Near Poor	Poor	Near Poor	Poor	Near Poor	Poor	Near Poor
Both sexes								
65 and older	10.1	6.3	33.8	11.3	22.5	11.0	12.2	6.8
65 to 74	7.6	4.9	29.6	11.0	20.6	10.4	9.7	5.4
75 and older	13.8	8.6	40.6	11.9	26.2	12.4	16.0	8.9
Male								
65 and older	5.6	4.6	27.8	10.7	18.6	8.4	7.6	5.2
65 to 74	4.5	4.0	24.6	10.1	18.0	8.0	6.4	4.7
75 and older	7.8	5.4	34.4	12.0	20.1	9.1	9.9	6.0
Female								
65 and older	13.2	7.7	37.9	11.7	25.3	12.9	15.4	8.0
65 to 74	10.2	5.6	33.6	11.7	22.7	12.3	12.3	6.1
75 and older	17.3	10.5	43.9	11.9	30.1	14.4	19.5	10.7

SOURCE: U.S. General Accounting Office (1992, p. 17).
a. Hispanics may be of any race.

Antecedents of Poverty in the Aging Population

Four factors equally contribute to the risk of poverty for men and women in later years: life expectancy, marital status, living arrangements, and work-life experience. Thus whether one is male or female, the chances one will face poverty in old age are increased by living longer, being widowed, living alone, or working in the secondary sector of the labor market. Yet, although there is no gender difference in the predictors of poverty, the data presented below will underscore that each of these four factors has an extraordinary impact on older women compared to older men.

Life Expectancy

It is common knowledge that women outlive men in developed or industrialized nations such as the United States. Less well known is that the gender gap in life expectancy has grown dramatically throughout the past century in the United States from a 2- or 3-year differential in 1900 to a 7-year one in 1990. In fact, it has been said that the principal problem of old age for men is that they die. The imbalance of the sex ratio is dramatic. Among persons age 65 to 74 there are 83 males to 100 females, while among the very old (85 years and older) the ratio is 43 males to 100 females (U.S. Bureau of the Census, 1987). It is important to underscore that life expectancy is not a measure of quality of life (Hess, 1990). As was noted in Table 13.1, living longer does not mean living better.

Marital Status

Because men's life expectancy is lower than women's and because men tend to marry women who are younger than themselves, most older men are likely to remain married until they die, while most older women are widowed. After age 40, there are five times as many widows as widowers. Moreover, while the divorced still represent only a small percentage of older persons, their numbers have increased four times as fast as the older population as a whole in the past decade. The divorce rate among older men and women is approximately equal, although the differences among men are remarkable. For example, older African-American males are twice as likely to be divorced as their white counterparts (American Association of Retired Persons, 1987). Yet whether widowed or divorced, given the opportunities afforded by the imbalanced sex ratio, older men are eight times more likely to remarry than older women (National Center for Health Statistics, 1987).

Of importance is that the poverty rates for older marrieds are quite similar and relatively low. Based on 1990 census data, among the older population, only 5.3% of married men and 5.7% married women are in poverty (U.S. Bureau of the Census, 1991). By contrast, men and women who are widowed, divorced, separated, or never married are at greater risk of being poor. The census data underscore, however, that in addition to marital status, gender has a separate and independent effect on poverty status. While 13.8% of widowed men are in poverty, 21.4% of widowed women are poor. Similarly, among divorced, separated, or never-married persons, 16.1% of older men and 24.3% of older women are poor (U.S. Bureau of the Census, 1991).

Living Arrangements

Older men as a consequence of both life expectancy and marital status are much less likely than older women to be living alone, in the home of another relative, or in a long-term care facility. Three quarters of men age 65 and older lived with their spouses as compared to only slightly more than one third (37%) of women of a similar age (U.S. Bureau of the Census, 1989). The risk of living alone increases with age. For men age 65 to 74, 12.3% live by themselves; for age 75 and older, 21.8% are living alone. By comparison, for women age 65 to 74, 33.5% live alone; for ages 75 and older, this figure rises to 51.1%. In fact, primarily because they live with their spouse, older men are also not at risk of institutionalization. Rather, older women are—approximately 75% of nursing home residents are women (Dolinsky & Rosenwaike, 1988).

Poverty is greater among all of the elderly—both men and women—living alone. These individuals are five times more likely to be living in poverty than elderly couples. Yet again gender exerts an independent effect. Of the elders living alone in 1987, 20% of women compared to 15% of men were in poverty (Davis, Grant, & Rowland, 1990). Ethnicity or race also has an impact on the poverty risk for elders living alone. White men age 65 to 74 have the lowest risk of poverty (9%), while Black women age 85 and older are at greatest risk (59%) (Davis et al., 1990).

Work-Life Experience

The U.S. economy is characterized as a dual labor market comprising a core or primary sector and a peripheral or secondary sector. The primary sector is composed of jobs that offer high salaries, job security, fringe benefits, and pensions. In contrast, the secondary sector is composed of jobs that offer low wages, little job security, and few, if any, fringe benefits and pension plans. It is common knowledge that women and minorities are disproportionately found in the secondary sector or the lower levels of the primary sector. Moreover, family caregiving responsibilities for children (Hochschild & Machung, 1989) and elderly parents (Stone, Cafferata, & Sangl, 1987) are still assumed primarily by women. These caregiving responsibilities often affect women's patterns of participation in the labor force or their career or job choices. Women may choose not to enter, to delay entering, or to temporarily or permanently leave the workforce to care for children, a spouse, or aging parents (Gonyea, 1993). These employment patterns have significant bearing on older men's and women's economic resources in later life.

For example, DeViney and O'Rand (1988) compared the labor force participation of American workers who were 55 to 64 years of age for the past three decades. They discovered opposite trends for men and women. While over the past 30 years older women increased their labor force participation, older men's presence in the workforce declined. These gender differences do not mean that women are displacing men. Rather, they reflect the sectorial evolution of the labor market and the lesser need of older men to maintain their employment for survival.

For the past 30 years, there has been tremendous growth in the service sector accompanied by a dramatic shrinkage in the industrial sector. Women who have predominately entered the service and retail professions have not forced out the men, who are disproportionately located in manufacturing jobs; rather middle-aged and older women seeking employment have found different employment opportunities. In addition, the decade of the 1980s brought plant closings, company downsizing, declining unionization, and rising levels of unemployment. For displaced older workers facing age discrimination in the labor market, the challenges of finding new employment are great. Once they lose their jobs, older workers are more likely to be unemployed longer, suffer greater wage loss in subsequent jobs, and ultimately give up looking for another position (Harris, 1981).

Because of the combined effects of the shifting labor market and gender differentials in pensions, the labor force participation of men age 65 and older has declined sharply over the past 30 years. In 1950, almost half (46%) of all men age 65 and older were in the labor force; by 1960, this figure declined to one third (33%); by 1970, this figure was again reduced to slightly more than one quarter (27%); and by 1986 only 16% of older men were in the workforce (U.S. Senate Select Committee on Aging,

1988). In contrast, the percentage of women age 65 and older in the labor force has remained fairly constant over the past three decades: In 1950, approximately 10% of older women were in the labor force, and by 1980 this figure declined to 7.4% (U.S. Senate Select Committee on Aging, 1988).

Sources of Income Among Elders

An analysis of the sources of income for the aging population underscores the importance of governmental transfer programs in the lives of older men and women (U.S. Government Accounting Office, 1992). However, the relatively large contribution of public programs in determining the economic well-being of the aged further emphasizes the need to examine whether these programs are, in fact, gender-biased.

Table 13.2 presents the various income sources for poor and nonpoor older households in 1990. For both economically advantaged and vulnerable elders, Social Security benefits are the largest source of income. For the poor elderly, however, Social Security represents almost three quarters (71%) of their income contrasted to 39% of the nonpoor elderly income. Following Social Security, the two largest sources of income for the poor elderly are also government programs—the Supplemental Security Income (SSI) program, which is a means-tested cash assistance program (9%), and public or subsidized housing assistance (9%). Interest and dividends, private pensions, and earnings contribute little to poor elderly's income. Conversely, for the nonpoor elderly, interest and dividends represent slightly more than one quarter (28%) of their income, and private pensions make up almost one fifth (18%) of the assets.

Because men are less likely to be among the ranks of the poor, it comes as no surprise that women are twice as likely to rely on Social Security as their only source of income. Men are twice as likely as women to receive a private pension (Hess, 1990). But, given the relative importance of Social Security and the SSI program in maintaining and improving the economic well-being of older Americans, the remainder of this analysis focuses on just these two public policies. Discussion will concentrate on exploring the value assumptions that underlie creation and implementation of these two programs and whether these judgments result in older men and women being treated differently in terms of either entitlements or allocation of resources. Although social definitions of masculinity have at times worked to both the benefit and the disadvantage of older men, "in

Table 13.2 Percentage of Poor and Nonpoor Elderly Household
Income From Various Sources, 1990

	Poor	*Nonpoor*
Earnings	1	12
Housing assistance	9	—
Interest/dividends	4	28
Pension	3	18
Social Security	71	39
Means-tested cash assistance	9	—
Food stamps	2	—
Other	1	2

SOURCE: U.S. General Accounting Office (1992, p. 17).

a society based upon the institutional power of men over women, men
benefit from inherited definitions of masculinity and femininity and
would be unlikely to change them—indeed, unlikely to even call them
into question" (Kimmel, 1986, p. 523). In the United States' development
of social policies, the normative standards of referent have been the
male-headed household and male labor force participation patterns. As a
result, men as a whole have typically experienced greater gains from
enacted programs than have women, and perhaps, as Kimmel (1986, p. 523)
suggested, "Men as a group have historically exhibited a smug satisfaction
with existing gender relations." Nonetheless, as comparisons across class
and ethnicity reveal, all men have not benefited equally.

The Social Security Act:
Old Age and Survivors Insurance (OASI)

Basic Assumptions of the Social Security Program

When enacted in 1935, the Social Security Act included a retirement
component, Old Age Insurance (OAI), to provide economic support to
retired workers age 65 and older. The adoption of OAI reflected the United
States' belated acknowledgment that in industrialized societies it was
necessary for governments to offer economic protection to persons who
were no longer productive members of society. It was recognized that

through no fault of their own those persons who lived to old age often had insufficient financial resources for their final years of life. In 1939, Social Security benefits were expanded to include dependents with a 50% spousal benefit and a widow's benefit (survivors insurance, now OASI). Three sets of assumptions about aging, work, and family underlie the creation of Social Security:

1. Only a small percentage of Americans would survive to old age to collect benefits, and those who did would receive benefits only for a brief time period. In fact, in the 1930s, for men who survived to the age of 20, their remaining life expectancy was approximately 42 years (Torrey, 1982).

2. Social Security would be only one of several sources of support—in addition to personal savings, pensions, interest and dividends, and other assets—in securing an economically viable future for the elderly. Social Security was never envisioned to be the sole source of financial support to older citizens.

3. The family would be the economic unit that receives the Social Security benefit. The typical family was viewed as being composed of a wage-earner husband and a homemaker wife, and marriage was regarded as a lifelong commitment. Women were seen as economically dependent on their husbands.

A key policy question as we enter the 21st century is whether these basic assumptions are still valid. Clearly, the average life expectancy of Americans has risen dramatically, and the fastest growing segment of the population is those over age 85, an age cohort that is predominantly female (Longino, 1988). The majority of Americans, both male and female, must now plan and save for at least 15 years of postretirement in which they will have few, if any, earnings. They also face declining physical health and thus fewer options for continuing employment as well as greater health-related expenses. Moreover, despite its original intent, for most persons—whether poor or nonpoor—Social Security benefits are their primary or only source of income in late life.

The traditional split-labor, two-parent household, in which the father is the "good provider" in the labor force and the mother is at home raising the children, now represents only a small segment—12%—of American society (Skolnick & Skolnick, 1989). There is a greater diversity in family structures, including dual-earner, single-parent, and gay and lesbian families. Within the United States, marital separation has risen from 35 divorced persons for every 1,000 married in 1960 to 100 divorced persons for every 1,000 married in 1980 (U.S. Bureau of the Census, 1985). Several amendments to Social Security, such as the extension of spousal benefits to divorced persons and the addition of base years to the calculation of benefits, have been enacted to respond to the changing economic and social conditions experienced by successive cohorts of the aging population. Despite these amendments, many gender inequities continue to exist in Social Security benefits.

Inequities in Social Security Benefits

Social Security is financed through a uniform payroll tax; in 1993 the wage rate was 7.65%, the wage ceiling was $57,600 of income, and there was a Medicare surcharge of 1.45% of income up to $135,000. Thus low-income workers—both men and women—pay a larger share of their earnings than do higher-income workers. To illustrate, while an employee earning $50,000 paid approximately 7.65% of his or her wages in Social Security taxes, an employee earning $200,000 paid approximately 3.18% of his or her income in Social Security taxes. However, benefits are based on the individual's wage and labor history. In general, full benefits are calculated on the assumption of 35 working years, and each nonworking year tallies as zero. Thus, although Social Security was designed as a progressive income-redistribution program, where there is a greater wage replacement for low-income workers relative to higher-income workers, the fact is that the working poor and persons with long periods of unemployment receive benefits that do not typically raise them above the poverty line (Olson, 1984). Higher-income workers are more likely to receive maximum annuities, compared to low-income workers who more often face longer bouts of unemployment, health disabilities, and greater pressures for early retirement (Olson, 1984).

Eligibility for Social Security can be based on either one's own wage-earning status or one's family status as the spouse of the wage earner. There is, however, a very significant gender difference in the use of this benefit. Few men receive Social Security based on a spousal benefit; the overwhelming majority of men collect benefits based on their own earnings record. By contrast, despite their massive entry into the workforce in the past three decades, the majority of women (60%) collect Social Security based on a spousal benefit.

Why is it in the interest of the majority of women to chose the spousal benefit which is just half of their husbands' wage-earner benefit? Clearly, it results from their significantly less economically rewarding work histories. Women are disadvantaged in the calculation of benefits based on their own labor history. The inequality is derived not only by their lower wages, but also by the years in which they delayed entry into or left the workforce to care for children, spouse, or aging parents. Social Security gives no economic credit for caring for family members or household management. Quadagno and Meyer (1990) refer to the spousal benefit as a "mixed blessing" for women. They argue that although the spousal benefit does provide women with a retirement income that is more generous than one based on their own work histories of no or low wages, "benefits based on family status are not earned and are always subject to change given a change in family status" (Quadagno & Meyer, 1990, p. 65). This is true in the cases of both divorce and widowhood. Dependent and survivor benefits (OASI) were originally restricted to just those persons who remained married. Recognition of the growing phenomenon of divorce, however, led to policy amendments that extended coverage to persons who had divorced after more than 10 years of marriage. However, a woman still cannot receive her benefits until her ex-husband applies to receive his, and she is entitled to only one third of the benefit while her ex-husband is alive. After his death, divorced women's benefits (like widows' benefits) are two thirds of the pension. If a women remarries, however, she forfeits the right to any spousal benefit from the previous marriage (Moon, 1990). Remarriage thus is not without its economic risks for older women.

Widowhood also may result in reductions in spousal benefits. If the primary breadwinner dies before retirement, the wage-earning record is indexed only to year of death. No projections are made in the calculation of benefits for earnings during the lost years. Should the surviving spouse choose to begin claiming benefits at age 60, the benefit is reduced by approximately 28% (Olson, 1984). It is important to underscore that under Social Security, family status is defined by the institution of marriage. This definition excludes a never-married mother or a homosexual partner from access to a spousal or survivor benefit.

One of the most hotly debated issues in Social Security is the dual-earner family. Under present Social Security laws, no person—whether man or woman—can collect full benefits as both a wage earner and dependent. Thus a two-income household may pay greater Social Security taxes but receive smaller benefits than a one-income household earning similar wages. For example, in a single-income household in which the wage earner earns $90,000, only the first $57,600 is subject to the 7.65% Social Security payroll tax; the remaining $32,400 is taxed at 1.45%. Thus the single-wage-earner household is subject only to a 5.4% overall tax. Conversely, in a two-income household in which a husband earns $50,000 and a wife earns $40,000, each partner must pay the 7.65% Social Security payroll tax on the first $57,600 of their respective incomes. Thus the dual-earner household ultimately annually pays $2,009 more in taxes than the single-earner home. Although advocates have urged Social Security to adopt an earnings-sharing formula in order to be responsive to dual-earner families, the program remains unchanged. Adoption of an earnings-sharing formula would be very costly to the government; and this option would help dual-earner households (i.e., working women) but penalize single-earner households (i.e., homemakers) (Moon, 1990).

In spite of these various flaws, calculations by Hurd (1990) suggest that if Social Security benefits were unavailable, the poverty rate for the elderly would increase from 12.4% to 45.9%. Axinn and Stern's (1988) analysis by gender and race demonstrates that Social Security lifts a smaller percentage of minorities and women out of poverty as compared to white men. For the young elders (those ages 65 to 74), Social Security kept 84% of white men out of poverty but only allowed 64% of African-American men to escape poverty. For white women, it was 69% effective in lifting them above the poverty line; for African-American women, it was only 48% effective. The effectiveness of Social Security to help the elderly escape poverty declines as age increases for all groups except white males (Axinn, 1989).

In fact, Crystal and Shea (1990) argue that the inequities experienced in the labor market are not only maintained or carried forward into the postretirement years, but rather are amplified in retirement. Using Bureau of the Census data, they found that economic inequality increased with each successive age group. For example, among adults age 35 to 44, the poorest 40% possessed only 18% of the total economic resources; by age 75, the poorest 40%'s share of the economic resources declined to 14%. For comparison, the richest 20% had 40% of these resources while age 35 to 44, and by age 75 their resources had grown to 47%. As Crystal and Shea (1990) stress, the equalizing effects of Social Security help individuals survive, but these effects are overshadowed by the weight of private pensions, interest and dividends, and other financial assets. Based on his analysis of the economic status of the elderly in five Western industrialized countries, Myles (1988) concludes:

> In sum, the United States does the most effective job of providing income security—continuity of living standards after retirement—but, because it has one of the least [egalitarian] systems of income distribution prior to retirement, it produces a very high level of relative poverty among the elderly after retirement. (p. 270)

Supplemental Security Income Program (SSI)

Basic Assumptions of SSI

In 1974, the Supplemental Security Income program (SSI), a joint federal and state program, replaced the federal and state old-age assistance welfare programs. SSI established a national means-tested cash assistance program for the country's most economically vulnerable elderly, blind, and disabled populations and provided a national guaranteed income. Several key assumptions shaped the nature of the SSI program:

1. Unlike the Social Security program, which is a contributory social insurance program, SSI is a welfare or public-assistance program. Eligibility for SSI must be proven (i.e., means-tested), based on one's economic and age or disability status. Receipt of SSI is not linked to one's work history.
2. As a joint federal-state program, states were allowed, but not mandated, to provide additional funds to eligible recipients.
3. The goal of SSI was to provide a guaranteed minimum level of income to the most economically needy. It was not mandated, however, that this minimum income should lift individuals above the official poverty line.

In 1990, more than 5 million persons received SSI benefits. Of these recipients, more than 20% (1.5 million) qualified because they were elderly (65 or older) and poor. Another 600,000 elders qualified as blind and disabled recipients (American Association of Retired Persons, 1992). The data reveal that both older women and minorities are disproportionately dependent on SSI as a source of income. Men constitute just one quarter of the elderly SSI beneficiaries, and 60% of these men are married. Analysis by race also reveals that approximately 25% of older Hispanics and 22% of older African-Americans, as compared to 5% of older whites, receive SSI payments.

It is estimated that approximately half of those eligible for SSI do not receive this benefit (Villers Foundation, 1987). A survey of persons age 65 and older who live near or below the poverty line revealed that more than one third had never heard of SSI (American Association of Retired Persons, 1992). Further, many elders are unaware that even though their income exceeds federal standards for SSI, they may still be eligible for a state supplement.

Inequities in SSI Benefits

Several aspects of the Supplemental Security Income program need to be called to attention. First, receipt of SSI does not allow individuals to escape poverty. The average monthly federal SSI benefit is only $190, and women constitute three quarters of the SSI beneficiaries. Although approximately half of the states supplement the federal SSI allowance, only four provide sufficient funds to lift recipients above the poverty threshold. Further, different benefit levels exist for individuals and couples; this has a discriminatory effect on women. The SSI benefit for elders living alone—80% of whom are women—is 76% of the poverty level. By contrast, the SSI benefit for couples—80% of older men are in a couple relationship—is 89% of the poverty level. Thus SSI is not gender-neutral in its impact (Moon, 1990).

Second, SSI income eligibility standards are set far below the official poverty line. Many elderly who are living in poverty are denied access to this program. Moreover, poor elders who struggle to save money for emergencies or to become more independent (e.g., to buy a car, to pay security deposits for rental apartments) may find that their meager savings place them in jeopardy of either having to return SSI benefits they were "overpaid" or facing termination of benefits. The SSI program has a stringent assets test. Except for the value of a home, a car with a market value of $4,500 or less, and a life insurance policy of $1,500 or less, families cannot possess assets exceeding $3,000, and individuals cannot have assets worth more than $2,000. If an elderly couple living in poverty, for example, owns an automobile worth more than $4,500 (unless it is essential for medical reasons), they will be deemed ineligible for SSI. Leavitt and Schulz's (1988) analysis of the Census Bureau's data reveals that approximately one third of the income-eligible population was asset-ineligible. Further, their analysis reveals the differences created by race and age. Approximately 40% of poor, income-eligible whites were asset-ineligible, whereas 28% and 15% respectively of impoverished, income-eligible Hispanics and African-Americans had sufficient assets to be deemed asset-ineligible. Among income-eligible individuals, assets disqualified one third (34%) of younger elders age 65 to 69, compared to one quarter (26%) age 70 to 74.

SSI also reduces a recipient's benefit by one third when he or she lives in the household of another family member or friend for a full month and receives in-kind support or assistance such as food or clothing. For many of the poor elders, this provision eliminates the option of living with other relatives, because they simply cannot afford to give up one third of their SSI income. For example, an individual who received the maximum benefit in 1992 of $422 dollars risked having this amount reduced to $281 if she or he chose to live in a daughter's household. By discouraging elders from seeking family support and hindering families from offering help, the SSI policy may contribute to premature institutionalization. Moreover, this policy may be especially hard-felt by minority elders who disproportionately live in the homes of other family members (American Society on Aging, 1992).

Conclusion

On the surface, similar factors contribute to the poverty that men and women experience in later life. For both sexes, poverty in old age is a function of living longer, being widowed, living alone, and having a work history of low wages and unemployment. Societal recognition of its responsibility to offer economic support to older citizens led to the creation of pubic programs such as Social Security and Supplemental Security Income. The evidence suggests, however, that these governmental programs have been differentially effective in lifting men from and keeping women and persons of color in poverty.

Moon (1990) makes the argument that we cannot base our decision on whether a policy is gender-neutral simply on its intent, we must also evaluate the policy's impact. Analysis of Social Security reveals that the program, especially OASI, is based on an outdated male model of both family and work. Enacted in the 1930s, the Social Security legislation perceived the "family" to be composed of a wage-earner husband and a homemaker wife who would remain married throughout their lives and would together share a brief period of retirement. The family was clearly a male-dominated household. A woman's proper role was to marry, bear and raise children, and be supported by her husband. Yet this vision of family is no longer the reality for the majority of Americans. The majority of women are now in the labor force, and for many, whether because of divorce or widowhood, marriage is not long-lasting.

Social Security legislation envisioned "work history" in terms of white male labor force participation. Men working in the primary sector of the labor market could be expected to earn good wages, receive fringe benefits and pensions, and have job security. Thus it was assumed Social Security would only supplement the elderly's own savings, interest and dividends, and private pensions. Yet this image of labor force participation does not pertain to many women and persons of color who find themselves in the secondary sector of the labor market. Low wages, little or no fringe benefits or pensions, and little job security have limited their ability to accrue sufficient economic resources to supplement Social Security in old age. Moreover, both the low earnings and periods of unemployment, whether voluntary (i.e., to raise children or care for aging parents) or involuntary (i.e., plant closings, seasonal unemployment, migrant labor), disproportionately experienced by women and persons of color have greatly reduced the dollar amount of Social Security benefits they receive. This image of high wages, good benefits, and steady employment is becoming less true for men as well. The economic climate of the 1980s and 1990s has led to a period of fiscal austerity, company downsizing, declining unionization, and job shrinkage in the manufacturing sector. Finally, for both men and women the postretirement period is no longer brief. Longer life expectancies mean that elderly often face 15 to 30 years in retirement.

There are two especially striking conclusions to this analysis. First, before the 1960s, both older men and women faced an almost equal 33% chance of living in poverty. Today, that is no longer true. Older men enjoyed a fourfold reduction in poverty over a 30-year period in contrast to the twofold betterment in women's poverty likelihood. Second, currently both older married men and women face a similar, very small poverty risk—5.3% and 5.7%, respectively. However, the poverty risk for women who are not married is four times as great, whereas the poverty risk only slightly more than doubles for men in the same situation. Why does this occur? Because both Social Security and SSI reward persons who remain in couple relationships throughout their lives. Women who violate the norm of being married, whether through divorce or widowhood, ultimately pay a much greater price than men, given that both Social Security is based on marriage as an economic partnership in which the husband is the breadwinner and SSI benefits to couples (which benefit older men) are greater than benefits to individuals (80% of which are older women).

Changes in our public perception of the aging population are important because these images shape the political environment in which policy decisions are made. Faced with a huge national debt, our society is increasingly likely to turn its attention toward instituting greater restrictions in federal entitlement programs such as Social Security, SSI, and Medicaid. Although the economic well-being of the aging population as a whole has improved, it cannot simply be assumed that all elders can afford reductions in these benefits. Rather, what is needed is a better targeting of public resources to the economically vulnerable. As serious review is given to Social Security and SSI, it must be acknowledged that these programs were designed for a time period in which the male single-earner family and marriage as a lifelong commitment predominated, and in which many fewer elders survived to experience late life. If we are to achieve greater gender and age equity in our public policies for future cohorts of aging populations, attention must be directed to redesigning these programs to be consistent with the greater diversity in living arrangements and work-life patterns that now exist.

References

American Association of Retired Persons. (1987). *A portrait of older minorities.* Washington, DC: Author.

American Association of Retired Persons. (1992). *Falling through the safety net: Missed opportunities for America's elderly poor.* Washington, DC: Author.

American Society on Aging. (1992). *Serving elders of color: Challenges to providers and the aging network.* San Francisco: Author.

Axinn, J. (1989). Women and aging: Issues of adequacy and equity. In J. D. Garner & S. O. Mercer (Eds.), *Women as they age: Challenge, opportunity and triumph* (pp. 339-362). New York: Haworth.

Axinn, J., & Stern, M. J. (1988). *Dependency and poverty: Old problems in a new world.* Lexington, MA: Lexington Press.

Binstock, R. H. (1983). The aged as scapegoat. *The Gerontologist, 23,* 136-143.

Catchen, H. (1989). Generational equity: Issues of gender and race. In L. Gray (Ed.), *Women in later years: Health, social and cultural perspectives* (pp. 27-34). New York: Haworth.

Crystal, S., & Shea, D. (1990). Cumulative advantage, cumulative disadvantage, and inequality among elderly people. *The Gerontologist, 30,* 437-443.

Davis, K., Grant, P., & Rowland, D. (1990). Alone & poor: The plight of elderly women. *Generations, 14*(Summer), 43-47.

DeViney, S., & O'Rand, A. (1988). Gender-based cohort succession and retirement among older men and women. *Sociology Quarterly, 29,* 525-540.

Dolinsky, A. L., & Rosenwaike, I. (1988). The role of demographic factors in the institutionalization of the elderly. *Research on Aging, 10,* 235-257.

Gonyea, J. G. (1993). Family responsibilities and family-oriented policies: Assessing their impact on the work place. *Employee Assistance Quarterly, 9,* 1-29.

Harris, L. (1981). *Aging in the eighties: America in transition.* Washington, DC: National Council on Aging.

Hendricks, J. (1990). Gender and aging: Making something of our chromosomes. *Generations, 14*(Summer), 5-11.

Hess, B. (1990). The demographic parameters of gender and aging. *Generations, 14*(Summer), 12-16.

Hochschild, A. (with Machung, A.). (1989). *The second shift.* New York: Avon.

Hudson, R. B. (1978). The "graying" of the federal budget and its consequences for old age policy. *The Gerontologist, 18,* 428-440.

Hurd, M. D. (1990, June). Research on the elderly: Economic status, retirement and consumption and savings. *Journal of Economic Literature,* pp. 565-637.

Kimmel, M. (1986). Introduction: Towards men's studies. *American Behavioral Scientist, 29,* 517-529.

Leavitt, T. D., & Schulz, J. H. (1988). *Time to reform the SSI asset test?* Washington, DC: American Association of Retired Persons.

Levy, J. A. (1988). Intersections of gender and aging. *Sociology Quarterly, 29,* 479-86.

Longino, Jr., C. F. (1988). Who are the oldest Americans? *The Gerontologist, 28,* 515-528.

Moon, M. (1990). Public policies: Are they gender-neutral? *Generations, 14*(Summer), 59-63.

Myles, J. (1988). Postwar capitalism and the extension of Social Security into a retirement wage. In M. Weir, A. S. Orloff, & T. Skocpol (Eds.), *The politics of social policy in the United States* (pp. 265-291). Princeton, NJ: Princeton University Press.

National Center for Health Statistics. (1987). Advance report on final marriage statistics, 1984. *Monthly Vital Statistics Report, 36,* 2.

Nelson, G. (1982). Social class and public policy for the elderly. *Social Service Review, 56,* 85-107.

Olson, L. K. (1984). Age policy: Who benefits? *Generations, 8*(Fall), 10-14.

Quadagno, J., & Meyer, M. H. (1990). Gender and public policy. *Generations, 14*(Summer), 64-66.

Skolnick, A. S., & Skolnick, J. H. (1989). *Family in transition: Rethinking marriage, sexuality and children* (6th ed.). Glenview, IL: Scott, Foresman.

Stone, R., Cafferata, G. L., & Sangl, J. (1987). Caregivers of the frail elderly: A national profile. *The Gerontologist, 27,* 616-626.

Torrey, B. (1982). The lengthening of retirement. In M. W. Riley, R. P. Abeles, & M. Teitelbaum (Eds.), *Aging from birth to death* (Vol. 2, pp. 178-205). Boulder, CO: Westview.

U.S. Bureau of the Census. (1985). *Money income and poverty status of families and persons in the United States.* Washington, DC: Government Printing Office.

U.S. Bureau of the Census. (1987). *Estimates of the population of the United States, by age, sex and race: 1980 to 1986* (Current Population Reports, Series P-25, No. 1000). Washington, DC: Government Printing Office.

U.S. Bureau of the Census. (1989). *Projections of the population by age, sex and race: 1988-2080* (Current Population Reports, Series P-25, No. 1018). Washington, DC: Government Printing Office.

U.S. Bureau of the Census. (1991). *Poverty in the United States: 1990* (Current Population Reports, Series P-60, No. 175). Washington, DC: Government Printing Office.

U.S. Government Accounting Office. (1992). *Elderly Americans: Health, housing, and nutrition gaps between the poor and nonpoor* (GAO/PEMD-92-29). Washington, DC: Government Printing Office.

U.S. Senate Select Committee on Aging. (1988). *Aging America: Trends and projections.* Washington, DC: Government Printing Office.

Villers Foundation. (1987). *On the other side of easy street.* Washington, DC: Author.

Name Index

Subject Index

About the Authors

Rebecca G. Adams (Ph.D., University of Chicago) is Associate Professor of Sociology at the University of North Carolina, Greensboro. Her major research interest is friendship patterns, especially as affected by geographic separation and cultural and structural context. She is coeditor of *Older Adult Friendship: Structure and Process* (1989), coauthor of *Adult Friendship* (1992), and author of numerous articles.

Jeffrey S. Applegate, D.S.W., teaches developmental theory and clinical practice at Bryn Mawr College's Graduate School of Social Work and Social Research. He has published many journal articles on men as caregivers across the life cycle, is coauthor of *Men as Caregivers to the Elderly* (1990), and is consulting editor for *Child and Adolescent Social Work Journal* and *Clinical Social Work Journal.*

Judith G. Gonyea, Ph.D., is Assistant Professor and Chair of Social Research at the Boston University School of Social Work. She is also a fellow at the Boston University Center on Work and Family. She has published extensively in the fields of gerontology, family, and gender studies. She currently serves on the editorial boards of *Research on Aging* and *Journal of Gerontological Social Work,* is a reviewer for *The Gerontologist* and *Social Work in Health Care,* and is writing *Family Caregiving, Policy and Gender Inequities* (with Nancy Hooyman) for Sage.

Theodore J. Gradman (Ph.D., University of California, Los Angeles) is a neuropsychologist at Mills Hospital in San Mateo, California. He also maintains a private practice in San Mateo specializing in short-term cognitive-behavioral psychotherapy with depressed and anxious adults. His research interests include the predictors of stroke rehabilitation outcome, psychotherapy with older adults, life span gender-role development, and intellectual functioning in diabetics.

Richard A. Greer, M.D., is Assistant Professor of Psychiatry at the University of Florida. His research interests include biological components related to geriatric sexuality, sleep disorders, forensic psychiatry, medication protocols for new psychiatric drug agents, and sexuality in couples with one spouse suffering from senile dementia. In addition to clinical and teaching responsibilities, he serves as an expert witness in both civil and criminal matters of law.

David Gutmann, Ph.D., a graduate of the Committee of Human Development at the University of Chicago, is currently Professor of Psychiatry and Education at Northwestern University, Chicago. He was one of the first American psychologists to question the conventional geriatric wisdom—namely, that the process of human aging is exclusively a tale of losses—and to explore the developmental possibilities for men and women in middle and later life. His American and cross-cultural studies on these matters were reported in his book *Reclaimed Powers: Towards a New Psychology of Men and Women in Later Life* (1987). He is Director of the Older Adult Program at Northwestern Medical School.

Margaret Hellie Huyck, Ph.D., is Professor in the Department of Psychology at Illinois Institute of Technology and a Fellow of the Gerontological Society of America. She is the author of *Growing Older* (1974) and (with W. Hoyer) *Adult Development and Aging* (1982), as well as chapters on gender and family relations during the middle years. Her major research has focused on young adult children and their parents in "Parkville," a study funded by NIMH. In addition, she has been examining the ways in which postgraduate physician education in geriatrics can facilitate broader perspectives of appropriate health care for older patients.

Lenard W. Kaye, D.S.W., is Professor at Bryn Mawr College's Graduate School of Social Work and Social Research. His research interests include men's elder caregiving experiences, community based and institutional long-term care services for the aged, marketing human services to older people, and the delivery of high-technology home health care services. He is author, coauthor, or editor of *Resolving Grievances in the Nursing Home* (with Abraham Monk and Howard Litwin) (1984), *Men as Caregivers to the Elderly* (with Jeffrey Applegate) (1990), *Congregate Housing for the Elderly* (with Abraham Monk) (1992), and *Home Health Care* (1992).

Pat M. Keith, Ph.D., is Professor of Sociology and Assistant Dean at Iowa State University's Graduate College. She is the author of *The Unmarried in Later Life* (1991) and coauthor of *Relationships and Well-Being Over the Life Stages* (1991). She is currently researching guardianship of older persons (with Robbyn Wacker) and assessing the relationship between legislative change and outcomes for proposed wards.

William Marsiglio, Ph.D., is Associate Professor of Sociology at the University of Florida. His current theory and research interests include men's issues as they relate to sexuality, procreation, contraception, child support, child care, parenting, and primary relationships of men of varying ages. He was recently guest editor for two volumes of the *Journal of Family Issues* devoted to fatherhood issues.

Sarah H. Matthews, Ph.D., is Associate Professor of Sociology at Cleveland State University. Her recent research has been published in family and gerontology journals and has focused on older families from the perspective of adult children. She also has written *The Social World of Older Women* (1979) and *Friendships Through the Life Course: Oral Biographies in Old Age* (1986).

Barbara Pittard Payne, Ph.D., is Emeritus Professor and Director of the Gerontology Center at Georgia State University. Her primary areas of interest are religion and aging, volunteerism, and faith development in late life. She has published many chapters and articles on religion and spirituality among older persons and has coedited two volumes of *Gerontology in Theological Education* (1989).

Kenneth Solomon, M.D., was Associate Professor of Psychiatry and Human Behavior and Associate Professor of Internal Medicine, St. Louis University School of Medicine. He was Director of the Geriatric Psychiatry Program at the St. Louis Veterans Affairs Medical Center, and Codirector of the Geriatric Psychiatry Fellowship Program in the Division of Geriatric Psychiatry, St. Louis Medical School. He authored or coauthored many publications that address the psychosocial factors associated with psychopathology in elderly men. He coedited *Men in Transition: Theory and Therapy* (1982). Kenneth Solomon died on April 12, 1994.

Peggy A. Szwabo, Ph.D., is Director of Geriatric Psychiatry Outpatient Services and Instructor in the Department of Psychiatry and Human Behavior, St. Louis University School of Medicine, and Adjunct Assistant Professor, St. Louis University School of Social Work. She has written about gender issues, psychotherapy, and caregiver concerns in the elderly and coedited *Problem Behaviors in Long-Term Care: Recognition, Diagnosis, and Treatment* (1993). Her research interests include gender issues in the development and treatment of psycho- pathology, clinical issues in long-term care institutions, and professional caregiver burnout.

Jeanne L. Thomas, Ph.D., is Professor of Psychology at the University of Wisconsin at Parkside. Her research interests include older parents' evaluations of adult children's assistance, concordance between older parents' and adult children's views of the affective quality of their relationships, psychosocial development in middle and later adulthood, and associations between grandparenthood and mental health. She is the author of *Adulthood and Aging* (1992).

Edward H. Thompson, Jr. (Ph.D., Case Western Reserve University) is Associate Professor of Sociology at Holy Cross College, Worcester, Massachusetts. His recent research has examined family caregiving, men's violence, and the masculinities of older men in public consciousness. His major research interest is the effect of masculinities on men's well-being, particularly middle-aged and elderly men. He has published in the fields of family, gerontology, and gender studies.

George E. Vaillant, M.D., is Professor of Psychiatry at Harvard Medical School and Director of Research for the Division of Psychiatry, Brigham and Women's Hospital. He is also Director of the Study of Adult Development at the Harvard University Health Services. His research interests include charting adult development, the recovery process of schizophrenia, heroin addiction, alcoholism, and personality disorder. He is author of *Adaptation to Life* (1977), *The Natural History of Alcoholism* (1983), and *The Wisdom of the Ego* (1993).